THE JAPANESE HOUSE

SINCE 1945

THE
JAPANESE
HOUSE

SINCE 1945

WITH 544 ILLUSTRATIONS

NAOMI
POLLOCK

FOREWORD BY
TADAO ANDO

Contents

Foreword
Tadao Ando

I began to be aware of architecture as a profession around the 1960s when Japan, embarking on a new start after the war, finally began to introduce genuinely modern architecture. The hero of that era was, of course, Kenzo Tange. Starting with the Hiroshima Peace Memorial Museum in 1955, the Kagawa Prefectural Government Office, which provoked controversy over its engagement with tradition, and the Yoyogi National Gymnasium, which marked the apex of structural expressionism worldwide, his works did not simply import a style, but proposed a uniquely Japanese form of modern architecture in a way that was both bold and beautiful. The works created by the talented young architects who gathered around him – Tange's disciples – were also truly brilliant.

Gazing from a distance at the receding figures of those star architects, I decided that I wanted to tread the same path, and in the late 1960s, I made an impulsive decision to make a start. However, the reality was not easy. The design of major public buildings was the job of elite graduates from prestigious universities, while self-taught, non-university-educated architects were only permitted to work on tightly regulated urban housing or on commercial buildings, both widely mocked at the time as not counting as architecture.

I think that the reason why I did not give up and was able to succeed despite these circumstances was that, alongside the achievements of Kenzo Tange, I was aware of the small residential works created by great modernist architects who had attempted to pioneer an architecture for the age of democracy using a different approach, such as Kiyoshi Seike, Kiyoshi Ikebe and Makoto Masuzawa. I was particularly struck by Makoto Masuzawa's home – a splendid fusion of modern construction methods and traditional Japanese beauty in a tiny space, even smaller than the nine-*tsubo* (approximately 30 square metres, or 320 square feet) Minimum House that he proposed as a solution to Japan's housing shortage. Then, in 1958, when Japanese society had regained its stability to the point that it was considered to have moved out of the post-war period, Kiyonori Kikutake's Sky House was completed. At the World Design Conference in Tokyo two years later, this house was praised as the most complete realization of the architectural style known as Metabolism. I am surely not the only one to have been moved and inspired by the important narratives contained in the tiny spaces of the residential architecture of that era.

The home is the building most intimately connected to the lives of human beings, and as such, it is the origin of architecture and the most effective means of capturing its essence. Consequently, tracing the residential buildings regarded as masterpieces of their time gives a sense of the social climate at that moment – or to put it another way, allows one to listen in on the true feelings of the community. In that sense, this book examining Japanese residential architecture in detail from 1945 onwards can be said to be a realistic history of post-war Japanese society, as seen through the filter of architectural design.

Even so, the opening pages looking at small homes from the 1950s appear fresh and radiant. I am sure this is partly because this period coincides with my own youth, but more importantly, it is perhaps a reflection of the sense of duty that architects of the era felt to provide people with excellent living environments as quickly as possible. These architects faced society head on with questions such as 'How should people live in post-war Japan?' and 'What kind of housing is needed to attain this lifestyle?', and they worked to realize those ideals despite restricted circumstances. Such high aspirations and pressures opened up great potential in tiny residential spaces.

As one turns the pages, one can discern a social trend towards increased diversity through the changing landscape of housing as it swings about the axis of modernism. During the past few decades, life has changed at an accelerated pace thanks to the digital network that now encompasses the entire world. As though reflecting these new circumstances, the pages in the latter half of this book present a state of chaos in which, for better or worse, the future is unclear.

In a society that has gone through a period of growth and entered a period of maturity, it is perhaps difficult to issue a message as strong as that made in the post-war years by the emergence of a new era in housing. Nevertheless, courageous architects will not stop creating. Going beyond the professional framework of designing the best building within a given budget and given conditions, architects will continue striving to capture an uncertain future through their buildings, however hard that is. The most important qualities required in an architect are not intellect or expertize, but mental strength and the ability to hang on to one's dreams!

The chain of creativity that began in the architectural world of post-war Japan remains unbroken – this book conveys that sense of hope.

The Japanese House
Inside and Out

Naomi Pollock

Over the years, many of the houses featured in the following pages have been praised and profiled in a variety of architectural and academic publications. Their experimental forms, inventive use of materials and unusual site conditions have been analysed and explained, photographed and sketched (left). 'The Japanese House: Architecture and Life after 1945', the 2017 touring exhibition curated by Yoshiharu Tsukamoto and Kenjiro Hosaka, is an excellent example of this scholarship. But what was it like to live in these homes? Since many of them are no longer extant, we may never know for sure. And, like private homes anywhere, those still standing are largely closed to the public. Taking a close look at Japan's architect-designed houses since World War II, this book probes that fundamental question.

In many respects, 1945 marked a point when Japan had to reset. Following the war, there was a new political order to establish, an economic crisis to overcome and physical devastation from which to rebuild. '2.1 million residences had been destroyed; with the addition of 640,000 households made up of demobilized soldiers and returnees from abroad, it's estimated that the housing shortage reached 4.2 million units,' writes Professor Yoshio Uchida.[1] In the following years, the Japanese government provided loans for building family homes, as well as for the construction of rental-apartment complexes, but 'the promotion of home ownership' was its end game, according to historian Laura Neitzel.[2] The unique circumstances of the post-war era resulted in a fresh start for the private home. Here was an opportunity not only to modernize housing, but also to rethink what a house could be. Due to the magnitude of upheaval to Japanese society, full-scale reconsideration was essential, and many of the ensuing changes departed radically from the past. Some came about in response to government initiatives, including a shift away from the standard social unit. Instead of the extended,

Completed in 2001, Jun Aoki's i takes its unique form from the legally permissible building volume.

multi-generational family, the nuclear family composed of parents and two children was promoted. Another major shift was the separation of eating and sleeping. These activities had previously taken place in the same space, but now this was considered unhygienic. In addition, the country's new constitution moved the status of women towards the centre of society and, therefore, towards the centre of the household. These changes all had profound implications for house design. Though traditional conventions were not cast aside entirely, referencing the past was considered 'taboo' in the face of Japan's defeat, according to Professor Shunsuke Kurakata.[3] Against this backdrop, Western models of convenient contemporary living became desirable.

'For Japanese architecture, the history of its modernization has also been a history of westernization,' explains architect Fumihiko Maki.[4] Prior to the war, Western design ideas were already circulating in Japan. Famously, Bruno Taut and Charlotte Perriand imported emerging European concepts in the 1930s and 1940s respectively. The exchange of ideas was also generated by Japanese architects going abroad, for instance Kunio Maekawa and Junzo Sakakura, who both worked for Le Corbusier in Paris, and Junzo Yoshimura, who followed his employers, Antonin and Noémi Raymond, to the United States. Upon returning to Tokyo, these designers shared their freshly acquired knowledge in both the studio and the university seminar room. Unsurprisingly, these new ideas surfaced in the design of their own houses, but also in the work of their architectural progeny. The passing of thoughts and theories from mentor to mentee is an ongoing process natural to the profession, with each generation adding modifications of its own. Le Corbusier's embrace of concrete appears in the work of Maekawa (right), who passed this know-how on to his students, such as Kenzo Tange, who then shared ideas with his own staff and students, including Fumihiko Maki and Kisho Kurokawa. Later, the airiness of Toyo Ito's steel-frame structures was rendered with an even lighter touch by his former employee Kazuyo Sejima, and lighter still by her disciple, Junya Ishigami.

The ease with which new architectural ideas took hold in Japan was partly due to the unprecedented design freedom that resulted from widespread devastation. Streets and property lines may have survived the conflagration, but the land itself was often left devoid of buildings, especially in major cities. As Japan began rebuilding in the early 1950s, efficiency was the aim of many architects' residential work. At that time money was tight, construction materials scarce and building size restricted for recipients of government loans. 'There was very little opportunity

The Tokyo Bunka Kaikan, built by Kunio Maekawa in 1957, bears the imprint of the architect's mentor.

for architects to do elaborate designing,' notes critic Noboru Kawazoe.[5] But Japan has proven again and again that size limits can be catalysts for invention. Some architects, like Kiyoshi Ikebe, were inspired by the concept of the 'minimum house' discussed at the 1929 Congrès Internationaux d'Architecture Moderne in Frankfurt. And, as the economy steadily improved, larger plots became affordable, manufactured materials, like concrete and steel, enabled new forms, and design possibilities expanded rapidly. Architects were keen to test out new concepts, and houses were the perfect medium for experimentation, be it for their own use or that of a willing client. Thanks to the country's astonishing economic recovery, by the 1960s houses were no longer just shelter. Many of those designed by architects had become highly personalized statements – a trend that continues to proliferate today.

While building codes still regulate matters of health and safety, aesthetic preferences are unrestricted. Where visual appearance is concerned, in Japan anything goes. Aside from select historic districts, unified street walls, continuous cornice lines and style consistency are all conspicuously absent. Even the address system – houses are numbered in the order that they are built – negates adjacency relationships. Along the same lines, contemporary party walls are very rare as they enable the quick spread of fire, a problem that plagued wooden houses of the past. These conditions have resulted in object-like detached homes that have little relationship to each other, let alone their surroundings. Making a bolder gesture still, some even front the street with windowless facades. A means of shielding the home from unpredictable urban development nearby, this strategy took off in the 1970s. More recently, some architects have begun to intentionally interact with the surroundings. Instead of shutting out the city, the sights, sounds and scenery outside become part of daily life inside (left).

The advent of computer-aided design (CAD) in the 1990s pushed the individualization of houses significantly further. 'For those…who spent a lot of time playing computer games as children and already had access to CAD in the beginning of their architectural studies, the computer is more than an aid for drawing: it serves to perfect their technique, it is even a source of ideas,' observes critic Shozo Baba.[6] Suddenly, organic shapes and complicated curves, which in the past took days to construct by hand, could be created with a series of mouse clicks. This technical freedom also eased the difficulty of designing for the small, awkward or downright strange sites being created just as the economic bubble burst in the early 1990s, and property became

Completed in 2004, the House in Ono by Suppose Design Office overlooks train tracks.

affordable again. Keen to cram as much house as possible onto these odd plots, many architects collaborated with engineers, whose structural prowess made it possible to build liveable homes on even the most challenged sites.

Materials are another area that evolved dramatically over the decades. In the war's immediate aftermath, timber was the only option for housebuilding. While wood remained a popular choice out in the country, non-burnable, mass-produced steel and concrete soon proliferated in cities. But in subsequent decades, architects' uses of materials became increasingly sophisticated and varied. Tadao Ando was the first to transform concrete from a rough industrial material into one of remarkable smoothness. Itsuko Hasegawa popularized the porosity of punched metal. Shigeru Ban proved the viability of paper tubes. And Kengo Kuma infused his work with the spirit of traditional craft – whether rendered in wood, stone or even corrugated metal. While the economic excess of the 1980s often gave birth to architectural extravagance, this triggered a reaction in the 1990s when lightness, transparency and minimalism emerged as guiding concepts for many architects. This paring-down reflected the belt-tightening caused by economic decline but also raised the aesthetic bar: is there such a thing as too thin?

One of the reasons why Japan is a hospitable environment for material experimentation is the independence of houses (top). The lack of relationships between buildings makes them extremely replaceable. If they aren't touching, they can be torn down rather easily. And this happens all the time. Though the number of renovations may be rising slowly, the lifespan of the average Japanese house is still a mere twenty-six years, observes architect Riichi Miyake.[7] The reasons for demolition include changes to the family's composition, the sale of the property or simply wear and tear. This short shelf-life gives architects the freedom to cater to the client's proclivities and the site's peculiarities, no matter how unusual (bottom). Since property values are generally tied to the land and not the building, few give a moment's thought to the impact on a home's resale value of having bathroom walls made entirely of glass, or a top-floor kitchen. Everyone knows that the house will likely be demolished when the property changes hands. For most homes, even those designed by well-known architects, the future is bleak. While this rapid pace of redevelopment sounds shocking, it is an accepted reality in Japan. 'Change is regarded as normal rather than exceptional,' comments author Chris Fawcett.[8] Yet constant renewal has its benefits. It infuses Japanese cities with vitality and, for better or for worse, provides work for architects.

Ecological and eye-pleasing, cork clads the Bay Window Tower House, built in central Tokyo by Takaaki Fuji + Yuko Fuji Architecture in 2020.

The crystalline form of Reflection of Mineral, a Tokyo home completed by Atelier Tekuto in 2006, is one of a kind.

Built in Tokyo in 2007, TNA's Mosaic House
is capped by the family's communal space – bathed
in daylight streaming in through its glass roof.

Despite their widely varying exteriors, Japanese homes accommodate a series of deeply engrained habits and rituals, beginning with the spoken greeting *tadaima* (I'm home) upon entry and the removal of outdoor shoes. These habits underscore the explicit divide between inside and out, and between family members and everyone else. Within the house, boundaries are fluid, personal space is limited and privacy a rarity. In fact, many parents continue to share sleeping quarters with their young children. Naturally, these conditions breed an informal, relaxed atmosphere centred on the combined kitchen-dining room – a necessity in the small urban house (left). While homes out in the countryside may have plenty of interior space, those in the city average only 100 square metres (1,080 square feet). And lots of people live comfortably with far less. Instead of a hardship, a compact dwelling is considered an acceptable trade-off for convenience and proximity. Bigger is not categorically better. In fact, many homeowners feel more at ease in a house where they can sense the presence of others and have their possessions at their proverbial fingertips. The functionality of these homes is often augmented by the city's resources. Public parks act like backyards, coffee shops and restaurants provide nearby venues for socializing, and the ubiquitous 7-Eleven convenience store is everyone's pantry. The space of a small home can also be expanded by the city itself, as many residential areas are knitted together by networks of narrow streets, some just wide enough for a car and others for pedestrians only. Like extensions of the home, they are swept daily by residents living nearby and beautified by their potted plants. These passageways are both components of the urban fabric and communal outdoor places where neighbours congregate, children ride bikes and stray cats scrounge for snacks.

Unsurprisingly, the urban architect-designed house is well represented in this book. This selection reflects the concentration of Japan's population, and therefore of architect-designed houses, in its cities. Aside from vacation homes, relatively few houses beyond the suburbs are designed by architects. In addition, the site conditions in metropolitan areas can be particularly extreme, which inspires the most innovative architectural responses – criteria for inclusion in this book. Exemplifying their respective time periods, the featured houses pushed limits and raised bars. Each one is documented with a text that incorporates interviews with the architects or their staff, with their family members or clients, or with architectural critics – people with first-hand knowledge and memories of the work – alongside a selection of photos and drawings. Together, words and pictures capture the spirit of the

architecture and help bring these homes to life. Bookended
by guest essays describing what came before and what might
be coming next, these house profiles are accompanied by
introductions to each decade outlining major events in Japan,
and Spotlights deconstructing specific house elements. In addition,
At Home essays – contributed by the architects, their children or
their clients – tell stories about the houses from the inside out.
Where the home is concerned 'there is no one right answer',
writes architect Kazuhiro Kojima.[9] Instead, this book shows
there are many.

A Brief History
of Japan's Housing
from 1910 to 1960

Hiroyasu Fujioka

An informal report issued in 1979 by the European Economic Community – the forerunner to today's European Union – stated that the Japanese were workaholics and their houses were like rabbit hutches. This description poked fun at Japan's typical townscape: rows of tiny single-family houses on tiny lots.

The reasons why the Japanese people stick to such housing are threefold:

1 The idea of owning a lot and building a house on it became popular in Japan after World War II, when land was regarded as the most reliable asset, and one whose value would continue rising.
2 As the population became increasingly concentrated in large cities during the post-war period, poorly planned housing developments arose in suburban areas. Their deficiencies led many people to prefer purchasing their own plots of land, however small, for building a house and garden.
3 High inheritance taxes introduced after the war resulted in the continuing subdivision of residential lots.

In Japan, the shared aspiration of 'building a house with a garden of one's own' dates back to the 1910s. It followed the emergence of a new social body, the middle class, which gradually took shape as modernization in education, business and industries progressed in the late nineteenth and early twentieth centuries. Members of the middle class were highly educated and held well-compensated posts in government, universities or major companies. They wanted single-family dwellings with gardens suitable to their modern lifestyle and status. Numerous house pattern books started circulating to meet their needs, such as *Saishin seiei wayou juutaku zusetsu* (Drawings and explanations of the latest and selected Western- and Japanese-style houses, right), published in 1920. As they were built at the behest of their owners, these houses are likely to have reflected their personal tastes. Incorporating Western or Japanese elements, or both, these dwellings had living rooms, drawing rooms, studies, dining rooms, kitchens, bedrooms, bathrooms and, in many cases, a maid's room with *tatami* mats. In 1920, the Japanese government even promulgated the House Building Association Act to help the middle class borrow construction funds more easily from banks.

The late 1920s was also the time when modernism, which started in Western Europe, was introduced into Japan. Some architects including Antonin Raymond (1888–1976), a Czech-American architect who started an architectural firm in Tokyo in 1920, and Kameki Tsuchiura (1897–1996), together with his wife Nobuko (1900–1998), applied up-to-date architectural trends to their house designs. The Tsuchiuras trained with Frank Lloyd Wright, while Antonin Raymond and his wife, Noémi, were also employed by Wright, initially at Taliesin in Wisconsin (although no trace of Wright's designs can be found in their residential works). It was easier to test out their new ideas in their own homes in Tokyo, which were not only rather small but also their personal property. The Raymond House was built in 1923 (right), and the Tsuchiura House (below right) was completed in 1935.

HOUSING CONDITIONS BEFORE WORLD WAR II

During the inter-war years, Japanese people commonly lived in small rental houses or apartments. According to a 1933 study by Tokyo Prefecture, about eighty per cent of Tokyoites lived in such housing. At that time, many Japanese landowners, both big and small, built rental houses and apartments on their land. By contrast, the super-rich lived in huge residences on vast properties of more than 70,000 square metres (750,000 square feet). At the time, Japan was a society marked by highly stratified class structures.

With the start of the Sino-Japanese War in 1937, the national government imposed material restrictions – steel bars and cement ceased to be available for private use. And, in order to enable tenants to remain in their homes, the Land and Housing Rent Control Act of 1938 ordered property owners not to raise rents.

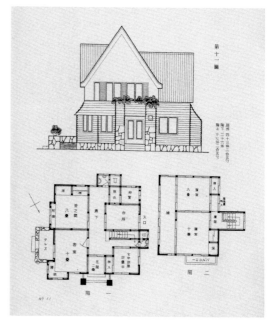

A page of *Saishin seiei wayou juutaku zusetsu* (Drawings and explanations of the latest and selected Western- and Japanese-style houses), published in 1920.

Antonin Raymond House, 1923.

Kameki Tsuchiura House, 1930.

After World War II, Japan's housing shortage became more acute due to several factors. In addition to the huge loss of urban dwellings caused by relentless air raids, the Land and Housing Rent Control Act meant landlords removed housing stock from the market, or left it unrepaired, because they could not raise rents to keep pace with the high inflation. Moreover, about 6.6 million Japanese, who had been fighting or living in former overseas colonies, were returning. Some built shacks with scrap lumber, others lived in abandoned buses. In the buildings that survived the air raids, multiple families often lived together under the same roof.

The Japanese government tried to alleviate these devastating housing conditions, but a lack of both building materials and budget limited its ability to do so. Consequently, the government had to restrict the floor area for new houses to 12 *tsubos* in 1947 (1 *tsubo* is 3.3 square metres or 36 square feet), rising, as circumstances improved slightly, to 15 *tsubos* in 1948.

Subsequently, the government tried to allocate funds to expand the supply of public housing, yet this was challenging in practice due to the difficulty in finding lots for building apartments. Local governments did supply some housing, but this was not enough to alleviate the shortage. Later, the Japan Housing Corporation, which was established in 1955, provided a fairly large number of rental apartments on the outskirts of big cities. Each unit was about 50 square metres (540 square feet) with a dining-kitchen room, two *tatami*-mat rooms, a small bath and a flush toilet.

The national government also founded the Housing Loan Corporation in 1950 to aid landowners in building small dwellings on their own property. This signified that the government had virtually abandoned its push to build public housing, changing its policy to help individual landowners instead. This shift encouraged common people to acquire land in order to build their own houses.

A policy of high inheritance taxes introduced right after the war made it difficult for property to pass from one generation to the next. Still today, many heirs must sell part of the lots they have inherited just to pay these steep taxes. Over time, this has caused the continuous subdivision of residential lots. The Building Act promulgated in 1950 soon abandoned a minimum buildable lot size for houses, and many people could not borrow enough money to buy lots large enough to build spacious homes.

To help tackle these difficult circumstances, after World War II some architects, including Kunio Maekawa (1905–1986), proposed various types of prefabricated housing. Maekawa's model, titled

PREMOS model7, housing for
Allied Occupation Forces officers in Tottori.

PREMOS (see image, page 17), could be assembled simply on site with standardized wood elements, and about 1,000 units were eventually produced. But the lack of sufficient building materials, funds and distribution strategies limited the proliferation of such prefabrication endeavours. One of the rare cases that succeeded was PRE-CON (Precast Reinforced Concrete Truss Construction), invented by Professors Heigaku Tanabe (1898–1954) and Kazuo Gotou (1913–1996) of the Tokyo Institute of Technology (right). These homes were framed by slender reinforced-concrete pillars and trussed beams, a comparatively inexpensive method that imitated the systems for fire and earthquake resistance used in traditional wooden construction. In 1970, one of the prefabricated-house builders, Sekisui Chemical Company, introduced its M1 prototype at the Tokyo International Good Living Show. Consisting of box-shaped units that could be transported by truck, it sold well.

As Japan's economy started growing rapidly in the late 1950s, many people rushed to big cities to find better-paid jobs. This led to another housing shortage, resulting in random developments with few government regulations in the further reaches of the suburbs. These developments enabled many Japanese to realize the dream of having a house, though small, on their own land. Privately owned, these reflected individual tastes. For some owners, this meant a little white cottage similar to those they had seen on American TV programmes.

PRE-CON house under construction. Heigaku Tanabe is on the far left in white overalls.

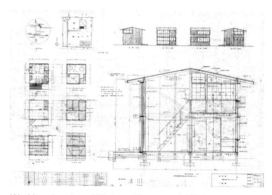

Working drawing of Makoto Masuzawa's Minimum House.

THE EMERGENCE OF JUUTAKU SAKKA

In the midst of the confusing period following the war, some Japanese architects designed 'minimum houses', including Makoto Masuzawa (1925–1990, see drawing middle right) and Kiyoshi Ikebe (1920–1979). Others, such as Kiyoshi Seike (1918–2005), proposed modern dwellings with free space surrounding a core containing a kitchen and a bathroom (right). This idea was based on the traditional house style, *shinden-zukuri*, but viewed through the filter of modernism. It became the new normal for architects to introduce contemporary American-style living, which was seen as functional, modern and family-oriented. But it took time for this lifestyle to catch on, because the appliances needed to live comfortably in such houses, for instance air-conditioning units and heaters, were not readily available.

During the rapid growth of Japan's economy in the late 1950s and 1960s, some young architects, who did not have opportunities

Associate Professor Saitou House, Kiyoshi Seike, 1952.

Kazuo Shinohara's Umbrella House interior, 1961.

House G (Nakamura House), Miho Hamaguchi, 1967.

to participate in big public or commercial projects, were able to explore their architectural ideas by designing small houses instead. One of them was Kazuo Shinohara (1925–2006), who advocated that 'the bigger the house is, the better', and criticized the commonly held belief that there should be an optimum scale for residences based on function – one of the primary notions of modernism. These architects were called *juutaku sakka*, literally 'house designers'. Among Shinohara's creations was Umbrella House (left).

Miho Hamaguchi (1915–1988) and Masako Hayashi (1928–2001) were among the first female architects in Japan, and designed many houses from a women-centric standpoint, including Hamaguchi's House G (below left). In those days, few cared for the housewife's comfort, and the conventional domestic kitchen was usually located in a dark, cold place, such as the northern part of the house. Hamaguchi proposed easy-to-use kitchens to help free the housewife from chores. In her book *Nihon juutaku no houkensei* (Feudal aspects in Japan's traditional houses), published in 1948, Hamaguchi advocated freeing women from time-consuming tasks by modernizing kitchens and minimizing the movements needed for cooking. Incidentally, washing machines, vacuum cleaners and other new products began circulating at this point.

The Building Sectional Ownership Act of 1963 prompted a new housing type known as a 'mansion', consisting of privately owned apartments, along the lines of a condominium. Such apartments gradually became popular, mainly because buying an affordable lot sized for a comfortable home within commuting distance became nearly impossible. Land prices in convenient areas have been incredibly expensive for many decades – it takes a fortune to buy and build a house in many parts of Tokyo, where land today can cost more than $14,000 per *tsubo*. Nonetheless, many people still prefer to live in an architect-designed house of their own.

1940—1949

1940s
Rising from
the Rubble

At noon on 15 August 1945, Emperor Hirohito proclaimed Japan's surrender to the Allied Forces in a speech recorded the previous day. Glued to their radios, the Japanese people heard their emperor's voice for the first time. His words marked the end of World War II. But also the start of Japan's recovery.

This began with a seven-year US occupation led by General Douglas MacArthur (left, pictured with Emperor Hirohito at the US Embassy in Tokyo in 1945). Under his aegis, fundamental changes occurred. The military was disbanded, a new constitution was drafted, which included greater rights for women, and a gradual process began whereby the nuclear family modelled after the West replaced the patriarchal, multi-generational household of old. Naturally, these changes had a profound impact on house design and construction, the need for which was urgent and extreme in the war's aftermath. For architects, these dire circumstances presented both an obligation and an opportunity.

With its vast tracts of open land resulting from the war's destruction, much of Japan's urban landscape had become a blank slate. Those with means were able to build homes, even during the war. But for most, money was scarce, and materials unavailable. In response, the Japanese government instituted house-size restrictions and sought some architect-designed solutions. These limitations, coupled with the changing family structure, were inspirational for some designers. And as early as 1948, the architectural journal *Shinkenchiku* hosted a competition for a minimal wooden house.[1]

Another source of inspiration came from the Allied forces themselves. To accommodate occupation officers and their families, the Japanese government was asked to provide 20,000 houses.[2] Size-wise, they were bigger than Japanese homes, and their construction expended valuable resources.[3] But the creation of these houses and their furnishings gave the local workforce a crash course in Western design, and Japanese citizens a close look at the American lifestyle.

The government-sponsored Industrial Arts Research Institute was tasked with producing American-style wood furniture for the US officers' homes.[4] Founded in the 1920s, the organization consisted of designers who, among other things, collaborated with craftsmen and small factories to develop export products. During the war, its focus shifted to military supplies but afterwards, with input from occupation officials, returned to developing household goods for overseas markets, such as cheese boards and salad servers.[5]

Similarly, in the immediate post-war period many Japanese manufacturers retooled their product lines, turning from ammunition and aeroplane parts to consumer goods. But it was also a time when new producers emerged. Catering to local needs, Sony got its start in 1946 repairing radios, and the Honda Motor Company launched its first motorbikes in 1949.[6]

The decade closed with the awarding of the commission for the Hiroshima Peace Memorial to architect Kenzo Tange. Though it would take several years to complete, the project ushered in a new era. It not only mourned the atomic-bomb victims, it also symbolized Japan's great resilience and readiness for rebirth.

1

Iihashi House
Junzo Sakakura
Tokyo
1941

businessman who commissioned this house, the architect's first residential work after opening his Tokyo office in 1940.

The house stood in western Tokyo, on an idyllic hilltop site overlooking a river. Though the land was lush and spacious, legal restrictions limited the building's size. On the ground floor, it featured a large living room with a high ceiling, a big fireplace set dramatically against a black slate wall, and a pivoting window-wall that opened onto a terrace and the garden beyond. While the kitchen, maid's room, tearoom and secondary spaces were at the back, the bedroom was upstairs, tucked beneath the higher half of the pitched roof.

Reflecting the influence of Le Corbusier, the Iihashi House was essentially a white box, both inside and out. But, as former Sakakura Associates staff member Noribumi Kitamura has observed, it was coated with traditional *shikkui* plaster and capped by an asymmetrical Japanese-style roof. It also bore the influence of the interior designer, architect and Le Corbusier collaborator Charlotte Perriand, whom Sakakura had first met in Paris.

In 1940, during the house's design phase, Perriand came to Japan as a guest of the Japanese government.[1] The purpose of her visit was to provide advice for turning Japan's traditional crafts into viable exports. During her stay, Perriand and Sakakura toured *minka* farmhouses, which may have influenced his design of the Iihashi House's roof. Inside, the French designer's presence was evident in a table that she had designed herself. In addition, the rotating movement of the gridded window-wall evoked her design sensibility, according to Kitamura. With a massive boulder from Sendai Prefecture as its doorstop, this movable, mullioned wall truly blended East and West.

2

Built during the war years, the Iihashi House anticipated the infiltration of European modernism and its impact on Japanese homes. In particular, it bore the imprint of the five years that Junzo Sakakura spent in Le Corbusier's Paris atelier. After returning to Tokyo in 1936, Sakakura's ties to France remained strong, resulting in an invitation from the Japanese government to design the Japanese Pavilion for the 1937 International Exposition of Art and Technology in Paris. Through that award-winning project, Sakakura met an established Japanese

❶ The pivoting window wall opened the living room to the terrace and garden beyond.

❷ Sunlight washed the south wall of the Iihashi House facing the garden.

1

1 Western-style doors stood adjacent to the *tatami* room and its wraparound *engawa* porch.

2 Plan: (A) entrance, (B) living, (C) kitchen, (E) sleeping, (G) *tatami*, (H) maid.

3 Elevations (clockwise from upper left): north, west, east, south.

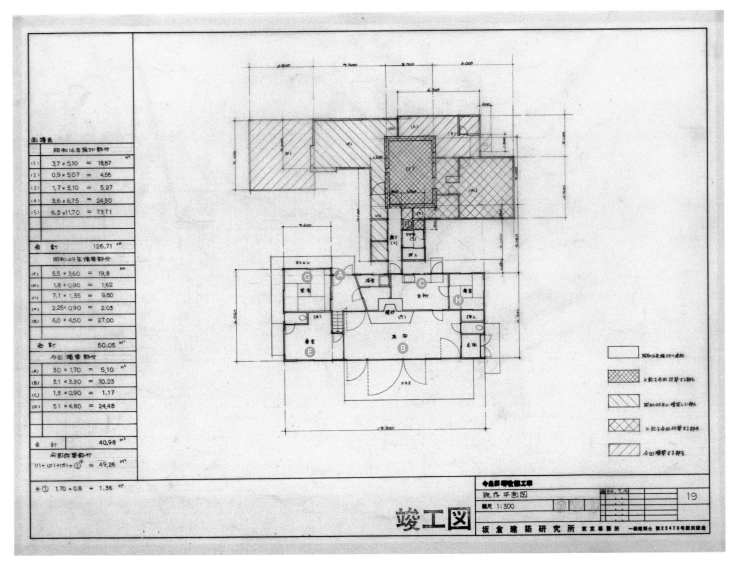

面積表		
昭和16年増築部分		
(1)	3.7 × 5.10 =	18.87
(2)	0.9 × 5.07 =	4.56
(3)	1.7 × 3.10 =	5.27
(4)	3.6 × 6.75 =	24.30
(5)	6.3 × 11.70 =	73.71
合計	126.71	
昭和49年増築部分		
(イ)	5.5 × 3.60 =	19.8
(ロ)	1.8 × 0.90 =	1.62
(ハ)	7.1 × 1.35 =	9.60
(ニ)	2.25 × 0.90 =	2.03
(ホ)	6.0 × 4.50 =	27.00
合計	50.05	
今回増築部分		
(A)	3.0 × 1.70 =	5.10
(B)	3.1 × 3.30 =	10.23
(C)	1.3 × 0.90 =	1.17
(D)	5.1 × 4.80 =	24.48
合計	40.98	
今回改築部分		
(1)+(2)+(ホ)+①* =	49.26	
*① 1.70 × 0.8 = 1.36		

竣工図

今度部増改修工事				
既存平面図			A 83.7.15	19
縮尺 1:300				
坂倉建築研究所 東京事務所 一級建築士 第23478号飯田誠造				

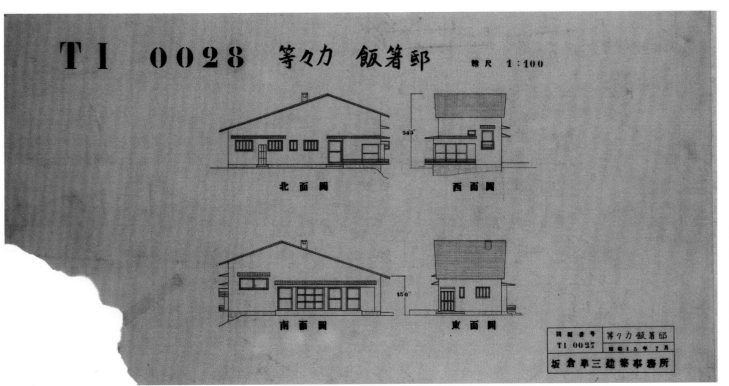

TI 0028 等々力 飯箸邸　縮尺 1:100

北面図

西面図

南面図

東面図

図面番号	等々力飯箸邸
TI 0027	昭和15年 7月
坂倉準三建築事務所	

Kunio Maekawa
Residence
Kunio Maekawa
Tokyo
1942

What makes a good house? In an essay on the topic written in 1947, Kunio Maekawa wrote: 'A modern house is a functional house that matches perfectly with how people live. The *zashiki* [formal sitting room] which had the highest status in the past, has given way to the living room, the centre of family life.'[2] At the time, Maekawa had already been living in the Toyko home he had designed for himself for several years. Though the wood exterior evoked traditional Japanese farmhouses, its interior centred on a spacious living room, exemplifying Maekawa's vision of the ideal house for the burgeoning modern era.

Maekawa's exploration of modern buildings began with a two-year stint in the Paris studio of Le Corbusier. After returning to Japan in 1930, he joined the Tokyo atelier of Antonin and Noémi Raymond, before launching his own studio five years later. In 1945 – the same year in which he married – his Ginza office was destroyed by firebombs. Consequently, he moved his practice into this house, with employees' desks occupying the ground-floor living room and mezzanine study for the next nine years – no doubt a cosy arrangement for the newly-weds.

The house was approached by a paved path with sequential 90-degree turns, requiring the body to repeatedly reorient, explains Isao Hashimoto, representative director at Maekawa Associates. Each turn offered a different view of the home's majestic front: a broad, gabled roof atop a tripartite facade, with a double-height bay and a solo column marking the middle – perhaps in homage to Japan's revered Ise Grand Shrine.[3] While sliding window-walls opened onto the gardens at the front and back, the entrance with its pivot-hinged door was tucked off to the side. Once inside, the glorious double-height space was revealed. Symmetrically arranged bedrooms, kitchen, maid's room and Western-style bathrooms stood on either side, with an open stair ascending to the mezzanine.

One of Japan's most beloved, as well as most analysed, buildings, the Maekawa Residence bore the imprint of the architect's mentors. The fluid interior and flat ceiling acknowledged the work of Le Corbusier, but the exposed post-and-beam structure may have reflected the Raymonds' influence. The house's timber construction also resulted from wartime limits on materials. 'The political climate of the day emphasized reviving Japanese tradition and culture,' explains Hashimoto. Neither purely modern nor straight-up historical, the Kunio Maekawa Residence bowed politely to both.

1

2

❶ The symmetrical southern elevation
overlooking the garden.

❷ Mr and Mrs Maekawa relaxing
at home with their dogs.

1 A continuous space, the living room segues into the dining area while open stairs ascend to the mezzanine.

1

1

① The double-height living room and
the dining area below the mezzanine.

② The north–south partial section.

③ Plan: (A) entrance, (B) living, (C) kitchen,
(D) dining area, (E) sleeping, (F) bath,
(H) maid, (I) study, (M) terrace.

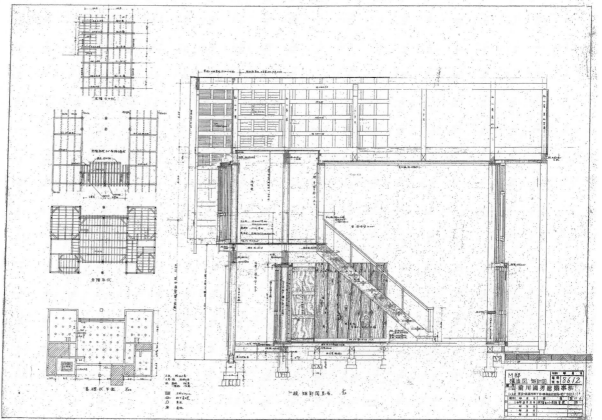

2

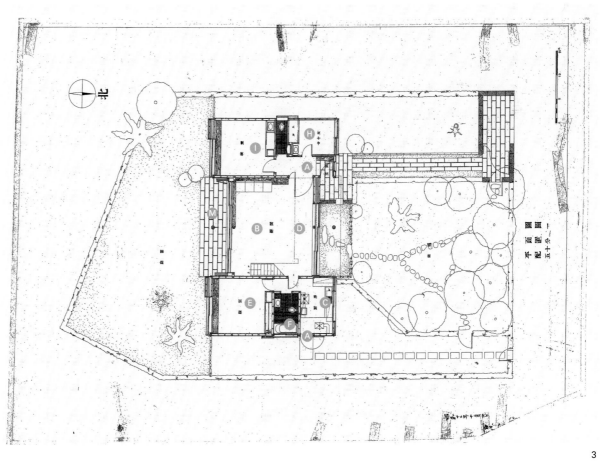

3

House No. 1
Kiyoshi Ikebe
Tokyo
1948

1

The period following World War II was one of urgent rebuilding in Japan, but also a time for rethinking the single-family home. These circumstances meant that architects had to contend with low budgets, widespread shortages of construction supplies, and rigid building-size restrictions, in addition to the national push towards modernization. Linked closely to Westernization, this overhaul had social, material and lifestyle implications. Many architects followed the example of their European peers by producing their ideal 'minimum house', which addressed these conditions and limitations. Though small,

inexpensive and quick to build, such buildings didn't skimp on design or function. But for Kiyoshi Ikebe, who worked under Junzo Sakakura on prefabricated houses during the war, industrialization was not the prime motive. Rather, he took this as an opportunity to rethink the disposition of space needed for a new lifestyle centred on the living room and kitchen. The first in a series of numbered houses, House No. 1 marked the beginning of what was to prove a lifelong quest.

Enclosed by a simple volume with a single slanted roof, the interior of No. 1 consisted of clearly defined but fluid functional zones that revolved around the stair core. While the living area, study, dining area and kitchen occupied the lower level, the bedroom and a workspace were upstairs. This efficient, pared-down plan made the most of the home's limited area while facilitating easy communication and a relaxed, family-oriented atmosphere. At the same time, the raised roof expanded the space vertically, providing space for the upper floor, which opened partially to below, and also for the high ceiling above the living area.

Ikebe's daughter Konomi, an urban planner, traces her father's interest in the minimum house back to tea. 'He really loved teahouses,' she explains, and it's easy to understand why they should hold this attraction. Created specifically for the carefully choreographed preparation and presentation of tea, some are no bigger than two *tatami* mats – just enough space for host and guest to serve and be served. Generated by a discrete sequence of actions, there is no need, or place, for anything more. This economy contributes to the exquisiteness of these miniature buildings, which have been an inspiration to many designers. According to the architect's architect granddaughter Mana, 'My grandfather wanted to incorporate the beauty of "no waste".'

1 A single, slanting roof united both levels
in a compact volume.

2 Upstairs, a small porch created a connection
to the outdoors.

3 Sections: (A) entrance, (B) living,
(C) kitchen, (E) sleeping, (F) bath, (I) study.

2

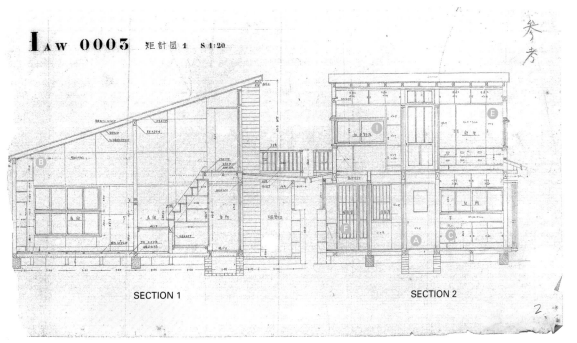

IAW 0003　矩計圖 1　S 1:20

参考

SECTION 1　　　　　　　　SECTION 2

3

Spotlight

The Site

Before construction of a new house commences in Japan, there is the land to consider. A common practice is to conduct the *jichinsai* ritual. This ceremony starts with designating a small portion of the empty lot with fresh bamboo stakes and rice rope. Here a Shinto priest presides over rites to purify the property, pray for the project's safe completion, and pacify the local deity that might be disturbed by the construction.[1] This ancient custom suggests the profound connection between homeowners and their land – no matter its size, shape or location.

But the value of property ownership in Japan is as much economic as it is spiritual. Though real-estate prices have dropped since their bubble-era highs in the late 1980s, they remain beyond the budget of many, especially in central Tokyo. Money is attached to the land, not the buildings. Families often struggle to keep their holdings – many must sell off parts just to cover the substantial inheritance taxes when property is passed down. If large homes hit the market intact, they are usually acquired by developers, who clear the site and divide it into as many saleable lots as possible. And then there are municipal projects, such as street widening, that slice through the urban fabric, often leaving awkward plots in their wake. For these and other reasons, peculiar conditions abound: the triangle; the long, skinny 'eel's nest'; the 'flagpole' connected to the street by a narrow lane; and parcels too diminutive for a crane or bulldozer.

Yet small sites are hardly new in Japan. For centuries, portions of Tokyo and other cities were riddled with narrow streets lined with tiny dwellings belonging to the lower classes. Many of these neighbourhoods were decimated by Allied bombs during World War II, which turned vast tracts of land into blank slates. While some architects envisioned grand rebuilding schemes, the web of streets remained largely intact and, bit by bit, new buildings filled the footprints of those destroyed during the war (opposite page). Over the years, redevelopment has been guided by numerous legal regulations. While rural sites face few limitations, lots in Tokyo are restricted not only by setbacks and curbs on the building's footprint, but also by the so-called 'sunshine laws' that preserve sunlight access for neighbours. Many of these laws chip away at the permissible building area. So does the municipal requirement for off-street parking for all car owners. But for architects, challenging site conditions can promote creativity.

1950s Restructuring and Recovery

The decade opened with the start of the Korean War. For Japan, this led to procurement contracts from the US military engaged in the conflict, boosting its economy as well as its steel production. These developments benefited the construction industry, even after the war ended in 1953.[1] By then the 1951 Treaty of Peace between Japan and the US had been signed, while the Allied Occupation had also concluded the following year.

Though the immediate post-war crises had passed, a significant housing shortage remained – even in 1955, some three million units were still needed. But this was partly because the expanding economy drew people to the cities.[2] Among other measures, the deficit was tackled with low-interest home-building loans provided to individuals by Japan's Housing Loan Corporation. Prior to the war, over seventy per cent of the housing in urban areas consisted of rental property; by 1955, sixty-four per cent was privately owned, reflecting post-war land reforms.[3]

Another intervention was the construction of subsidized *danchi* apartments by the Public Housing Authority.[4] These concrete complexes contained standardized, single-family units centred on the dining-kitchen area. This marked a decisive break from the traditional home, where eating and sleeping took place in the same space, and the kitchen, and therefore the housewife, was relegated to a dark corner. Labelled with the term 'nLDK' – an abbreviation for living, dining, kitchen plus an unspecified number of bedrooms – this plan type envisioned a new, modern lifestyle. And that spilled over into the form of architect-designed houses.

The 1950s was also the decade when Japan began recognizing the value of new notions of design, which separated conception from construction. A relatively recent import, this way of thinking dovetailed well with the growing production of consumer goods needed for a modern lifestyle prioritizing convenience, comfort and Western furnishings. Even houses themselves began to be mass-produced after the introduction of the so-called 'housemaker' prefabricated homes, for instance the Midget House produced by the Daiwa House Industry Co., Ltd from 1959.[5] Among the icons that debuted in the 1950s were Isamu Noguchi's Akari Light Sculptures, the repackaged Peace cigarettes fittingly authored by the American designer Raymond Loewy, and the electric rice cooker introduced by Tokyo Shibaura Electric Co., Ltd. In celebration of the country's emerging design culture, the Japanese government launched the Good Design awards in 1957.[6]

In architecture, the decade brought about many important buildings, mainly at home yet also abroad. In 1954, New York's Museum of Modern Art opened the Japanese Exhibition House, a wooden building designed by architect Junzo Yoshimura but based on sixteenth- and seventeenth-century prototypes. Meanwhile back in Japan, modernism was taking shape with the completion of Antonin Raymond's Reader's Digest Building, Kenzo Tange's Tokyo Metropolitan Government Building and Le Corbusier's National Museum of Western Art. But one of the most visible and emblematic monuments of the new era was Tokyo Tower, the red-and-white Eiffel Tower look-a-like completed in 1958 (opposite page).

1

Kano House
Junzo Sakakura
Tokyo
1950

factories and other building types that could be mass-produced by the military during the war. Subsequently, the architect repurposed his knowledge of prefabrication to help Japan rebuild its civilian housing stock.[1]

One of Sakakura's first ventures was the Kano House, which demonstrated the suitability of the easy-to-assemble A-frame to mass production. Fittingly, the client was the first president of Japan's public housing authority.[2] The building's most distinctive visual feature was the A-frame at either end, which both supported the weight of the pitched roof's ridge beam and stood strong against lateral forces – a chronic concern in an earthquake-prone country.

Inside, the layout was compact and efficient. The ground floor held a generous double-height living room – a luxurious touch in a house of modest stature – plus the kitchen and a bedroom, with the bath and lavatory in between. Connected by an open stair with an elegant curving rail, the first floor contained storage and a multipurpose space overlooking the living room. Ceiling-mounted light fixtures, dark wood trim, and furnishings designed by Sakakura all embellished the interior. A model for Japan's mass-produced housing, it graced the cover of the architectural journal *Shinkenchiku*, which resumed publication in 1946, shortly after the modest home's completion.[3]

2

From the 1940s onwards, the skills of many Japanese architects and designers were enlisted by the country's military. For Junzo Sakakura, this process began with investigating prototypes for prefabricated architecture for the Imperial Japanese Navy. Sakakura's introduction to prefabrication can be traced back to the A-framed construction system developed in France by Le Corbusier, Jean Prouvé and Charlotte Perriand, the last of whom brought drawings of this system to Sakakura when she travelled to Japan in 1940. Based on these, Sakakura developed barracks,

❶ The double-height living room from above.

❷ The home's distinctive A-frame structure expressed on the front elevation.

Raymond House and Studio in Azabu
Antonin and Noémi Raymond
Tokyo
1951

Antonin and Noémi Raymond were the first, and remain among the most successful, foreign designers to set up shop in Japan. And not just once, but twice. In part they were in the right place at the right time – first when Japan was developing rapidly in the 1920s, and then again shortly after World War II. Over these two periods, the duo produced a wide range of well-received buildings, including schools, hospitals, churches, embassies and, of course, houses.

Five of those houses were built for themselves. Most incorporated design studios as well as dwelling space. Perhaps this combination was an outgrowth of their days spent working with Frank Lloyd Wright at Taliesin, his home-studio in Wisconsin where they were invited to work in 1916. Later, it was Wright who brought the Raymonds to Japan to work on his Imperial Hotel in Tokyo.[5]

In 1921, the Raymonds parted from Wright but remained in Tokyo to open their own office. Shortly after, they built their first Tokyo home, a multi-storey reinforced-concrete edifice with modernist flare (see page 16). That house was sold before the couple exited Japan, just prior to the outbreak of World War II.[6] After returning in 1951, they completed their second Tokyo home, a modest timber structure in keeping with Japan's sombre mood and the scarcity of construction materials.

Located in the city centre, the site was expansive but littered with debris and rubble. 'In spite of this desolate appearance, I could see its advantages and possibilities,' wrote Antonin.[7] The house had two wings: the street-facing atelier in front and the residence at the back, with a covered walkway and a shared garden in between.

The house component was further divided into two parts. Flanking a covered terrace where the Raymonds dined in warm weather, one half held the bedroom, bathroom, kitchen and other private areas. The other contained the living room with its wood-burning fireplace, followed by a small studio. Transitioning from residence to workplace, this adjoined the office wing, which featured a large drafting room plus related functions.

The entire building was unified by a post-and-beam frame made of logs planed smooth but otherwise unfinished. As in traditional Japanese homes, this structure enabled window-walls of wood and glass that could be opened freely, merging inside and out. High clerestory windows washed the interior with soft daylight, while built-in furniture and textiles turned the rustic building into a relaxed home.

1 Muted sunlight bathed the dining area and covered terrace.

2 Deep roof eaves shielded the *shoji* screens on the south elevation facing the pool and garden.

2

1

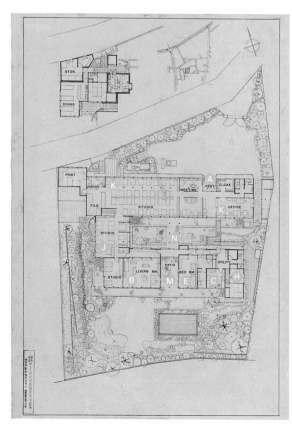

1 Looking out towards the pool and garden from the living room.

2 Plan: (A) entrance, (B) living, (C) kitchen, (E) sleeping, (H) maid's room, (J) studio, (K) office, (M) terrace, (N) courtyard.

3 The terrace doubled as the Raymonds' outdoor dining area in the warmer months.

2

Minimum House
Makoto Masuzawa
Tokyo
1952

and, separated by sliding *fusuma* panels for privacy, the family bedroom at the back. Off to the sides were the bath and the staircase up to the top floor. This loft-like space was open to below, and contained his-and-her work areas: the architect's study and his wife's sewing space. Conspicuously absent was anything *tatami*-covered. With beds for sleeping and chairs for sitting, the Minimum House maximized the modern Western lifestyle.

In the early 1950s, the Japanese government helped address the housing deficit by offering home-building loans. One catch was that any new construction could not exceed 50 square metres (538 square feet). Unsurprisingly, this limitation spawned numerous case studies for compact dwellings built from readily available materials. Many of these experimental homes were designed by architects for use by their own families.

At the time, Makoto Masuzawa was working for Antonin Raymond, himself a prolific residential designer. On his own watch, Masuzawa created this home for his wife and son on a generous property in central Tokyo. Like many of his mentor's works, Masuzawa used an exposed timber frame, a cost-conscious solution that enabled the construction of a two-storey dwelling. 'This was a rarity in Japanese homes, but stacking floors reduced the size of the foundation as well as the cost,' notes designer Makoto Koizumi, who has devised a contemporary version of Masuzawa's Minimum House. Expanding vertically also made the home seem bigger, an idea reflected in the facade. Drawing the eye upwards, the building front was composed of six panels – four of them sliding *shoji* screens – arranged in a square formation. These movable panels could be pushed aside to open up the interior.

The end panel also doubled as the main entrance (a side door for deliveries opened directly into the kitchen). A shoe cupboard marked the foyer, where the open floor plan was revealed. The ground level held the kitchen and the double-height dining area in the front,

❶ The facade was composed of six panels, four of them sliding *shoji* screens that opened the interior when pushed aside.

1 The double-height dining area was washed in soft daylight passing through the *shoji* screens.

2 The loft-like study area upstairs.

1

2

3

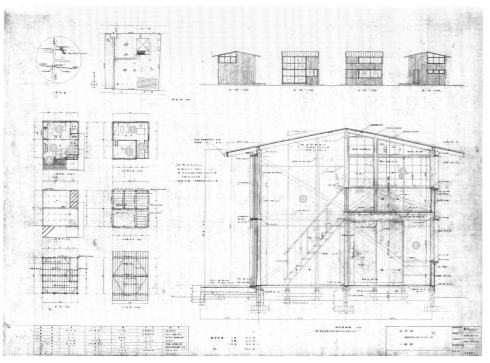

4

❸ Though unusual at the time, stacking two floor levels was an economic solution that reduced the size of the home's overall footprint.

❹ Ground-floor plan (left), first-floor plan (right), elevations and section: (A) entrance, (C) kitchen, (D) dining, (E) sleeping, (I) study, (J) studio, (L) void.

1

SH-1
Kenji Hirose
Kanagawa Prefecture
1953

Hirose's impetus for the construction was his recent marriage. Keen to make a home of their own, the newly-weds chose a property in Hirose's hometown, Kamakura, and the architect got to work on a modest house and garden. 'Basically, it was one room divided by furniture,' explains Ryunosuke Hiraga, an architect and former student of Hirose's. Only the bathroom and closet had bona fide walls and doors. Everywhere else, built-in elements such as the large *petika* – a Russian-style radiant heater made of brick – and the three-quarter-height shelving units separated functional areas. This resulted in a sparely appointed but fluid space. 'It was a minimal house with very simple details,' comments Hiraga.

The divide between inside and out was similarly ambiguous. Complemented by segments of brick wall, the south and west sides opened to the garden with sliding glass panels supported by a lightweight steel frame and X-shaped tension rods. By 1953, steel was readily available in Japan but had yet to be used much for houses. Strong, affordable and machine-made, it was an industrial material with great architectural potential – Hirose recognized these qualities, and their significance for an important growth area for his profession. '[Hirose] felt keenly that mass production of houses was an absolute necessity given Japan's post-war circumstances,' writes Professor Shin-ichi Okuyama of the Tokyo Institute of Technology. '[He made] a system that was cheaper than wooden construction and capable as well of mass production.'[8] In so doing, Hirose laid the groundwork for many architects who followed.

2

During World War II, the skills of designers of all sorts were called up by the military. Joining their ranks, the architect Kenji Hirose was tasked with designing aeroplane hangars – simple, utilitarian structures made with a limited material palette. Perhaps this experience influenced the design of his own house, built shortly after launching his practice in 1952. The first of seventy-two projects in his 'Steel House' series, which lasted almost twenty years, Hirose dubbed it 'SH-1'.

❶ Occupying a narrow slot of space, the kitchen was sequestered behind the brick *petika* radiant heater.

❷ Light-weight steel and glass formed the thinnest of barriers between inside and out in the living room.

1

1. The solid brick wall panel on the east side enables the transparency elsewhere.

2. Plan: (A) entrance, (B) living, (C) kitchen, (D) dining, (E) sleeping, (F) bath.

3. The living room was loosely partitioned with well-placed furniture.

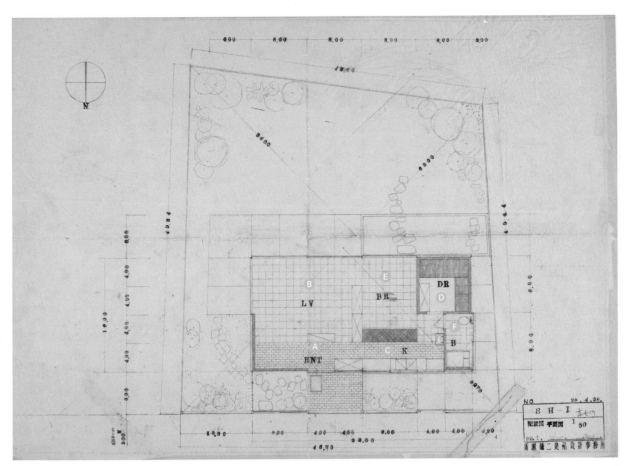

2

3

Tange House
Kenzo Tange
Tokyo
1953

Among Japanese architects, few, if any, have had the impact of Kenzo Tange. Early in his career, he emerged as a leader, garnering commissions for the Hiroshima Peace Memorial and Museum in 1949; the Tokyo Metropolitan Government Building, completed in 1957; and the Yoyogi National Gymnasium for the 1964 Tokyo Olympics. His influence extended even further through writing and teaching. Among his University of Tokyo students were Fumihiko Maki, Arata Isozaki and Kisho Kurokawa – all became luminaries in the field. Though residential work was not a Tange mainstay, the home he designed for his young family shares ideas with his large-scale works. Perhaps more importantly, it is a superior example of the push and pull of Japanese tradition and Western modernism,

a theme throughout architecture in Japan at that time.

The family home was in Tokyo's Seijo area, standing towards the back of the plot, facing a large lawn. Consistent with community norms, there was neither fence nor wall. Instead, a grassy berm loosely defined the property, but welcomed the neighbourhood children – with ginkgo trees to climb and a sandbox beneath the house, it was a popular spot. 'Even when it rained, I could play outside,' recalls Tange's daughter, Michiko Uchida.

This outdoor area resulted from elevating the house on piloti columns – also an important strategy at the Hiroshima Peace Memorial and the Tokyo Metropolitan Government Building. From here, stairs ascended to the living space: one big, mainly *tatami*-floored room, with the sleeping quarters at one end; Tange's study at the other; and the kitchen, bath, sitting and dining areas in between. The only private place was the maid's room behind the stair. The spaces were partitioned by sliding paper panels, or *shoji*, facing the *engawa*-like porch outside and the opaque *fusuma* panels inside. Some of the latter were coloured, others white, and a couple were adorned with paintings by the artist Toko Shinoda.

While Tange drew from a traditional vocabulary, many components were rendered in a modern way. As in historic homes, he used a measurement module, but he adjusted the proportions, with a ripple effect throughout the house. Architectural historian Saikaku Toyokawa explains that standard dimensions could not accommodate both the *zabuton* floor cushions and low-scale chairs that marked Tange's desired lifestyle.[9] In turn, the sight lines from these seated positions determined the heights of railings and other horizontal benchmarks. Visually, these bands tied the house together in a unified whole.

1 Sliding *fusuma* panels, adorned with an abstract painting by artist Toko Shinoda, in the architect's study.

2 Mixing Japanese- and Western-style furnishings, the Tange family, seated on *zabuton* cushions and a chair, gathered around a short-legged *chabudai* table.

2

1

UPPER LEVEL

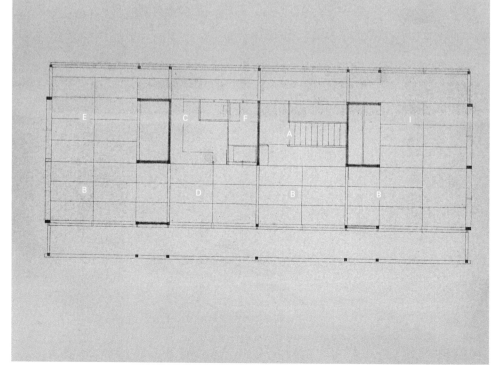

❶ Stairs in the covered piloti space lead up to the entrance.

❷ Plan: (A) entrance, (B) living, (C) kitchen, (D) dining, (E) sleeping, (F) bath, (I) study.

❸ A gentle berm drew a soft boundary around the house and its expansive lawn.

❹ Site plan including the ground-floor area under the piloti.

2

3

SITE PLAN

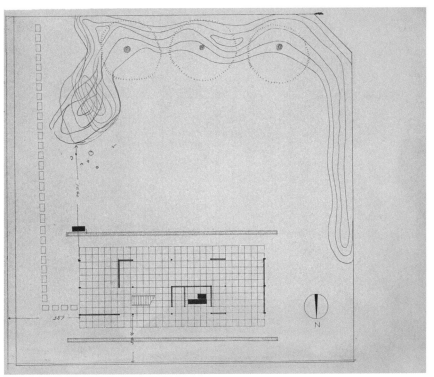

4

At Home Tange House

Michiko Uchida

I moved to that unconventional house in Seijo, a residential neighbourhood on the west side of Tokyo, at the end of 1953, just as I became old enough to be aware of my surroundings. Designed by my father, this house formed the backdrop to my childhood and is packed with memories of the formative years I spent there until the age of seventeen.

The Seijo area was created when the parents of students moved there to build the Seijo Gakuen educational institute. My mother's family moved there when my mother was of kindergarten age. Among these parents were many celebrated academics and intellectuals, and in those days Seijo was populated by people who identified with the free-thinking that flourished at Seijo Gakuen. My family's home there was the first and last house my father ever designed. This was at around the same time as he produced the Hiroshima Peace Memorial Park, having won the design competition, and I see some similarities.

For a child, the house was heaven. Consistent with the philosophy of the educational institute, there was a rule forbidding the construction of high walls in Seijo in those days. Rather than an imposing front gate, each house had just a low hedge. The town had an open atmosphere, and everyone could casually drop by one another's houses. My father followed the rules and created an artificial hill rather than a wall. This hill surrounded an expanse of lawn. There were no trees or bushes apart from three large ginkgo trees that had been on the land for many years, as well as a small amount of bamboo and bamboo grass. The garden was just like a small public park – anyone could freely enter.

When I got home from school I would run around the garden, climbing the ginkgo trees and the hill, which seemed like a huge mountain to me at the time. I remember hiding treasures in a biscuit tin and burying it at the base of the middle ginkgo tree. Beads I had found, marbles, sweets – trifling little things, but they were my prized possessions. In December, when the ginkgo trees lost their leaves, the entire lawn turned a beautiful bright yellow, and playing in those leaves is one of my happy childhood memories (left).

The house was raised on piloti (opposite page left), which I think was unusual, or perhaps the first example, at that time. There were no rooms on the ground floor and life went on upstairs on the first floor. The space around the piloti provided a wonderful play area where we had a sandpit with blocks and could ride our bicycles and play outside even when it was raining.

The entry hall was up the stairs in the centre of the piloti area. There were entrances on both the left and the right, and opening the left-hand door gave an expansive view over the garden. Going inside, there was a living area that extended around a central core, and when all of the *fusuma* sliding doors were opened, the entire house became a wide open single space. The floor was *tatami*, but unlike ordinary Japanese-style rooms, the *tatami* mats were laid out in straight rows.

The width of the mats was also slightly narrower than the standard, and we used chairs rather than sitting on the *tatami*. My father wrote somewhere that, when designing the house, he contemplated where to situate the centre of the space and decided that eye level, when sitting in a low chair, was the most pleasing. This appears to be the height at which the windows and the handrail of the *engawa* were placed. Also, if you look closely at the grid of the *shoji*, you will see that the spacing of the bottom three levels is slightly different in order to match that line. I think that it is this kind of attention to detail by my father (right) that made the house beautiful.

The *fusuma* dividing the rooms were also non-standard dimensions, and they were colourful – vermilion and indigo. Even though the architectural details were the same as those used in other Japanese houses of the time, the house had a completely different feel. Red-canvas lounge chairs and other furnishings gave it a very modern look.

I had several favourite places in the house. One was the maid's room behind a sliding door on the right-hand side of the entry hall. The space was like an extension of the hallway, but there was a desk and a closet with a pull-out bed inside, and as the only partitioned space in a house without any private rooms, I was a little envious of it. Another favourite place was the bathroom. Opening a sliding door allowed conversation with people in the dining area, and I enjoyed sitting in the bath watching TV or chatting with my father as he ate dinner after coming home late from work. Later, I was pleased to recognize what must have been his inspiration in a similar open bathroom connected to the living room in Le Corbusier's Villa Savoye in France.

The house had many visitors. Not only architects but artists and designers from Japan and overseas gathered there. International visitors included Walter Gropius, Charlotte Perriand and Isamu Noguchi. As well as a place for socializing, the house was used as a workplace, and I will always remember Kenzo Tange Laboratory staff working through the night as a deadline approached.

I regret that the house no longer exists, and I feel an odd affection for my childhood self, who grew up thinking that it was normal. I think that my ideas of beauty and comfort have their origins in that beautiful house and garden in Seijo. Perhaps my father's perfect modules were unknowingly ingrained in my consciousness – from the spaciousness created by the whole house being one open space, to the height of the windows and railings, the subtle spacing of the *shoji* screens and the size of the *tatami* mats.

Some people say that the house should be rebuilt, but my view is that the architecture existed together with the atmosphere and personality of the town of Seijo as it was in those days. Townhouses now stand on the site of the house. However, the three ginkgo trees remain. I wonder whether the treasures I buried as a child are still there.

My Home I
Kiyoshi Seike
Tokyo
1954

1

The story of My Home I begins in 1935, when Kiyoshi Seike's father purchased a plot of land in Tokyo with a two-storey wooden house in situ. As adjacent lots became available, he bought those too, eventually accumulating a property of 1,000 square metres (10,800 square feet). On a portion of this land, perpendicular to his parents' home, Seike built this 50-square-metre (538-square-foot) home – the maximum size permitted for recipients of a government-issued loan. Though intended as retirement quarters for his father, it became the home of the architect, his wife and their

growing family. And there they remained until 1970, when Seike replaced his parents' house with My Home II (see page 132), and the family joined his mother and father next door.

Essentially a one-room dwelling, My Home I is a simple rectangular building enclosed within concrete walls on three sides and glass on the fourth, where sliding doors, which double as the home's entrance, open the compact interior to the expansive garden. Initially conceived as a shoes-on house, there is no traditional foyer. Instead, the garden's stone-paved terrace steps up and continues inside as the floor.

Within the house, the only fixed partitions are two short structural wall segments. Flanking the central living-dining area, one separates the kitchen and bathroom, the other the master bedroom and study. The latter served as the architect's office early on, with staff members plying their trade as the family ate breakfast a few steps away. Doors are conspicuously absent, even in the bathroom. 'When I was small, it was really very comfortable; I liked being able to chat with my father about school while he was shaving,' recalls the architect's daughter, Yuri Yagi. For the most part, functional zones are defined by cabinetry and curtains – airtight privacy was not a priority. But when his teenage daughter requested space of her own, the architect converted the bomb shelter below the house into bedrooms for the children.

Though rendered mainly with industrial materials and Western furniture, the flexible interior epitomizes Seike's embrace of *shitsurai*. This traditional use of movable furnishings to reconfigure rooms makes the most of the home's small space. Extending that idea, the *tatami*-covered platform Seike created for the house was a mobile mini room that could even be rolled outside. Playing multiple roles, this versatile piece served as seating (especially for those wearing *kimono*), a table when entertaining student groups, and even a bed for Yuri's younger sister.

2

❶ The house opens onto an expansive garden.

❷ A nighttime view looking into the living and dining area (left) and the study (right).

❸ A storage unit and curtain loosely partition the public and private zones within the house.

3

1 A mobile mini room, the *tatami* platform can be moved anywhere within the house or even outside.

2 Plan: (A) entrance, (B) living, (C) kitchen, (D) dining, (E) sleeping, (G) *tatami*, (I) study.

1

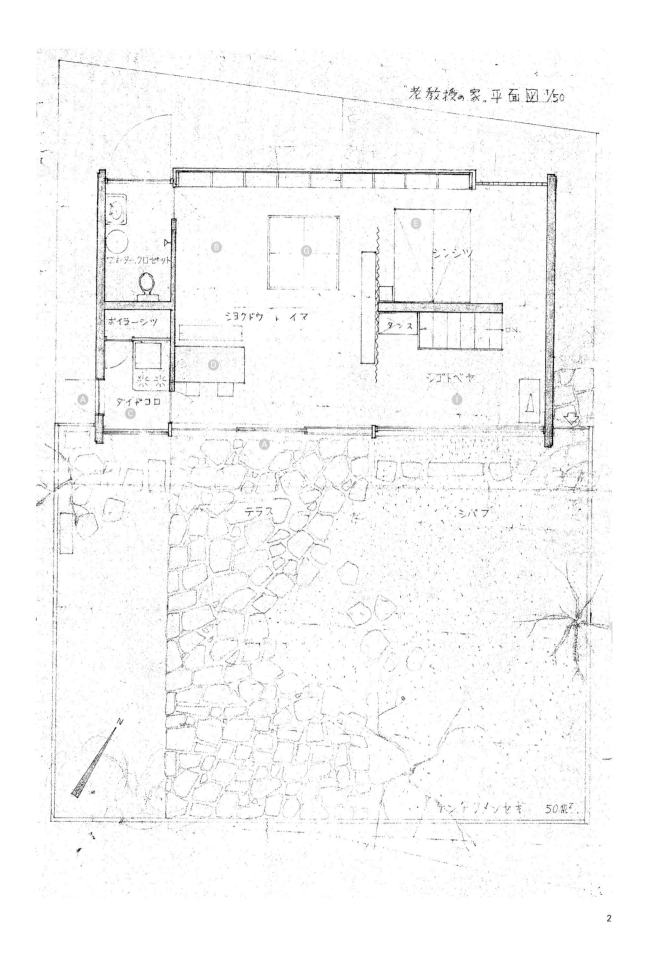

"老教授の家" 平面図 1/50

1

No. 17
Kiyoshi Ikebe
Tokyo
1954

chance not just to revisit the idea of connected dwellings – the two halves shared a common wall – but to try out other innovations, including a centrally located kitchen and the extensive use of glass. Modified with subsequent additions, the T-shaped building was a living, breathing architectural laboratory.

Prioritizing freedom of movement, the open-plan interior had few partitions or doors. Instead, furnishings – most created by the architect's wife Masako, who was also a designer – defined functional areas, with curtains to separate the bath and toilet, and glass walls to blur the divide between inside and out. 'He believed that lifestyle creates the space,' explains Ikebe's granddaughter Mana, herself an architect. A keen observer of human movement and activity, Ikebe continually promoted the reduction of women's housework by designing convenient kitchens in the middle of the house. In his own home, this took the form of a U-shaped kitchen and living room, which extended out into the garden, with the sleeping quarters upstairs. In 1968, the house was expanded by adding a second bedroom upstairs, plus an atrium, greenhouse and other modifications below.

Throughout the building, transparent walls were a defining feature – the house was affectionately known in the neighbourhood as the 'Glass House'.[11] 'My father really loved the primitive experience,' says Ikebe's daughter, Konomi. 'When it's cold, it is OK to feel a little cold.' In practice, however, the glass yielded warmth in winter and, with the help of *yoshizu* bamboo shades, coolness in summer. Another benefit was the close connection to the pond and garden beyond. Home to more than two hundred plant species, plus an array of birds and other creatures, No. 17 championed flora and fauna throughout the property. 'In contrast to a public garden, having a garden where you can plant trees and flowers and place stones as you like is especially important in terms of family life,' explained the architect.[12]

2

Over the course of his career, Kiyoshi Ikebe created some one hundred numbered houses. Among the most experimental was No. 17, a test case for a two-family home – one half belonged to an architect friend and the other to Ikebe, his wife and their daughter. 'When I designed my own house, I wanted to deal with as many problems as possible that I could not address when creating other people's houses,' wrote Ikebe at the time.[10] This was a

❶ The architect with his plants and bird in the greenhouse.

❷ Largely enclosed with glass, the sleeping quarters were upstairs, and the living room extended out into the garden below.

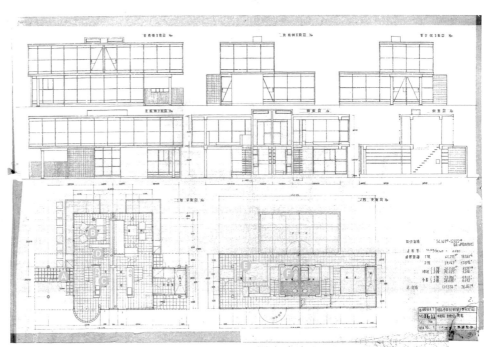

1 Viewed from the garden, the living room with chairs and other furnishings designed by Masako Ikebe.

2 Elevations, sections, ground-floor plan (left) and first-floor plan (right): (A) entrance, (B) living, (C) kitchen, (D) dining, (E) sleeping, (F) bath.

2

At Home No. 17

Konomi Ikebe and Mana Ikebe

The work of my father, Kiyoshi Ikebe, is often described using two terms: 'minimalist housing' and 'postmodernism'. Kiyoshi (above, with me on his lap) was a great lover of Japanese culture and nature. The rationality of the tea-ceremony room, and its ability to cultivate beauty in a small area, must have been his definitive model for architectural design that combined functionality with minimal space.

My father coined several terms, although 'small is beautiful' was his fundamental belief. The word 'small' here means 'refined' and refers to design devoid of unnecessary decoration. He wanted his designs to be modern, but at the same time elegant – a word he used to describe the beauty that he found in his wife's (my mother's) work (she was a textile designer) – and in the fashion choices of both his wife and daughter. He also liked to use the term 'sporegant' to describe a style that was both sporty and elegant. Ultimate elegance based on function was the ideal of beauty that he sought.

My father kept over thirty species of animals in his house, including seahorses and an owl. Years after the house was built, it was expanded to include my mother's studio and an atrium with a gum tree that had been planted when the house was first constructed. On days off, I let the owl, large parakeets and parrots loose in this atrium, which was separated from the living room by a glass wall. The atrium was always filled with life, and from the living room we could see the flowers and birds. My father did not have a study, preferring to sit in his living room, where his dog was always by his side.

On Sunday mornings, he worked in his garden. The plants came from Hakone, and later from other plant markets. Deciduous trees were planted near the pond that surrounded the house, and the garden was intended to be cool in summer and sunny in winter. He and my mother sometimes read *haiku* and *tanka* poems, and they cherished the changing of the seasons. It is a pity that the houses that Kiyoshi built are often perceived as inorganic, just because they are made of concrete and glass.

The house was filled with many pieces of furniture that he and my mother had designed together. The shelves that doubled as large partitions, along with casements designed by my mother, were decorated with reds, blues and yellows. The space he created was open, comfortable and inviting, with no corridors or doors.

Early on, the house was protected from the western sun by a screen, but my mother later created custom roll curtains for the space. Most of the motifs in these textiles were modelled after plants and birds. My mother also designed cubes made of cardboard and wrapped in colourful vinyl, which could be used to hold children's toys or books, and could also be stacked atop one another. Some of these pieces have been preserved in the house.
KONOMI IKEBE

I was born in 1988, ten years after my grandfather passed away. The house that he designed and constructed in Tokyo was the place where some of my fondest memories took shape. I made a sport of climbing up the concrete columns and fishing for frogs in the pond. The open-plan house gave me the freedom to build a LEGO railroad that stretched through two rooms. Even before I have any visual memories of the house, I remember pressing my fingertips on rough concrete walls and running my feet over the thick, threaded, colourful carpet. These textures from my childhood moulded the paths I would later pursue.

'Pirrrrrr-kekkyo, kekkyo.' In the spring, Japanese bush-warblers, white-eyes and tits would come by our cherry-blossom trees. My grandmother and I offered them leftover food on a plate balanced on a branch. At other times, we sat on the swings, enjoying a morsel of *akebi* fruit with the birds, who loved being around the pond. The pond continued into our neighbour's house, who, like my grandfather, was an architect and loved the idea of a simple terrace house structurally supported by our shared wall and columns.

I used to take naps on the carpet in the living room, which felt like an extension of the garden. Before falling asleep, I would stare in wonder at the abstract pattern on the curtains my grandmother had designed. Was it a sleeping dove? Or a *Cyperus* leaf turned upside down? Once I started elementary school, my grandmother showed me her pattern books, in which she catalogued and critiqued patterns from Japan, the rest of Asia, the Silk Road and the Muslim world. She loved to talk about civilizations across the globe.

One day, I heard a loud thud. A brown-eared bulbul had crashed into the glass. My grandmother rushed to calm me; she had been doing laundry in the greenhouse, where the orchids were in full bloom. 'Remember,' she said calmly, 'nature is your teacher. Rule number one: observe. Rule number two: observe more.' When my mother was a child, there were almost twenty birds in the greenhouse, including Chao the owl (below left, with my grandparents). They never kept Chao in a cage. Just as Kiyoshi intended, nature and humans coexisted in our glass house.

Come summer, the rough concrete on the dining-room floor was cool to the touch, a soothing reprieve from the heat. The east-facing windows were covered with a bamboo screen, and the light coming between the narrow wooden blinds was as delicate as the linen weaving through it. My grandmother was a talented cook, and she spent most of her time cooking in a beautiful U-shaped white kitchen. She recalled, 'Women used to cook in the northern part of a house, away from the sunlight, in cold kitchens where they were hidden from view. After the war, your grandfather and I suggested that kitchens be moved closer to the middle of the house. Sometimes, I had ideas that were different from your grandfather's. I integrated a small alcove into the design of our kitchen for my child to sit in so that I could watch her while I cooked. I was more intuitive in my designs, while Kiyoshi was more rational. He and I stayed up late arguing about which method was better.' I often did my homework across from the kitchen while the earthy aroma from freshly chopped leaf buds filled the whole house.

We had guests once in a while, mostly my grandmother's art students. 'Back when we were young, we all thought we had to choose between a design career or being a wife. But after I met Ikebe-sensei and your grandmother, I realized I had more freedom to follow my passion,' a guest of my grandmother's once told me with a smile. 'And I never wanted to leave Ikebe-sensei's house. There was always music, animals [opposite page, left], crafts and beautiful colours.'

Jumping into a thick pile of autumn leaves was pure joy. My grandmother revealed to me,

'When we first arrived, there was nothing but dirt, but we planted our first tree....Then we started going to the plant market every week. I had to keep a record, and in the end, there were two hundred kinds of trees.' My grandfather's love for the interesting coherence formed between rough primitiveness and nature was embodied in our house. He believed that the home was the critical nexus between humans and nature (below right), and because of that, we must be mindful of the resources and energy we use in order to keep the whole ecosystem in balance. Kiyoshi himself described the importance of this relationship:

'Nature is what gave birth to human beings, and it should naturally have equal or greater value than we do. However, our cities are being constructed in a way that implies that nature is merely a slave to serve human life. Such actions are threatening to exterminate the original nature and transform it into an artificial one. If such a pattern continues, humanity will go down a dangerous path in turning against the nature that originally supported us.'

My favourite thing about being in the house was that a sense of freedom permeated the space. There was no door in the bathroom. Almost every house in Japan had a *genkan*, an entryway just inside the front door to take your shoes off; we chose not to have one.

When I needed a break from the world, I would find solace in the arms of this house.

I can still hear my grandfather say, 'As long as you are doing your best to think things through, trying to find an answer, do not worry yourself with opinions that are assumed right by society. Regardless of your status, anyone can make strong decisions through effort and experimentation.'

Twenty years later, I am spending a winter in my childhood living room. The house and its vicinity have completely changed, and many apartments have replaced the former natural surroundings. My grandmother's table, chairs, counter, carpet and tapestries – all the interior elements my grandfather called 'unchanging things' – were moved to our new house, which utilized a barrier-free design. My grandfather believed in an organic relationship between 'changing' things and 'unchanging' things. Architecture should continue to evolve as society evolves, but we should strive to preserve the interconnectedness of humans, nature and energy consumption. The philosophy that Kiyoshi adopted and helped sustain continues to be an important contribution to people's lives in this modern age.
MANA IKEBE

1

Taro Okamoto
House
Junzo Sakakura
Tokyo
1954

keen to rebuild on the site, this time with a combined home and studio. Despite his strong aesthetic leanings, he gave the architect free rein over the building's design. As expressed by the roof's unusual construction, Sakakura's two-part building was divided vertically into a home and a studio. The latter was a soaring double-height space that faced the garden to the north, but was enclosed with smoked glass that admitted soft daylight – a priority for the artist. 'Clear glass would have been too bright,' explains former Sakakura Associates staff member Noribumi Kitamura.

Upstairs, a narrow book-lined gallery partially ringed Okamoto's workspace. Adjacent to this was the primary living space, the main areas of which were located on the first floor. Accessed by a run of straight stairs up from the studio, or by a sculptural spiral from the ground-floor entry foyer (perhaps a polite nod to Sakakura's mentor), these included the kitchen and sleeping areas as well as a multipurpose space overlooking the studio. Serving as a study as well as the dining room, it featured a free-form table plus chairs designed by Okamoto. Weighing in on the tile colours and other details that were to tailor his new space, the artist was known to pay daily visits to the construction site.[13]

2

Capped by a double-barrelled monocoque roof, the Taro Okamoto House makes a bold statement. Given the persona of the client, an avant-garde artist known for large murals and public sculptures, this comes as no surprise. Among Okamoto's best-known works is the colossal Tower of the Sun statue (see page 130), the centrepiece of Osaka's Expo '70, which was laid out by Kenzo Tange. For his residence, Okamoto enlisted his friend Junzo Sakakura – they had first met in Paris while the young architect was working for Le Corbusier.

Okamoto's childhood house had been destroyed during World War II, and he was

❶ The artist working at the free-form table of his own design.

❷ The monocoque roof quietly defines the studio and home as seen on the rear elevation.

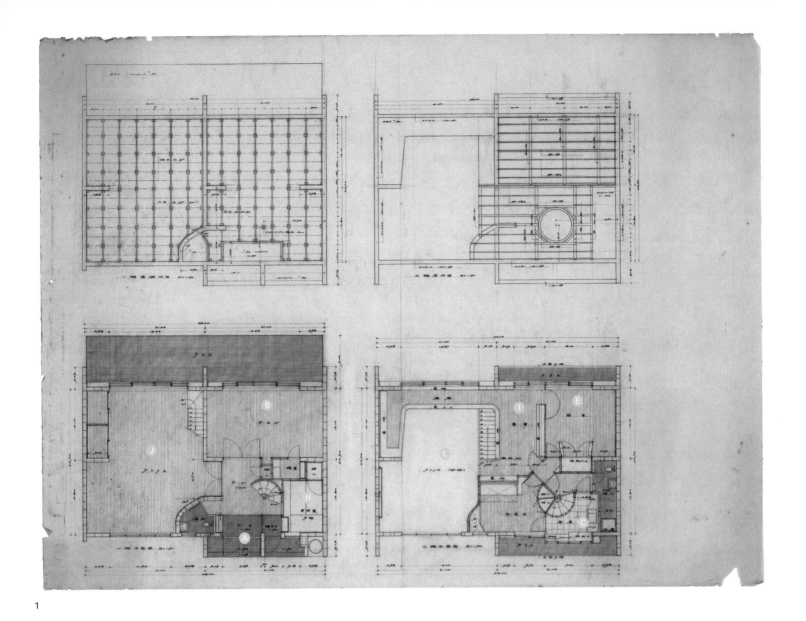

1

1 Ground-floor plan (left) and first-floor plan (right): (A) entrance, (B) living, (C) kitchen, (E) sleeping, (H) maid, (I) study, (J) studio, (L) void.

2 The artist's double-height studio with floor-to-ceiling filtered glass.

2

77

Ura House
Takamasa Yoshizaka
Hyogo Prefecture
1956

1

It was in Paris that Takamasa Yoshizaka and his client first met. Both had come from Japan to advance their careers, the designer as an apprentice in the atelier of Le Corbusier and the client as a student of mathematics. During visits to buildings by Yoshizaka's employer, the two cemented their relationship. After returning to Japan, the mathematician asked his architect friend to design his home. Inspired by his experience overseas, the client wanted a shoes-on home perched on piloti, with separate areas for communal and private spaces.

Giving form to these requests, Yoshizaka proposed two single-storey boxes elevated by columns, four per box. One volume holds the kitchen, living and dining rooms (plus a Japanese-style room for the client's mother) and the other the bath and bedrooms. Between the boxes is the entrance hall, where stairs lead down to the ground level, a covered but exterior space. Instead of sequestering the home, this design connects it to its surroundings, a residential area near the client's Kobe University workplace.

In part, Yoshizaka achieved this openness by placing the columns in the middle of the walls. This freed up the corners, making the area below the boxes less room-like and more a continuation of the outdoors. Extending up two storeys, these smooth concrete pillars are flanked by rough, red-brick walls. This highly textured surface creates shadows and controls heat gain, according to Yuko Saito, a former staff member at Yoshizaka's practice. Inside, bricks are recast as an interior finish, alongside exposed concrete and, at the entrance, a stained-glass wall arranged in an abstract composition of red, blue and yellow rectangles. Like Le Corbusier, Yoshizaka designed everything, down to the details and furnishings, including cabinetry and a vanity mirror whose organic shape recalls the freeform geometry of his mentor.

For Yoshizaka, this commission was not just a chance to design a dwelling. It also had urban implications. 'The individual house is an important component of the townscape,' explains Saito. Like building blocks, Ura House's boxy units were designed to be repeated, replicated, and used to create a welcoming residential neighbourhood.

❶ Clad with textured brick, the house consists of two cubic volumes perched on piloti columns.

❷ The stained-glass window-wall in the entrance.

❸ Plan: (A) entrance, (B) living, (C) kitchen, (D) dining, (E) sleeping, (F) bath, (G) *tatami*.

2

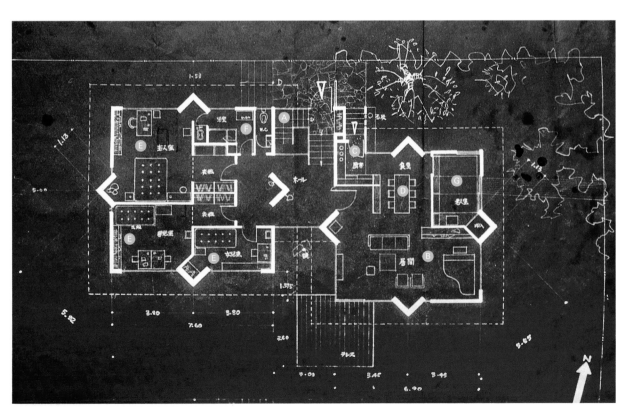

3

House at
Minami-Dai
Junzo Yoshimura
Tokyo
1957

Approached from the car park by a stone path, the house is entered on the north side. Located in the middle of the house, the foyer segues into the living room – the home's centrepiece, ringed by the music and dining rooms, the kitchen and a covered *engawa* porch. 'When the windows are open, we sense the seasons from the sounds,' says Takako. Instead of corridors, rooms connect to rooms, with sliding *fusuma* and *shoji* panels to partition spaces when needed. Mediating between interior and exterior, the wood deck opens onto the carp pond and an expansive garden beyond. 'In the winter, we made snowmen in the garden,' recalls Takako. 'In the summer, we converted the pond into a small children's pool.'

The home's horizontal flow evokes the spirit of historic houses, but it is punctuated by moments of well-placed verticality. Used for practice as well as performances, the music room is topped with a high slanted ceiling. 'Maybe that's why the acoustics are so good,' speculates Takako, also a professional musician. A later addition was the double-height kitchen, where the void space above promotes air circulation in the middle of the house and allows daylight to filter down – a sharp contrast with the dark kitchens of traditional Japanese homes. 'The morning sun coming in from the high east-facing window is particularly pleasant,' says Takako.

1

With much of Tokyo levelled by fire bombings, few houses in the city were left standing at the end of World War II. One exception was a two-storey hilltop home with a river below and rice paddies nearby. In 1946, the property was purchased by the architect Junzo Yoshimura and his wife, a professional musician. Over the next ten years, they conducted a sequence of renovations as rooms were added, subtracted and reconfigured. Among the first additions were a new music room and a bedroom for the couple's young daughter, Takako. An elegant blend of Japanese and Western lifestyles, the house soon became a gathering place for friends and family, as well as the setting for small concerts.

❶ Full-height sliding doors connect the living room to the garden.

❷ Crossing cultures, *shoji* screens and an expressed wood frame defining the living-room space coexist amiably with Western-style furniture.

❸ The architect (left) with relatives in front of his house.

❹ Plan: (A) entrance, (B) living, (C) kitchen, (D) dining, (F) bath.

2

3

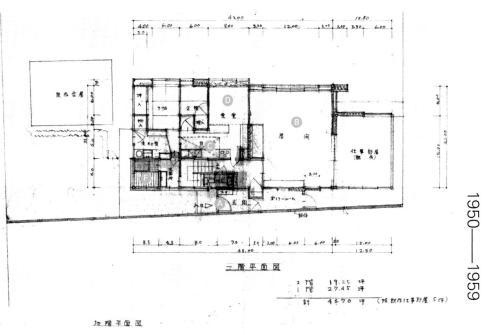

一階平面図

2階　19.25　坪
1階　27.45　坪

計　46.70　坪　(別棟仕事部屋 5坪)

初階平面図

4

1

Sky House
Kiyonori Kikutake
Tokyo
1958

2

Square in plan and elevated by massive piers at the midpoint of each of its four sides, Sky House has a pure geometry not often seen in Tokyo houses. There is nothing missing from its balanced, symmetrical and stable form. But this house was earmarked for change even before its concrete had cured. Unsurprisingly, it was designed by a leader of Japan's Metabolist movement, which promoted architectural schemes with a built-in capacity for renewal. Sky House was a chance for Kiyonori Kikutake to prove his point but, more importantly, to enjoy a home that could grow, as well as shrink, in harmony with his family.

Aided by his mother-in-law, Kikutake chose a hilltop site with splendid views of Gokokuji Temple nearby and, at that time, the Diet Building in the distance. Elevating the single-storey house maximized these vistas, but also provided a separate space between the piloti piers below for the architect's studio. Initially, the house consisted of one large room rimmed by a covered porch that opened the interior like a traditional *engawa*. 'It was a great place for moon-viewing,' recalls the architect's daughter, Yuki. Within the room, Western-style furniture defined functional areas, but these pieces, along with parts of the building itself, could easily be rearranged. Located on the porch, the galley kitchen and compact bathroom were contained within 'movenett' units – a term coined by Kikutake to describe the house's movable (and replaceable) mini rooms – so they could be popped out or plugged in at various points along the building's perimeter.

When children came along, more movenetts were added. Wooden boxes were suspended below the main room, each with a single window and just enough space for a bed, table, closet and a window. 'It was extremely small but extremely fun,' explains Yuki. But by the time Yuki turned five, the house needed enlarging and the hanging movenetts had to go. 'As our family grew, we didn't want to stop living in Sky House, so we expanded the space beneath the house instead,' explains Yuki. At first, this area held a sunroom and bedrooms, with the living room taking over the top floor. A second renovation transformed the sunroom into the living room, and the upper floor into a place for formal events – a nod to Kikutake's childhood home, where a large sitting room had been the scene of many neighbourhood gatherings.[14]

1 Initially, the house consisted of one single-storey, square space wrapped by a covered porch.

2 Suspended boxes, called 'movenetts', were added later for children's bedrooms.

1

2

❶ The living area.

❷ Housed in 'movenett' boxes, the kitchen (shown above) and bathroom could, in theory, be moved around the house perimeter.

❸ A cosy, child's bedroom inside a 'movenett'.

3

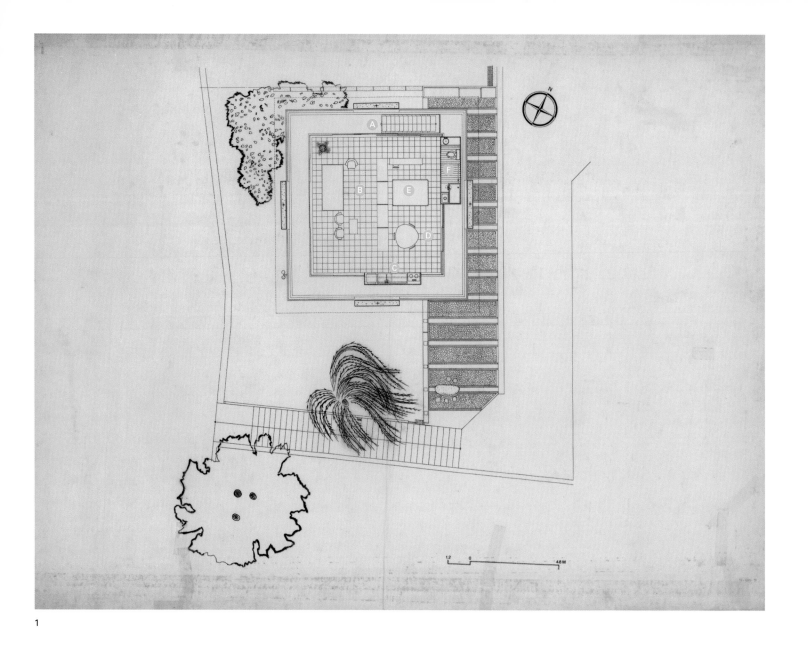

1 Plan: (A) entrance, (B) living, (C) kitchen,
(D) dining, (E) sleeping, (F) bath.

At Home
Sky House

Yuki Kikutake

Sky House is a house with a system that allows for free expansion and renovation. Throughout my father's life, he experimented with living, function and space as its inhabitants grew from two people to a family with three children and a dog named Mary (above). Through Sky House, he showed the ideal form of a house: make an indoor space with a large degree of freedom for living; use movable and variable devices (he called them 'movenetts') as the kitchen and bathroom; and open up the space to the outside with a garden and pilotis located below.

When the building was completed, the pilotis were lined with stones to create a space for barbecues, while the rest of the space around the house was planted with bamboo and other plants. By the time my siblings and I were in elementary school, egg-shaped swings made of woven rattan had been hung and playground equipment such as iron bars set up in the piloti area, so we could play to our heart's content every day regardless of the weather. At the time, my father took seriously our innocent suggestion that we wanted a swimming pool with a slide, and tried to build one. Of course, my mother rejected our idea.

The exterior plantings were also modified little by little. Starting with the addition of the *tsukubai* stone washbasin and a bamboo channel called *shishi-odoshi* or 'deer scarer' (a traditional device for startling animals), a small water stream was created with a gentle curve. Beside the stream, azaleas from my father's hometown, Kurume, were planted, and a wisteria trellis was built on the southwest side of the property. The shape of the wisteria trellis has changed, but it still exists today.

What was special for the children was the planting of the willow tree, the symbol of Sky House. The willow, which grew nearly 7 metres (23 feet) tall, was a reminder of the four seasons. The sight of the buds swelling up on the fallen branches in spring, and the leaves flourishing and fluttering in the wind, was a pleasant one, and is vividly etched in my mind as the original scenery of my childhood. One summer in the 1970s, a typhoon brought down a willow tree. I clearly remember the whole family praying through the shutters on the balcony that the willow would not fall over and watching the moment it did. My father's sketch of the willow can be seen on the floor plan of Sky House from that era. After that, he covered the pilotis with glass and made a greenhouse as an experiment in passive solar energy, but now it is used as a living space.

The most striking feature of the exterior is the bamboo rain gutter. It blends in with the concrete walls in such a way that it is hard to imagine any other material but bamboo. Freshly cut bamboo is always beautiful, but I am fascinated by this old, faded bamboo gutter. Looking back, I realize once again that my father had a deep appreciation for Japanese trees, flowers and the four seasons.

Last but not least, I still encounter geckos at Sky House. Although they were unpleasant reptiles for children, my parents taught us that geckos are important and auspicious creatures. I believe that, whenever a gecko is around, it will protect Sky House as long as I can see it.

Spotlight

The Roof

Whether hipped or pitched, thatched or tiled, the roof of the Japanese home has historically been a strong visual feature symbolizing the domain of the extended family. But it has also been, and remains, a defining architectural element of the country's villages, towns and cities. Despite the rise in skyscrapers and vast urban developments, low-scale buildings and single-family homes dominate Japanese cityscapes. From above, even Tokyo seems to be blanketed with small roofs as far as the eye can see.

The primacy of the Japanese roof can be traced back to the pit dwellings of the Jomon period (10,500–300 BCE), which had the appearance of a roof sitting directly on the ground. Over the centuries, a wide range of residence styles, and therefore roof forms, developed. While *machiya* townhouses congregated in the cities, *minka* farmhouses dotted the countryside. Constructed in response to local climates, materials and, in the case of *minka* especially, agricultural practices, all were topped with angled roofs (opposite page).

The development of new construction materials and methodologies, which ramped up after World War II, led to the proliferation of house types topped by an assortment of roofs. Among the most dramatic changes was the rise of the flat roof, which accompanied the introduction of steel and concrete. Coupled with computer technology, these materials subsequently yielded entire buildings topped by sculptural forms, fragmented planes or tent-like covers. Despite the country's long predilection for slanted roofs, formal, material or stylistic constraints seldom limit architects in Japan when it comes to topping out.

Instead, legal restrictions have the greater impact on roof design. In addition to numerous setback regulations, houses in urban areas are subject to the so-called 'sunshine laws'. Introduced in the 1970s, these rules protect neighbours' access to sunlight, which is often threatened by new construction.[1] But these limits often result in awkwardly shaped buildings, especially when paired with the small lot size typical in cities such as Tokyo. Squeezing as much house as legally possible onto these properties can lead to unusual building profiles, pointy tops, or shapes that are barely recognizable as roofs.

But the roof can also enlarge the client's usable space. For many, a house is not a home if it does not have a place to air *futon* bedding, dry laundry or tend potted plants. In addition to serving these specific functions, the roof can also provide outdoor space when there isn't room at ground level. And all within the privacy of one's own home.

1960—1969

1960s
The Economic
Miracle

The 1960s was a period of meteoric growth for Japan. At the start of the decade, the size of the national economy was just ten per cent of that of the United States. By the end, Japan had the second largest gross domestic product in the world.[1] The population of the greater Tokyo area grew past twenty million in 1965.[2] And, with economic prosperity, consumer goods proliferated countrywide – the TV, refrigerator and washing machine were lauded as the 'three sacred treasures'. Leaving both defeat and recovery behind, it was the decade of Japan's rebirth: Tokyo hosted the 1964 Olympic Games, the Beatles played the Tokyo Budokan in 1966, and the novelist Yasunari Kawabata received Japan's first literature Nobel Prize in 1968. Once again, the world began turning its attention to Japan. This time with awe and admiration.

The decade kicked off with the World Design Conference in 1960. During this landmark event, architects and designers from Japan, Europe and the United States congregated in Tokyo. It was here that Japan's Metabolists debuted their home-grown approach to urban and architectural development. Promoting design that could evolve, or metabolize, over time, their concept stemmed in part from Japan's traditional embrace of nature. But their forms were decidedly futuristic. Extending out into Tokyo Bay, architect Kenzo Tange's Metabolism-infused 'Tokyo Plan, 1960' featured a highway spine encircled with rings of civic and commercial facilities.[3]

Though few Metabolist projects made it off the drawing board, the decade gave rise to an unprecedented building boom. The revision of the Building Standard Law in 1963 relaxed height restrictions, which enabled the construction of Japan's first skyscraper – central Tokyo's thirty-six-storey Kasumigaseki Building – to begin two years later.[4] Also, the New Urban Housing Act of 1963 promoted the development of suburban 'bedtowns', such as Senri New Town at the edge of Osaka.[5] For architects of private homes, it was a time of liberation. They had access to emerging technologies, a broader variety of construction materials, and clients with discretionary income. Conceptual expression was no longer eclipsed by practical need.

As in other parts of the globe, the 1960s were also a decade marked by social unrest. The evolving military alliance with the United States, affirmed by the US–Japan Security Treaty of 1960, provoked repeated student protests decrying the permanent US military presence within Japan. A series of environmental pollution crises, including the Minamata mercury poisonings, underscored the costs of rapid industrialization.

But the seminal event of the decade was the 1964 Tokyo Olympics. Much more than an international sporting competition, it invited the world to experience the new Japan. In preparation, the country undertook transformative redevelopment projects, including the erection of Tokyo's elevated expressway system and the launch of the Shinkansen bullet-train network (opposite page). In a first for the games, a specially appointed design committee oversaw the production of Sori Yanagi's Olympic torch; Masaru Katsumi's pictograms intended to assist non-Japanese speakers; and Yusaku Kamekura's iconic poster featuring Japan's red sun hovering over the interlocking Olympic rings. Like Tange's Yoyogi National Stadium, an engineering feat defined by a swooping tensile roof, these endeavours welcomed the crowds and proclaimed Japan's creative might.

1

No. 58
Kiyoshi Ikebe
Tokyo
1960

technological departure, No. 58 was his first curvilinear roof.

Located in a residential Tokyo neighbourhood, the single-storey house was designed for a pair of painters who wanted to live and work in one place. 'The focus of their life was their studio, which forms the spatial centre of the house,' noted Ikebe.[2] Coming in from the carport, the entrance led to the kitchen, which segued into the dining area. Partially sequestered behind a three-quarter-height storage wall, the bedroom stood on one side and the studio on the other. Here the ceiling soared up, skylights admitted plenty of daylight, and pegboard walls held art and various accoutrements of daily life. The bathroom, maid's room and storage were concentrated at the back, while south-facing sliding glass doors opened the living and work spaces to a narrow terrace. Jutting out beyond the exterior wall, the roof hovered overhead, providing a degree of protection from sun and rain.

In many ways, the roof's distinctive shape was an expression of the time. With the difficult recovery from World War II receding and the economy growing steadily, the 1960s were ripe for experimentation and the emergence of new technologies, among them the bending of laminated wood to make curved forms. One famous example, Sori Yanagi's now iconic Butterfly Stool made of moulded plywood, debuted in 1954. Similarly, but on a much larger scale, the roof of No. 58 was made by bending synthetic slate panels, normally used for industrial buildings.

The furniture and textiles in No. 58 were designed by the architect's wife, Masako. Echoing the roof, a curved wooden coffee table and rattan chairs exemplified her design talent and aesthetic sensibility. 'They really cupped the body,' recalls the architect's daughter, Konomi.

2

'The roof is the real symbol of the house,' wrote Kiyoshi Ikebe in 1954.[1] Indeed, the roof of No. 58 – a name designating its position in an ongoing series of experimental houses – was its defining feature. Its corrugated surface rose straight up to form a double-height end wall, and then angled down dramatically to enclose the interior, before cantilevering out over the carport. Though Ikebe was no stranger to curved forms, which he had previously used for staircases and other discrete elements, his earlier houses had favoured rectilinear volumes, topped by a flat or pitched roof. Marking a point of aesthetic as well as

❶ Soaring, skylit space was used for the artists' studio.

❷ The monolithic roof yielded deep eaves above the terrace and provided passive sun screening.

1

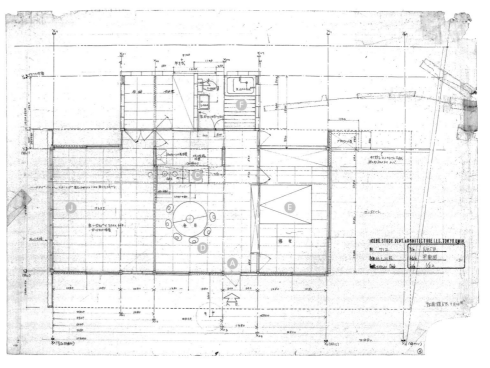

1 The combined kitchen and dining area, with furnishings designed by the architect's wife Masako, formed the centre of the house.

2 Plan: (A) entrance, (C) kitchen, (D) dining, (E) sleeping, (F) bath, (J) studio.

3 Pegboard partitions held works of art in the studio (beyond), as well as all manner of household goods in the kitchen.

2

3

1

Umbrella House
Kazuo Shinohara
Tokyo
1961

Though initially drawn to mathematics, Shinohara changed direction in 1950 when he began studying architecture under Kiyoshi Seike.[3] This was a critical time for an architect to come of age, since World War II had ended only five years earlier, and Japan's meteoric economic growth was about to take off. As the urgent need for reconstruction receded and technology advanced, houses could be conceived as something beyond a roof and four walls. '[It was] the transition from mere shelter to art form,' explains Professor David B. Stewart of the Tokyo Institute of Technology.

For Shinohara, this shift was initially manifested in his interest in the traditional and its relation to the contemporary – the theme of his 'First Style'. 'In 1960, I wrote an article for *Shinkenchiku* in which I said that though tradition may be a person's starting point, it is not always the point to which he returns,' stated Shinohara.[4] Evoking history, but in a distinctly modern way, Umbrella House is one example.

A simple square building with a pyramidal roof, Umbrella House originally stood in a residential neighbourhood west of central Tokyo, where agricultural fields mingled with homes. Upon entering, the roof's spectacular support system revealed itself in one fell swoop. Radiating out from a square steel frame at the pyramid's apex, the spoke-like beams were modelled on a traditional Japanese umbrella. Set against a white background, this web of dark wood unified the entire space. At room height below, the rafters were secured by an asymmetrical cross-shaped framework, loosely dividing the interior into quadrants containing the wood-floored living room, eat-in kitchen, a bathroom, and a *tatami*-mat room for the clients and their daughter. A ladder led to a storage area above. Sliding *fusuma* paper panels, *sudare* blinds and a subtle change in the floor level both separated and connected the rooms.

2

Among designers of residential architecture in Japan, few have been as influential as Kazuo Shinohara. The subject of numerous exhibitions, books and articles, many authored by the architect himself, Shinohara's opus is also among the most studied and analysed. Divided into four self-proclaimed styles, his output consisted mainly of houses for much of his career. His practice, and the thinking behind it, have influenced generations of architects, many educated at the Tokyo Institute of Technology, his own alma mater.

1 Resembling the spokes of an umbrella, the exposed roof structure hovered protectively over the living (background) and dining (foreground) areas.

2 A simple square building with a pyramidal roof, the home's clean geometry stood out from that of its neighbours.

1

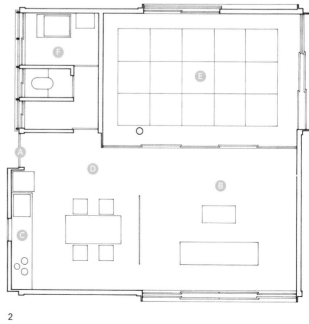

2

3

① One quadrant of the home's square plan
held the kitchen and dining areas.

② Plan: (A) entrance, (B) living, (C) kitchen,
(D) dining, (E) sleeping, (F) bath.

③ The *tatami*-floored sleeping quarters
(background) were separated from the
living area (foreground) by sliding *fusuma*
screens and a subtle level change.

1960——1969

No Front House H
Junzo Sakakura
Architects
and Engineers
Hyogo Prefecture
1962

Located in a densely built area of Nishinomiya City, No Front House H was a low-slung, single-storey building that abutted the street with a long concrete wall. The roughly textured surface was articulated with a sequence of scored geometric figures, and punctuated with a variety of small windows plus the doorway. The latter led into a small, concealed entry garden – a place to pause and change shoes before proceeding inside. But from the street, the only clues about the home's inner workings were the triangulated skylights poking up behind the wall.

Though completely isolated from the built environment, the interior enjoyed a close connection to the natural environment. The L-shaped plan flanked two sides of the courtyard, with the communal rooms occupying one leg and the bedrooms the other. Incorporating trees, plants, a pergola and a small pond, the outdoor space was visible from the main rooms but especially from the living room, which jutted out into the garden and opened completely to covered, brick-paved terraces on two sides.

While the perimeter walls, horizontal layout and integration of exterior space may echo historic *shoin*-style homes, the building was realized with industrial-grade concrete, accompanied by brick, wood and glass. These were complemented by furnishings designed by Sakakura himself. Like his mentor in Paris, Le Corbusier, the architect worked on multiple scales. His interest in furniture design began with drafting tables for his own use, but expanded into other pieces, including the broad-backed side chairs used in the dining room of No Front House H.

1

In response to the rapid and rampant construction that took place as Japan recovered from the devastation of World War II, the Osaka office of Junzo Sakakura's architectural practice created a series of 'No Front Houses'. Organized around a central courtyard, each one was inwardly focused and enclosed by walls on all sides, a strategy that protected the living space from anything undesirable or unpredictable beyond the property's perimeter. Turning its back to the neighbourhood, each house lacked a strong facade, hence the 'No Front' name.

❶ The living room with seating designed by the architect.

❷ The combined kitchen and dining areas.

❸ The concrete facade and front door.

❹ Plan: (A) entrance, (B) living, (C) kitchen, (D) dining, (E) sleeping, (F) bath, (G) *tatami*, (N) courtyard.

2

3

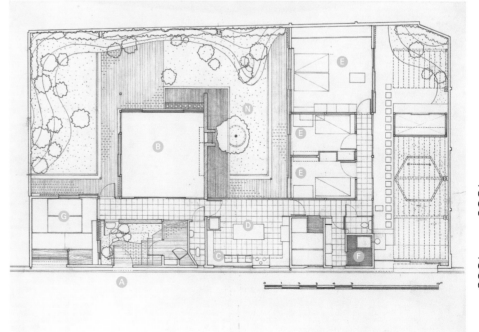

4

1

Mountain Cottage in Karuizawa
Junzo Yoshimura
Nagano Prefecture
1963

2

A counterbalance to Junzo Yoshimura's Tokyo residence (see page 80), this country home sits on a gently sloping site surrounded by dense forest. As the architect wrote, 'Looking skyward and seeing the greenery of the trees, I thought of building a house where I could live like a bird atop a tree.'[5] Instead of spreading horizontally, he expanded the house vertically, placing the wood-encased living space on a concrete base and topping it with a tilted roof. His first foray into the elevated-house type, this configuration enabled Yoshimura and his family to integrate the natural environment with daily activity at every level.

Unsurprisingly, Yoshimura chose to build his retreat in Karuizawa, where he had spent several summers working for the designers Antonin and Noémi Raymond, who had clients as well as a home and studio in the town. Defined by rustic lanes and a quaint shopping street, Karuizawa is a comfortable trip from Tokyo – close enough for the architect to summon his staff when needed, and for his violinist wife to host a music camp for her students. But mainly, it was a private getaway. 'One of the first things my father did was to heat the wood-burning bath and then go out and buy groceries,' recalls his daughter, Takako Yoshimura.

A short distance from the town centre, the house is ringed by a ground-level terrace where meals could be taken alfresco and the outdoor fireplace enjoyed. From there, stairs inside the concrete base ascend to the main floor: a compact arrangement of bedrooms, eat-in kitchen and bathroom surrounding two sides of the wood-clad living room. A square within a square, this communal space centres on a large fireplace but opens to a narrow porch partitioned with sliding *shoji* screens and glass doors. Blending indoors and out – the only separation is a simple log guard rail – the porch extends the room while filling it with daylight, fresh air and views to copious foliage. Upstairs on the mezzanine are a study, a *tatami*-mat room and a ladder to the roof terrace. 'When you go up there at night, you can only see the sky,' says Takako. 'I enjoy the stars and sound of trees moving.' From top to bottom, the connection to nature is always present.

1 Like a treehouse, Mountain Cottage perches on a concrete base, immersing the living space in the forest.

2 The cosy, sun-filled living room centres on its fireplace.

1

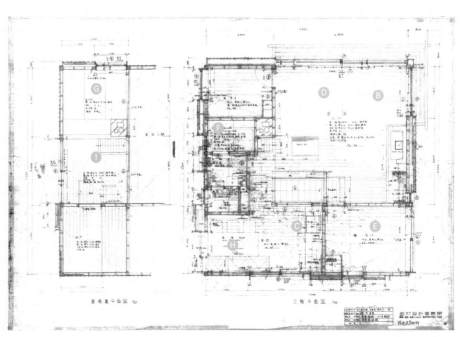

2

1 *Shoji* screens can be pushed aside to completely open the living area to the porch and tree-studded landscape beyond.

2 Second-floor plan (left) and first-floor plan (right): (B) living, (C) kitchen, (D) dining, (E) sleeping, (F) bath, (G) *tatami*, (H) maid, (I) study.

At Home Mountain Cottage
Takako Yoshimura

My parents loved Karuizawa. They got energy and physical strength from their summer stays there. Our house was used mainly as a place to relax, recuperate and immerse ourselves in nature so that we could face our busy Tokyo life for another year.

For father, the house was a place to contemplate and concentrate while working on his projects. Almost every weekend, he went there alone straight from his office, and then on Monday, he went from there back to his office. Mother was busy teaching at her small music school, and I was busy with this and that in Tokyo. He cooked, kindled a fire for the bath (*goemon-buro*), and enjoyed listening to music, mostly Beethoven. The greengrocer and the butcher in town got well-acquainted with him.

Sometimes, the house turned into father's 'Karuizawa Branch Office'. When there was a big project going on and intensive work was necessary, the staff would come up, a few drafting boards would be installed and the place would become his office for several days. The house also became a classroom once a year when father was still teaching at the university. He invited newly enrolled students of architecture for an overnight stay.

They made meals, had discussions and played Chinese chequers together by the fireside.

For mother, the house provided a place to hold a summer music camp. The entire house – even a storage room and two tents set up outside near the house, where students slept and played cards at night – was lively and filled with music all the time. The living room upstairs was for lessons with piano students and the veranda was for string students. The rest of the space was used for practising, even the roof deck. We had concerts and invited friends (left). Mr and Mrs Kenzo Tange and Mr and Mrs Genichiro Inokuma were among them. The veranda would become a stage and the ground in front of it was turned into makeshift seats for the audience.

Although it is a small house, it is very flexible. Even when as many as thirty people are inside, we did not feel too crowded. But the best was when we used it privately and quietly for ourselves! We felt the woods and nature were very close all the time. We appreciated the change of light throughout the day, the moonlight, the sound of wind in the trees, and the murmuring of nearby streams, birds, insects and animals.

We were blissful, and we felt safe in this house.

1

Adachi Villa
Antonin and
Noémi Raymond
Nagano Prefecture
1966

2

A spacious second home nestled among a trio of large trees, the Adachi Villa was created for an American family living in Tokyo. The clients, a husband and wife who began working in Japan during the Allied Occupation, were long-term residents of the country. At the time, many members of Tokyo's foreign community chose Karuizawa to escape the city's summer heat – a practice started by missionaries in the late nineteenth century. Quaint, countrified yet fashionable,

the town contained a mix of wooden cottages, stylish hotels and social clubs.

Like their clients, Antonin and Noémi Raymond called Japan home, and they had two home studios in Karuizawa. Built before World War II, the first was capped by distinctive angled roofs, while the second, built in 1962, was defined by a twelve-sided studio centred on a fireplace. Shortly after that, the designers got to work on the Adachi Villa.

'What my parents wanted was to create a structure where you can be inside and outside at the same time,' recalls Cathy Adachi. The Raymonds responded with an arc-shaped plan oriented towards a hillside that sloped southwards to a creek. The string of spaces inside consisted of the living and dining rooms, followed by the master bedroom and two children's bedrooms. 'Our rooms were teeny, just big enough for a bed,' recalls Cathy. 'But the house was geared towards entertaining and being with other people.'

Separated by a long corridor, the kitchen, bathroom and maid's quarters were at the back of the home, while a covered porch lined its front. This was, in effect, an outdoor room – it was here that the clients would read, enjoy the quiet and sip cocktails. 'The foxes and flying squirrels which came in the evening were real gourmets,' recalls the family housekeeper, Kazuko Mori. '[The Adachis] would throw them hors d'oeuvres.'

A seamless extension of the exterior, the interior was characterized by the Raymonds' refined rusticity, manifested in the fluid floor plan, natural materials and built-in furnishings. Complementing the timber beams and columns, as well as the wood ceiling and walls, paper lanterns and *shoji* screens offered soft light. A fieldstone fireplace dominated the living room, while the custom cabinetry and shelving held the clients' collection of *mingei* folk art. 'It was a Raymond house, but it was really a Noémi Raymond house,' explains Cathy. 'She clearly understood how people occupy space.'

1 The Raymonds' vocabulary of natural materials blends well with the wooded site.

2 The view from the corridor into the dining and living room (beyond).

2

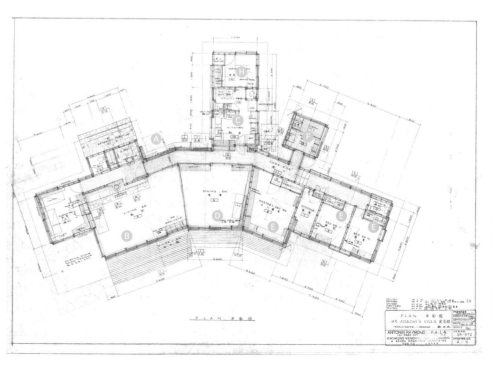

1 The master bedroom with its built-in furnishings.

2 The arc-shaped home opens to the sloping hillside and creek below.

3 Plan: (A) entrance, (B) living, (C) kitchen, (D) dining, (E) sleeping, (F) bath, (H) maid.

3

1960——1969

Chalet Moby Dick
Mayumi Miyawaki
Yamanashi
Prefecture
1966

The first house designed by Mayumi Miyawaki, the project was the result of a commission to design a menswear boutique. After creating a shop for its stylish owner, Miyawaki was then charged with designing his weekend house overlooking Lake Yamanaka, a popular location for vacation homes at the base of Mount Fuji. '[The client] liked well-designed, beautiful things; he wanted something different, so he picked this young architect,' comments Miyawaki's daughter, Sai. He also wanted a second home for year-round use – a rarity in Japan where vacation houses are usually intended for the warm-weather months only.[6]

Miyawaki responded by orienting the building towards the lake but enclosing it with solid walls and its distinctive roof. Shaped like an hourglass, the main level was entered at the side, where the middle of the plan cinched in. To the left was a guest room, to the right was the living-dining room, which flowed out onto a deck facing the water. Directly ahead stood a compact three-storey core – on its main level were the kitchen, the stairs and a cosy conversation pit with a fireplace. Above and below, this mini tower held the bedrooms and bathrooms.

Overhead, the three-part plan was unified by the dynamic ceiling and its exposed structure, consisting of over one hundred differently shaped rafters.[7] These held up the roof, recalling the matrix of beams seen in many historic *minka* farmhouses. The wood members tilted inward towards the central ridge, and were arranged in a fluid, undulating formation that reached its apex above the core. In contrast to this skeleton, the roof's outer surface was smooth and sculptural. Supported by plain concrete walls on the sides, the roof ended in a *minka*-like pitch at either end.

1

With its humpbacked roof and angled exterior walls, Chalet Moby Dick was a house ahead of its time. Remarkably, its organic form was conceived before the advent of computer-aided design – the structure had to be calculated and constructed by hand. It took an architect with a taste for the eye-catching and a client in the fashion world – assisted by a skilled builder of traditional shrines and temples – to bring this unique building to life.

2

① The home's monolithic, abstract form bore a resemblance to a great white whale.

② Angled, rib-like rafters unified the interior, with the dining area in front and the conversation pit in back.

③ The deck overlooked Lake Yamanaka.

3

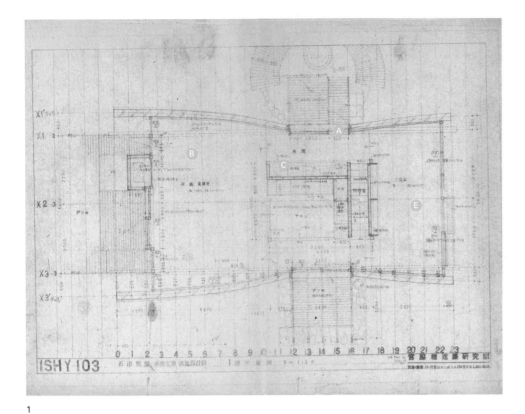

1

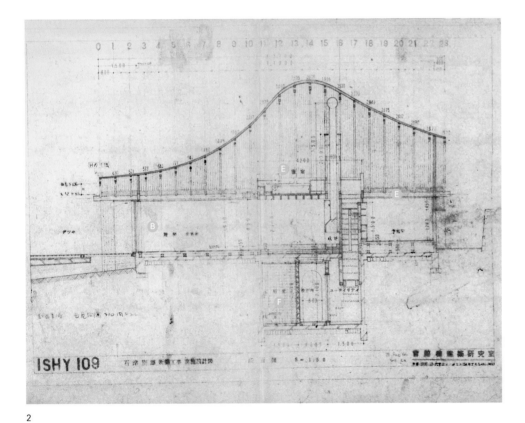

2

❶ Plan: (A) entrance, (B) living, (C) kitchen,
(E) sleeping.

❷ Section: (B) living, (E) sleeping, (F) bath.

❸ The view from the conversation pit to the
living, dining and outdoor deck areas.

3

1

House in White
Kazuo Shinohara
Tokyo
1966

2

Shortly after completing Umbrella House (see page 96), Kazuo Shinohara made his famous declaration in the architectural journal *Shinkenchiku*: 'A House is a work of art.'[8] This loaded statement set up a distinction between the homes he was creating and the one-size-fits-all, mass-production houses that had been on the minds of many architects since the end of World War II. It also distinguished the private residence from other forms of architecture. '[The house] must be shifted to the realm of art, where it belongs together with painting, sculpture, literature, and so on,' wrote Shinohara.[9] But whether a house is indeed a work of art has much to do with its architect. The purity of its shape, the abstraction of its expression and the quietude of its space squarely place the House in White in that category.

This project began after the client, a leading publisher of children's books, encountered Shinohara at a 1964 art exhibition presented by Tokyo's Odakyu Department Store, according to Professor Shin-ichi Okuyama of the Tokyo Institute of Technology. Moved by the architect's first book, *Jutaku Kenchiku* (Residential Architecture), the client commissioned Shinohara to design a house for his family not far from Tokyo's Tama River. As with Umbrella House, Shinohara responded with a simple square building topped with a pyramidal roof. Inside, capped by a high but flat ceiling, are the living, dining and kitchen areas to one side, as well as a small box holding the bathroom. On the other side, behind a partition, are the stacked bedrooms, with one sleeping area below and a second tucked beneath the sloping roof above.

Throughout the house, the ceilings and walls, both inside and out, are pure white, creating a sense of scaleless abstraction consistent with modernist design. Even the windows, which are covered with *shoji* paper screens, are milky white. But against this pale, pared-down backdrop, key elements stand out. Most notable is the single cedar column marking the centre of the floor plan. Evoking the *daikokubashira* – the structural as well as symbolic centrepiece of many traditional houses – this column supports concealed diagonal bracing. It culminates at the apex of the tiled roof, the gently sloping surfaces of which yield deep eaves on all four sides.

❶ In the double-height living room, a solo cedar column marks the centre of the square floor plan.

❷ Deep roof eaves provide plenty of shade at the house perimeter.

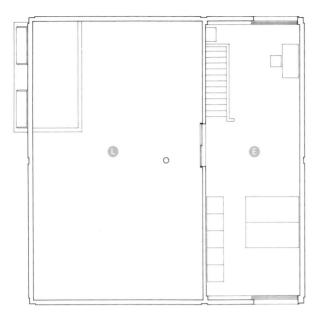

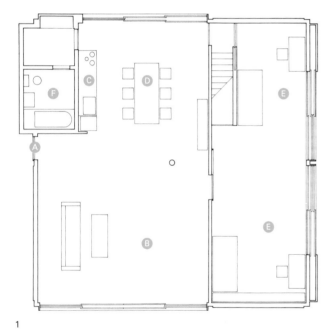

1

1 Plans: (A) entrance (B) living, (C) kitchen, (D) dining, (E) sleeping, (F) bath, (L) void.

2 The combined kitchen and dining areas with *shoji* screens beyond.

2

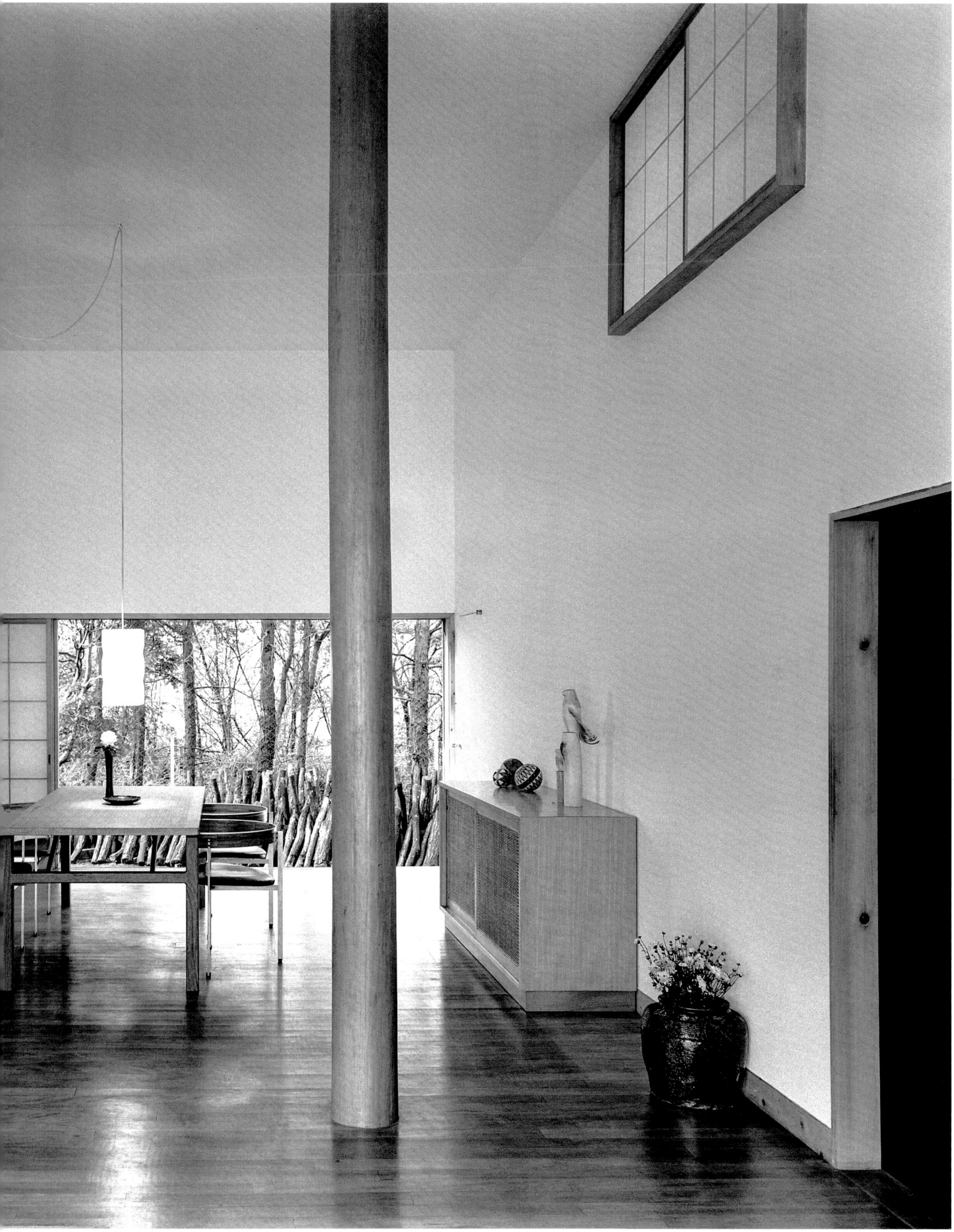

JOH House
Makoto Suzuki
Tokyo
1966

architectural lineage: Suzuki trained under Takamasa Yoshizaka, who was apprenticed to Le Corbusier. For the two-storey JOH House, Suzuki devised a cube wrapped on two sides by an L-shaped volume, with skylit circulation space in between. At ground level, the cube housed a spacious square living room with sliding window-walls on two sides that both opened to the expansive walled garden. 'It felt like it was half-outdoors,' recalls Naiki. Above the living room was an enclosed roof terrace (which was later converted into a solarium). By contrast, both floors of the L-shaped volume were filled with small rooms. Downstairs, these included a carport, an eat-in kitchen, and a *tatami*-floored room where, according to Naiki, the client was fond of playing mahjong. Upstairs were bedrooms, a walk-in closet, and little balconies at either end where stairs connected to the roof terrace.

More than a mere corridor, the open circulation zone doubled as functional space. Downstairs it was an extension of the living room, and upstairs it expanded into a book-lined study where the children were known to play. But it was also an essential means of bringing daylight into the heart of the house. Angled at 45 degrees, its glass skylight allowed soft light to filter all the way down to the ground floor. 'My impression is that light enters indirectly in Japanese architecture,' comments Naiki. But Suzuki, and no doubt his client too, wanted something more dramatic.

1

Many architects launch their careers with commissions from friends or family. But Makoto Suzuki's first house was created for a movie star with a sizeable plot in western Tokyo, a growing family, and a Dobermann. A play on the client's name, JOH House was the elegant, concrete conclusion of their collaboration.

Like the work of some of his architectural peers, Suzuki's basic scheme was driven by geometry. Hiroki Naiki, a long-time member of Suzuki's practice, speculates that this approach may have reflected his mentor's

1 Aerial view of the house and garden.

2 The double-height living room with the study visible above.

3 Plans: (A) entrance, (B) living, (C) kitchen, (D) dining, (E) sleeping, (F) bath, (G) *tatami*, (I) study, (M) terrace.

2

GROUND FLOOR

FIRST FLOOR

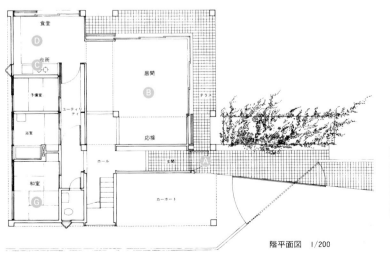

階平面図　1/200

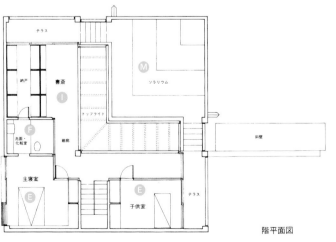

階平面図

3

Tower House
Takamitsu Azuma
Tokyo
1966

But these amenities could not lure the Azumas. 'I like the city life…I like to meet people and have access to new information, traditional culture, and the many things that happen in the city spontaneously,' said the architect.[10]

With those intentions as his guide, Azuma selected a central Tokyo property abutting a four-lane thoroughfare, which had been widened in the run-up to the 1964 Tokyo Olympics (many of the athletics events were held nearby). Transforming a quiet residential neighbourhood, this road redevelopment left tiny triangular lots in its wake. Measuring a mere 20 square metres (215 square feet), one of those lots gave rise to the Azumas' concrete mini tower.

Separating the home from the street, a short run of stairs ascends to the entrance, with parking for a compact car tucked behind. Inside, additional steps lead to the basement, where the architect had his office, and up to the combined kitchen-dining-living room. Overlooking the street, a picture window gives the compact cooking area a bit of breathing room, while a double-height ceiling adorned with a long paper lantern augments the living area. Upstairs, the bathroom with its wooden tub occupies the second floor; the master bedroom the third floor; and Rie's room, plus a roof terrace, crowns the building. In lieu of corridors or doors, stairs both separate and link rooms, enabling a sense of space and allowing sound and people to travel effortlessly from top to bottom.

In due course, Azuma moved his growing practice to an office nearby, freeing up a room for the studio of his wife, an accomplished weaver. For the most part, the house contains little discretionary space or even storage, but the family favoured daily visits to local greengrocers and bakers, as well as outings to cafés, concert halls and museums.

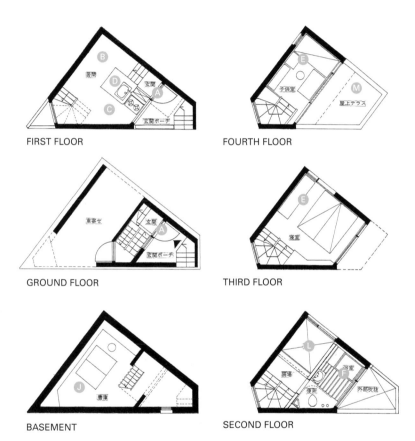

FIRST FLOOR

FOURTH FLOOR

GROUND FLOOR

THIRD FLOOR

BASEMENT

SECOND FLOOR

2

In Japan, it is the quality, not quantity, of space that matters. With just 65 square metres (700 square feet) of floor area, Tower House is a case in point. Spread out over six levels, it holds only one room per floor. But that was more than enough for architect Takamitsu Azuma, his wife and their young daughter, Rie.

The little family could have built a bigger home plus a garden out in the suburbs, allowing the Western-inspired lifestyle that was all the rage in Japan by the mid-1960s.

❶ Rie Azuma in front of Tower House shortly after its completion.

❷ Plans: (A) entrance, (B) living, (C) kitchen, (D) dining, (E) sleeping, (F) bath, (J) studio, (L) void, (M) terrace.

1 Compensating for the small floor area, a long paper light fixture draws attention to the height of the living and dining areas.

2 The concrete stair treads double as informal seating.

2

At Home
Tower House
Rie Azuma

My parents grew up in the centre of downtown Osaka, where many of the wooden houses had attached workplaces, such as shops, small factories or offices. So when they came to Tokyo, they wanted to live in the centre of town too, without the need to commute. I remember visiting apartments in Harajuku and a house in the suburbs that was in the middle of being built, but nothing was quite right. Finally, they made the decision to live in the centre of Tokyo, but on a very small site.

When our family (above) moved to Tower House, which was designed by my father, Takamitsu Azuma, I was still in elementary school. On the first day, we kept our shoes on because the floor was not yet finished – it was just a rough concrete surface. This was unusual because Japanese people normally take their shoes off at home. My new home was a wonderful spatial experience for me. The top room became my room, and I became the princess who lived at the top of the tower!

Many people and journalists have visited Tower House since it was built. Most of them have been interested in what my childhood there was like, given that there are no internal doors, and I've often been asked if living there

was problematic. I have always answered 'no', and said that I didn't really understand the meaning of 'ordinary'. For a six-year-old child, everything is a new experience, and moving into Tower House was all just so exciting and cool.

When I was a college student at architecture school, I stayed at a traditional Japanese wooden hotel called a *ryokan*. Early in the morning, while lying on my *futon*, I heard the sound of muffled footsteps and smelled breakfast being prepared by the staff. I thought about how similar this experience was to Tower House. Each one of us felt the presence of others in the house, which shaped our interactions and revealed something specific and essential about the way we communicate in Japanese culture. When I heard the sound of my mother climbing the stairs to hang the laundry on the balcony, I hid my comics and pretended to study. If the TV downstairs was too noisy, I told my parents to turn it down, or I joined them. If the conversation between guests downstairs sounded fun, I went down to join in.

When my father was busy and came back late, I would often sit on the steps of my parents' bedroom and talk to him before going to school. Sometimes I would sit on the bathroom steps listening to a record and talking with my mother in the kitchen. On a sunny spring Sunday, I would lie down in my parents' room to enjoy the view of a big tree outside. I lived everywhere in Tower House. It always seemed to me that this was just like living in a traditional wooden house.

Life in Tower House was central to our family relationships – the house itself almost became a fourth family member for us. Now more than fifty years old, Tower House is a home that makes you think about living. I hope that, even after the Azuma family moves on, another will move in to enjoy Tower House's many charms.

1

Katono House
Tetsu Katono
Sapporo
1968

2

All architects' self-designed homes are experiments of one sort or another. Katono House, a modernist gem in Sapporo, right in the heart of the island of Hokkaido, is no exception. At the time of its conception, Tetsu Katono was designing big buildings made of glass, steel and brick for the Sapporo outpost of the construction company Takenaka Corporation. Keen to repurpose his technical know-how, Katono reasoned that what was good for hospitals and hotels might work well for homes too. 'My father wanted to use the detailing and materials of commercial buildings in designing our house,' explains Katono's architect son, Koku.

Initially, Katono envisioned living in the centre of Sapporo. However, land on the outskirts of the city was cheap, plentiful and empty. 'There were no houses nearby, only farms and a few temples,' recalls Koku, who was then a high-school student. Over time, more houses cropped up, but carefully positioned trees preserved the family's privacy.

A single-storey rectangular volume, the house originally held an entry hall, living room, dining room, *tatami*-floored room, master bedroom and two children's bedrooms at its perimeter, with a kitchen and bathroom forming its core. In 1982, the rooms were modified (as reflected in the drawings) and a two-storey addition was built at the back. This contained the architect's study and book-storage area, plus a *tatami*-floored tearoom upstairs for his wife, a tea-ceremony enthusiast.

Though residential in scale, the house is made of industrial-strength materials to withstand the harsh winters and heavy snows. Sapporo gets more than a metre (3 feet) of snow yearly, so Katono responded with a flat concrete roof that was strong enough to support its weight until the springtime thaw. Though common elsewhere, a pitched roof would have been problematic since it would allow the snow to slide off and accumulate around the house, explains Koku. Equally well suited to the climate, insulated walls of locally made brick encase three sides of the house. But the south face, which opens onto a raised deck, is almost entirely transparent. To fend off the cold, Katono used double-paned glass for the window walls and lined them with double-layered *shoji* paper screens plus curtains to keep the interior warm. But when the mild weather returns, the curtains are taken down for the season and the window walls pushed aside to let in the fresh Hokkaido air.

❶ The entry hall with built-in shoe storage.

❷ Sapporo's heavy snow is left to accumulate on the roof until the springtime thaw.

1

1 Double-paned window-walls help keep the living area toasty even in the dead of winter.

2 Plan: (A) entrance, (B) living, (C) kitchen, (D) dining, (E) sleeping, (F) bath.

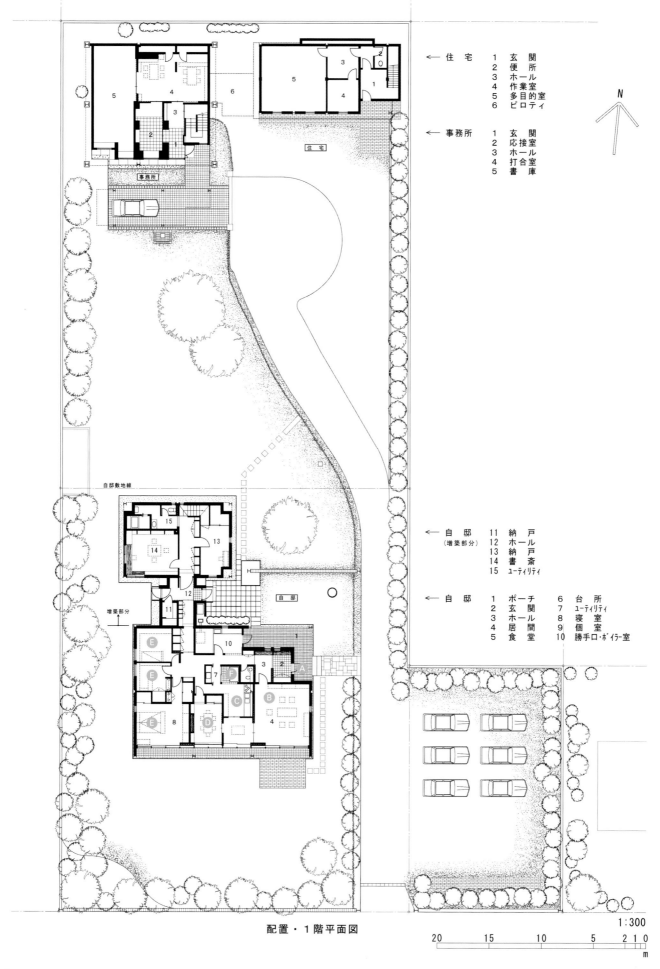

N

← 住　宅　　1　玄　　　関
　　　　　　2　便　　　所
　　　　　　3　ホ ー ル
　　　　　　4　作 業 室
　　　　　　5　多 目 的 室
　　　　　　6　ピ ロ ティ

← 事 務 所　　1　玄　　　関
　　　　　　　2　応 接 室
　　　　　　　3　ホ ー ル
　　　　　　　4　打 合 室
　　　　　　　5　書　　　庫

← 自　邸　　11　納　　　戸
（増築部分）　12　ホ ー ル
　　　　　　13　納　　　戸
　　　　　　14　書　　　斎
　　　　　　15　ユーティリティ

← 自　邸　　1　ポ ー チ　　6　台　　　所
　　　　　　2　玄　　　関　　7　ユーティリティ
　　　　　　3　ホ ー ル　　8　寝　　　室
　　　　　　4　居　　　間　　9　個　　　室
　　　　　　5　食　　　堂　　10　勝手口・ボイラー室

配置・1階平面図

1：300

20　　　15　　　10　　　5　　2 1 0
　　　　　　　　　　　　　　　　m

1960—1969

2

Spotlight

Floors and Ceilings

Entering a *tatami*-floored room is a total body experience. The sight of the tidy rectangular mats pleases the eye, the fresh smell of rice straw awakens the nose, and the thick, cushiony pads give slightly with each stocking-footed step. For centuries, mats in various forms were one of the three main flooring elements in Japanese homes, alongside wood and earth. Each correlated with a different function. Dirt floors frequently appeared in transitional spaces between indoors and out, such as doorways and *doma* work areas, while raised wood floors defined spaces for daily life. A level change divided the two, enabling the separation of clean and dirty areas by the swapping of outdoor shoes for slippers – a custom that still remains deeply entrenched. Positioned on top of the wood floor, woven mats originally marked individual places for sitting or sleeping, but eventually evolved into a continuous floor covering composed of rice-straw blocks. Proportionate to the human body, *tatami* became, and continue to be, the means of measuring room size, despite a recent decline in their use.

Unlike Western floors, which are passive surfaces on which to walk or place furniture, the Japanese floor is a platform for various activities related to the human body. In a matter of minutes, folding *futon* mattresses or flat *zabuton* cushions can convert any space into sleeping quarters or a sitting room. Since World War II, a variety of durable materials has largely replaced the *tatami* mat, yet the floor's primacy in the Japanese house remains – nothing conveys the feeling of 'being home' more than slipping off one's street shoes. And for Japanese designers, floors are important variables. Even a level change of a step or two can subtly differentiate one space from another.

Historically, the floor and ceiling sandwiched a single-storey, horizontal swathe of space (opposite page). But the ceiling played a supporting role in relation to the floor. It was the position of the human body seated on the floor that determined a room's height – typically less than 2.4 metres (8 feet) in homes. In addition, ceilings were not essential for post-and-beam structural frames. Consequently, they could be highly decorative, as in traditional tearooms, or entirely absent, as in *minka* farmhouses, where hulking roof beams hovered in the semi-darkness overhead. With this legacy, the ceiling remains a malleable element that can be lifted to make a cramped interior feel bigger, or used to create space for a loft, or even be punctured with skylights.

1970s
Expo and Exports

The decade opened with Expo '70 on the outskirts of Osaka. Its symbol, the Tower of the Sun (opposite page), was created by the artist Taro Okamoto. Though less impactful than the 1964 Tokyo Olympics, this futuristic event heralded Japan's emergence as a technological leader. And with the reversion of the island of Okinawa to Japanese sovereignty in 1972, the most prominent vestige of the Allied Occupation was removed.

But, in many ways, the 1970s was a decade of unrest. It witnessed a global energy crisis, an economic downturn, and angry protests about a variety of issues. Among the most astounding of these protests was the public suicide of author-turned-right-wing-activist Yukio Mishima in 1970, an act expressing his rejection of Japan's rapid modernization and post-World War II demilitarization. Dependent on imported petroleum, Japan was hit hard by the global oil shock of 1973, which slowed economic growth and triggered belt-tightening by consumers, many of whom used oil products to heat their homes, as well as power their vehicles. It also encouraged the development of fuel-efficient cars in Japan, which proved a sales success overseas, where many of Japan's major automobile makers had begun to make significant inroads.[1] However, the proliferation of factory-made goods posed a serious threat to Japan's deeply rooted craft culture. To save this legacy from obsolescence, many contemporary designers, most notably Toshiyuki Kita, initiated collaborations with the makers of paper, lacquerware and other traditional goods.

Despite its economic ups and downs, the decade was ripe with creativity. In 1970, Issey Miyake established the Miyake Design Studio in Tokyo, launching one of Japan's most esteemed fashion houses. Two years later, the Museum of Modern Art in New York hosted Tadanori Yokoo's solo show, garnering international attention for the graphic designer's avant-garde works. And in 1974, Hello Kitty arrived, making her first appearance on a vinyl coin purse.[2] Epitomizing Japan's love of all things cute, this endearing cat, with her round face, red bow and smile-less expression, soon developed a huge fan base among adults and children across the world.

Opening a door to rising globalization, a major new airport for Tokyo – Narita International Airport – started operations in 1978, despite the protests of the local rice farmers and their radical student allies, who had opposed its construction vociferously. And in 1979, the Sony Walkman debuted. A runaway success both at home and abroad, it revolutionized the way the world listened to music and paved the way for hand-held devices of all sorts.

My Home II
Kiyoshi Seike
Tokyo
1970

Like My Home I, the new house has a simple rectangular footprint. Though both homes were originally conceived as one-room dwellings, they are more different than similar. The new version is not just bigger, it is spread out over two storeys, with stairs at the centre dividing the plan into two square spaces. And, unlike his earlier design, Seike included an entry foyer. This leads to the mother's area on one side and the family living room on the other. From here, a small change of level separates the dining room and kitchen. 'Guests couldn't see if they would be eating French food or Japanese *ochazuke*,' recalls Yuri Yagi, the architect's daughter. Between the living and dining areas, the open stairs connect to floor levels above and below. Originally, the architect's study was downstairs while the upstairs was for sleeping. Clad with eighteen *tatami* mats, the main room was divided by movable cabinetry. 'From time to time, my father used to change the layout,' remembers Yuri.

Being able to adjust one's space according to function, season or even time of day – the traditional Japanese idea of *shitsurai* – appealed greatly to Seike. Professor Hiroyasu Fujioka of the Tokyo Institute of Technology credits him as the first to introduce the concept, which dates back to aristocratic *shinden-zukuri* residences of the Heian period (794–1192), into contemporary house design.[1] Recalls Yuri, '[H]e loved this thinking – people who live there can decide how to use the space.'

1

Sixteen years after completing My Home I for his young family (see page 64), Kiyoshi Seike was back at the drawing board. His neighbourhood had developed, making the openness of the house less desirable. His family had grown and could benefit from more space. And the physical needs of his mother and father had changed. Seike addressed these concerns by replacing his parents' original wood home with a two-storey dwelling for his immediate family, along with separate single-storey accommodations for his mother and father at opposite ends.

1 A stone path leads to the front door, which is flanked by the architect's mother's quarters (left) and the main house (right).

2 Open stairs ascend from the living room to the sleeping quarters upstairs.

3 Reminiscent of My House I, full-height sliding panels open the living room to the garden.

4 Plans: (A) entrance, (B) living, (C) kitchen, (D) dining, (E) sleeping.

2

3

FIRST FLOOR   BASEMENT

GROUND FLOOR

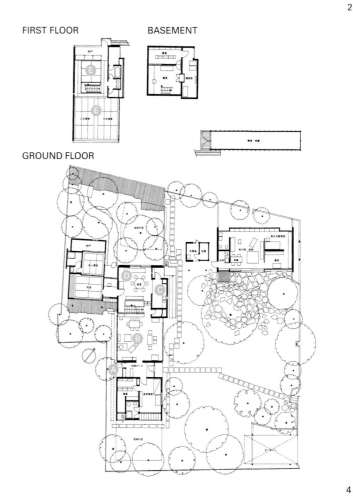

4

1

Blue Box House
Mayumi Miyawaki
Tokyo
1971

A bright blue box popping out from the side of a steep hill, this house epitomizes cool. Its bold geometry and brilliant colour contrast sharply with the conventional, pitched-roofed neighbours. This unique structure resulted from the perfect pairing of an avant-garde architect and his equally cutting-edge client. Both had participated in international events hosted by Japan – Expo '70 in Osaka and the 1964 Tokyo Olympics respectively. A well-known photographer, the client had taken the striking shots of sprinting athletes that graphic designer Yusaku Kamekura turned into his iconic posters for the Tokyo Olympics.

Right off the starting block, Mayumi Miyawaki wanted to use a basic form and a strong colour. 'In a cluttered city, primary architecture can have a strong identity,' explains Eizo Shiina, who was the house's project architect. The challenge was how to build on the site's 34-degree slope. The architects began with a cantilevered cube, which they manipulated in multiple ways, such as slanting the front wall or incorporating a built-in balcony. But the eureka moment came when Miyawaki excised the cube's bottom quadrant. This sophisticated form was further enhanced by cutting a cylindrical hole in the quadrant above, enabling bamboo to grow straight up through the building.

Approached from the street, the house is visually anchored by a shell-like garage built into the base of the hill. Inside this garage, the back wall was originally covered with a phantasmagoric mural created by the illustrator Yuzo Yamashita. Alongside, outdoor steps ascend to the entry foyer on the side of the building. The lower level contains the communal areas, including a sunken 'lounge pit'. Covered with carpet and throw cushions, this groovy circular seating element echoes the cylindrical hole. The upper level holds bedrooms, a bathroom and a *tatami*-floored room. These private quarters are arranged in an L-shape around the roof garden, where the bamboo pokes up. Walled on the sides but open to the sky, it is the ideal outdoor space for a house on a hill.

1 An exterior stairway connects the garage with the house that cantilevers out from the hillside.

2 The view from the living room's sunken lounge pit towards the dining area.

2

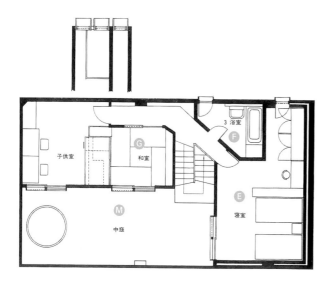

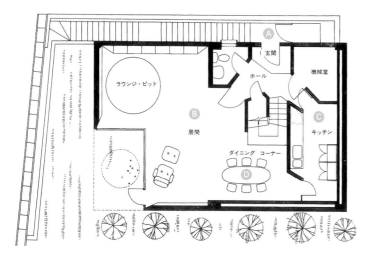

1

1 Plans: (A) entrance, (B) living, (C) kitchen,
(D) dining, (E) sleeping, (F) bath, (G) *tatami*,
(M) terrace.

2 The circular shape of the lounge pit is
echoed by the opening that allowed bamboo
stalks to grow from ground through to the
roof terrace.

2

Capsule House K
Kisho Kurokawa
Nagano Prefecture
1971

2

The Capsule House K may look like the setting for a sci-fi film, but its amazing form – a concrete core with four protruding Corten-steel capsules – can be traced back to the traditional Japanese teahouse. The home is the product of Kisho Kurokawa, who was a proponent of Japan's futuristic Metabolism movement, yet grew up in a historic house in the countryside of Aichi Prefecture. As private space was scarce within this family home, the young Kurokawa took to the teahouse, an independent structure out in the garden. This direct experience of one of Japan's most distinctive building types had a profound impact. It instilled a lifelong appreciation of the carefully choreographed tea ceremony, but also moulded Kurokawa's sense of proportion and space, ultimately becoming the inspiration for the capsules he created for this house in Nagano Prefecture, and then for Tokyo's Nakagin Capsule Tower, which was dismantled in 2022.

Intended as much as a demonstration of the applicability of Metabolism to residential design as a country retreat for Kurokawa and his staff, the house sits on a steeply sloped site amidst a vacation-home development. Taking advantage of the terrain, the two-storey dwelling is approached from above by exterior stairs that lead down to the entry foyer embedded in the core. The core also contains the living-dining room and, connected by a spiral stairway, the man-cave-turned-master-bedroom below. Attached to the core upstairs, the four capsules hold the kitchen, two bedrooms and a tearoom respectively.

Jutting out from the core in three directions, each of the 4.2 by 2.7 metre (13 foot 9 inch by 8 foot 10 inch) capsules could, in concept, be moved, as per Metabolist doctrines. But their small size, efficiency and self-sufficiency stem from teahouse architecture. For example, the bedroom is equipped with a 'unit bath' plus a wall incorporating electronic equipment, lighting, cabinetry and a fold-down desk in a manner similar to the Nakagin Capsule Tower. Because conventional contractors baulked at all the built-ins, a yacht manufacturer was enlisted for the interiors in both buildings. 'They had the technology needed to cram in a lot of stuff,' explains the architect's son, Mikio. Three of the home's capsules terminate in a dome-shaped window, contributing to its unique appearance while maximizing views. Over the years, trees filled the site, but the glorious Mount Asama was once the focus.

① Four capsules containing the kitchen, two bedrooms and a tearoom jut out from the building core.

② Inside, the *tatami*-floored tearoom capsule with its round window is a curious blend of futurism and tradition.

1

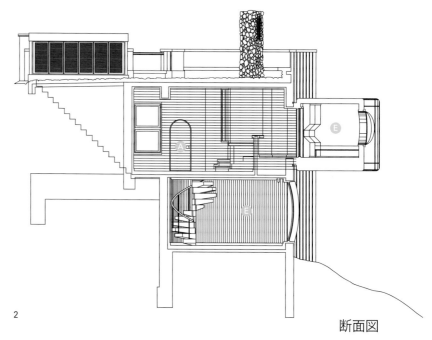

① The wood-clad man-cave-turned-master-bedroom, whose large round window looks out at the landscape.

② Section: (A) entrance, (E) sleeping.

③ The kitchen is the only capsule without a round window.

④ Plan: (A) entrance, (B) living, (C) kitchen, (E) sleeping, (G) *tatami*.

2

断面図

3

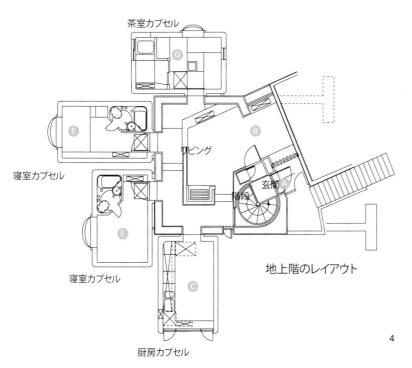

茶室カプセル

寝室カプセル

寝室カプセル

厨房カプセル

リビング

玄関

階段

地上階のレイアウト

4

1

Anti-Dwelling Box
Kiko Mozuna
Hokkaido
1972

A pair of nesting cubes, the Anti-Dwelling Box neither looks nor sounds like a house. In addition to its unusual name, the structure's abstract form is devoid of both scale and typical domestic features, such as room-sized windows or a slanted roof. Plus the exterior was originally painted yellow. But this bold, brawny building is the home that Kiko Mozuna designed for his mother.

Experimental architecture such as this might not stand out so much in Tokyo or Osaka, but in Kushiro, a small port city on the southern coast of Hokkaido, the Anti-Dwelling Box looms large. In a place where summers are blissfully cool and winters brutally cold, however, the house is right at home thanks to its concentric organization and generous use of glass. Integrated with the roof and two exterior walls, triangular expanses of glass admit copious daylight. 'When you first come inside, it still seems like you are outside, but it is very warm, like a sunroom,' comments the architect's architect son, Kozo.

Inside, the smaller box, which is on the upper level (or ground floor), contains the living-dining room. Echoing the building's skin, its enclosure incorporates a triangulated arrangement of windows that fill the room with light and air. Between the two boxes, a narrow layer of space insulates the interior like a traditional *hanten* padded jacket. It holds the entrance, kitchen, bathroom, and a labyrinthian arrangement of stairs leading up to a small *tatami* room, or down to the bedroom. Partially embedded in the ground, the sleeping quarters are cosy and protected. 'It was a very special place, which felt like a ship's hull,' recalls Kozo, who slept there during childhood visits.

For Mozuna, the idea of living in a cube was natural. 'Usually there are many boxes within a house, for example, the television, jewel box, room – in a house one is always in boxes, between boxes and outside of them,' he commented in 1975.[2] But, as its name suggests, this interpretation of what a house could be was a break with the past. 'Instead of normal dwelling patterns, he wanted to create something new,' explains Kozo.

BASEMENT   GROUND FLOOR

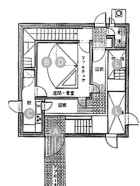

3

1. An inner layer of triangulated windows enables sunlight to bathe the interior in a soft, warm glow.

2. Bands of glass admit copious amounts of sunshine and daylight.

3. Plans: (A) entrance, (B) living, (C) kitchen, (D) dining, (E) sleeping, (F) bath, (L) void.

1

Hara House
Hiroshi Hara
Tokyo
1974

the house is organized along a central corridor with rooms mirroring each other on either side.

But the interior also has a distinctive urban character consistent with Hara's predilection for embedding the city in his buildings. Resembling a little village for four people, the circulation spine is like a street, dotted with pedestal-mounted light fixtures and flanked by building-like rooms. Entered from above, this promenade begins at the foyer, where leafy greenery is visible through the glass doors at the opposite end. As it descends, the hallway repeatedly narrows and widens. Each of its levels holds a pair of rooms: the children's bedroom and the *tatami*-floored guest room at the top; the kitchen-dining room and the combined bath and utility room in the middle; and then the two-room master suite. The corridor culminates in the double-height living room opening onto the balcony.

Overhead, this central spine is illuminated by a clear glass skylight running much of the building's length. Composed of two layers, one half round and the other with angled planes, it keeps moisture out but reveals the constant play of light and shadow. 'It's a little like being outside – it's cold,' laughs Hara. 'But Japanese houses are like that.' In part, this is mitigated by the milky cloud-shaped ceilings topping the individual rooms. Made of acrylic, a new architectural material in the 1970s, they admit natural light into each room by day, but in the evening, when their occupants are home, they emit a soft glow.

2

'Japan is a valley culture,' says Hiroshi Hara. Having grown up in a small city amidst the Japanese Alps, he has personal experience of this way of life. But, as he explains, Japan's valleys are human-sized and friendly, in contrast to those in Switzerland or Colorado. This makes them suitable models for Hara's buildings, which he views as outgrowths of natural topography. Unsurprisingly, when it came time to build a home for his young family, the architect chose a hillside site at the western edge of Tokyo. Following the lay of the land, he created a long single-storey building that incorporates the site's 3-metre (10-foot) drop, utilizing floor planes that step down gradually. Much like an artificial valley,

❶ Like an indoor street, the stepped central corridor leads down from the entrance to the living room.

❷ In contrast to the roof's straight ridge line, the floor plane follows the land's gentle, downward slope.

1

1. The living room segues into a deck overlooking the landscape.

2. Upper-level plan (below): (A) entrance, (C) kitchen, (E) sleeping, (F) bath, (G) *tatami*. Lower-level plan (above): (B) living.

3. Symmetrically placed globe lights and cloud-shaped acrylic ceilings enliven and lighten the interior.

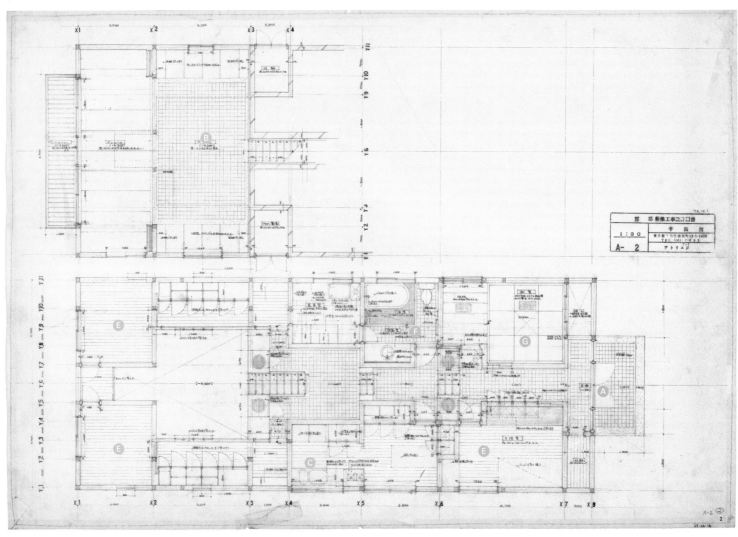

2

3

House in Uehara
Kazuo Shinohara
Tokyo
1976

Initially, the columns seem oversized for the building's modest square base. But there is a logic behind this discrepancy. In addition to minimizing the depth needed for the floor slabs (which helped its architect, Kazuo Shinohara, meet the building code's height restriction), they support the cantilevered covering above the car park. From there, it is possible to enter directly into the studio of the husband, a professional photographer. Alternatively, stairs go up to the main living floor containing the family spaces, the master bedroom, and a *tatami*-mat room designed for the husband's mother. Added late in the design process, the third floor holds the children's bedroom, which is enclosed with a semicircular vault.[3] Like eyes, its two round windows peer out towards the street.

Located up the hill from a commuter train station, the house fronts a narrow road, with homes chock-a-block on either side. Though close to the city centre, this is the kind of tight-knit Tokyo neighbourhood that feels like a small village, where residents and shopkeepers know each other well. Against this backdrop, the geometric expression of Shinohara's design stands out. Though the house abuts the street, privacy is hardly an issue thanks to Shinohara's use of triangular windows upstairs. Of her favourite place, the second-floor living room, the wife says, 'You can see the sky from there, through the triangular window. You could see birds fly down and alight in our trees.'[4]

1

The most astonishing feature of this house is the forest of concrete columns that holds it up. Like tree trunks with bifurcating boughs, their angled limbs define the interior space as well as the exterior elevations. The boldest of the bunch stands in the middle of the communal area, with daily activities occurring all around. Creating an ambiguous boundary between the kitchen and the living-dining area, its tripartite shape is the first thing one sees after ascending the stairs, and its rough surface is, perhaps, the last thing touched before descending. Instead of accommodating to user needs, the column requires users to accommodate to its massive form, walking under or climbing over to get from one side of the house to the other.

❶ A studied composition of squares, triangles and circles, the house stands out from its neighbours.

❷ Stairs leading up from the car park face the massive concrete support partitioning the communal space.

2

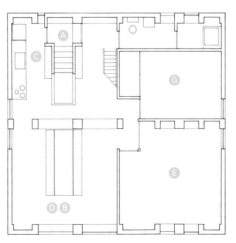

1

GROUND FLOOR   FIRST FLOOR   SECOND FLOOR

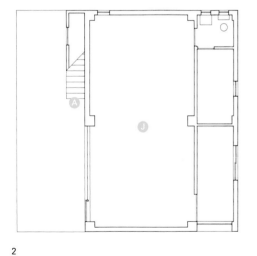
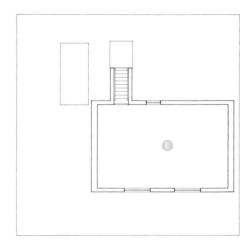

2

① The massive concrete support must be negotiated to get from the kitchen (background) to the living and dining area (foreground).

② Plans: (A) entrance, (B) living, (C) kitchen, (D) dining, (E) sleeping, (G) *tatami*, (J) studio.

③ A door set into the wall's wood infill panel.

1

Row House
in Sumiyoshi
Tadao Ando
Osaka
1976

Ando.[5] Little did he know that this bold move would kick-start his career, and result in many subsequent house commissions. This job came from a couple who wished to replace the middle of three rowhouses in an old Osaka neighbourhood that had survived the war. Hugged by party walls on either side, the site was less than 4 metres (13 feet) wide. Instead of filling the narrow property to the max, Ando opened it in the middle. This not only relieved the tightness, it also created direct contact with nature where least expected.

While greenery and plantings are nowhere in sight, sunlight and sky, as well as wind and rain, activate the courtyard. This pared-down version of nature is echoed by Ando's abstract forms and planar surfaces – mainly concrete, glass, slate and, in areas that are frequently touched, wood. Enclosing the courtyard at either end, glass walls enable plenty of contact between the two halves of the house, as does the connecting bridge. At the same time, the courtyard's physical separation of rooms instils a sense of privacy.

In contrast to the transparent walls encasing the courtyard, the boundary with the street is a completely windowless facade – a gutsy move by Ando. While the imprint of the wood formwork and the round rebar indentations articulate the wall's surface, its only opening is the symmetrically placed entry vestibule. Within this recessed nook, the door stands off to the side, keeping the interior well hidden.

2

On rare occasions, the completion of a new house sends a jolt. Making a clean break from convention, this two-storey concrete box is one of those houses. Concealed behind a poker-faced front elevation, the house consists of four rooms, two per floor, with a courtyard in the middle. Embedding a small garden is an age-old Japanese strategy for bringing light and air into the heart of the house. But here the outdoor space itself is the heart of the house. To get from one room to another the owners must cross their courtyard, regardless of the weather.

'The building was made possible by the reckless courage of youth,' writes Tadao

1 Aside from the entry vestibule, the house is fronted with a completely blank facade.

2 Separated by the courtyard, the two halves of the house are connected on the first floor by a bridge.

1

FIRST FLOOR

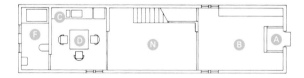

GROUND FLOOR

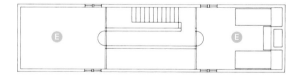

SECTION

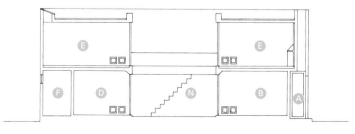

1 Looking from the dining area into the courtyard.

2 Plans and section: (A) entrance, (B) living,
(C) kitchen, (D) dining, (E) sleeping, (F) bath,
(N) courtyard.

3 Shades screen the bedroom for privacy
and sun control.

2

3

1

White U
Toyo Ito
Tokyo
1976

2

A concrete-encased tube of space, White U was as much a memorial as a single-family home. The house, which Toyo Ito terms 'a subterranean space above ground', was designed by the architect for his elder sister, shortly after her husband had died prematurely. 'It was a sad time,' recollects the architect. The couple and their two school-aged daughters had been living in an apartment nearby but, after her husband's death, the client wanted to be closer to her extended family. And she wanted to be closer to the earth. Fortunately, she was able to build on a central Tokyo site adjacent to the family homestead, a modest wooden house where she had lived prior to her marriage.

Sitting directly on the ground, White U's monolithic form didn't look like a domestic dwelling. 'At first, the neighbours thought it might be a church rather than a house,' recalls Ito. Though it surrounded a courtyard, the single-storey home had few openings and little contact with the outdoors. Instead, its enclosure offered a much-needed feeling of protection. The house was entered through a vestibule on its north side that led into the communal area, a continually curving space where functional zones were loosely defined by furniture. At either end, it terminated in a narrow corridor leading to walled-in rooms: the kitchen and bathroom in one direction; two bedrooms (plus an additional toilet and a storage room) on the other; and a study spanning the two sides.

In contrast to the grey exterior, the equally abstract interior was pure white – from carpeted floor to painted ceiling. But four carefully placed skylights animated the plain surfaces with ever-changing light, shadow and darkness. Joining the inner wall with a gentle curve, the angled ceiling tilted towards the courtyard's centre. Windows provided glimpses of this outdoor space, but access was limited – its earthen surface was intended primarily for the eyes.

After living in the house for twenty years, the family was ready for a change. Both daughters had grown up and were ready to live independently. Plus all three no longer felt the need to live in a home built in response to their great loss. Yet they could not imagine anyone else occupying such a personal space. Instead, demolition seemed like the best option, and the house was taken down in 1997.

❶ Inwardly focused, the house maximized privacy and offered a sense of protection.

❷ Inside, furniture designated functional zones, such as the dining area pictured here.

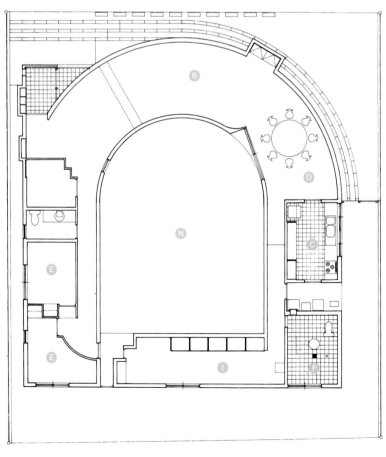

1 A large window connected the dining area to the courtyard.

2 Plan: (B) living, (C) kitchen, (D) dining, (E) sleeping, (F) bath, (I) study, (N) courtyard.

3 Carefully placed skylights and windows animated the interior with light, shadow and darkness.

3

House 2 in Yaizu
Itsuko Hasegawa
Shizuoka Prefecture
1977

whose only requests were high ceilings. But perhaps its main purpose was to provide a hands-on building experience for Hasegawa's students at the Tokyo Institute of Technology. Under her guidance, they erected a sequence of triangular frames, each one an assemblage of square-section wooden beams joined at the apex with 45-degree-angled metal hardware manufactured by a local ironworks. Standing the frames in parallel formation resulted in the house's bold profile. Afterwards, a carpenter was brought in to add walls, windows and the shimmery skin.

Inside, the dominant feature is the wooden framework that creates the scaffolding for the three floor levels. The ground floor holds the living, dining and kitchen areas as well as the bath. Shortened at either end by the triangular geometry, the first floor holds the bedroom, and storage occupies the top floor – the smallest space of all. Admitting fresh air and daylight, windows are positioned between the diagonal bracing embedded in the side walls. Additional wooden frames can be added on either side, should the owner ever wish to expand their Silver Triangle.

1

Affectionately known as the Silver Triangle, this house sits directly on the ground like an ancient Japanese pit dwelling. Yet its gleaming metallic exterior gives it a distinctly futuristic aura. Located in Itsuko Hasegawa's hometown of Yaizu, the property is about 200 metres (656 feet) from the coast, but was surrounded by open land at the time of construction. In contrast to the tight sites typical of Tokyo, here there were no neighbours or rigid legal restrictions to hamper creativity. In short, it was the perfect backdrop for a house that looks like it could have fallen from the sky.

The house was initially conceived for the architect's mother, an amateur artist who specialized in Japanese-style painting, and

2

1 A bold, silver triangle, the home evokes the shimmer of the sea nearby.

2 The house in model form created by the architect's students.

3

GROUND FLOOR

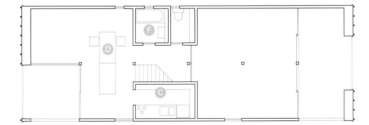

FIRST FLOOR

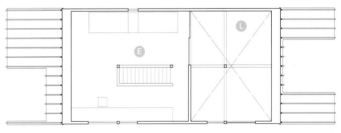

4

SECOND FLOOR

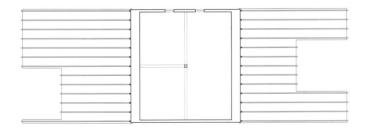

3 The exposed structural frame evokes the traditional Japanese farmhouse.

4 Plans: (C) kitchen, (D) dining, (E) sleeping, (F) bath, (L) void.

Yamakawa Villa
Riken Yamamoto
Nagano Prefecture
1977

A house without walls, the Yamakawa Villa was designed as a summer getaway for a 'salaryman' and his family. It consists of three main elements: an elevated floor, a pitched roof and a series of six white stucco boxes. Aside from the roof's deep eaves, which shut out sun and rain, there is no exterior wrapping. There are no screens, shutters or security devices. The house is simply open to the natural environment. 'Wild boar and other animals are free to come in,' says its architect, Riken Yamamoto. While the boxes contain discrete functional components – bedroom, bath, toilet, eat-in kitchen and storage closets – the semi-outdoor space in between is where the family gathers. Clearly, the void space is as important as the solid.

The project began after the client acquired a property located within a planned vacation-home community at the base of Mount Yatsugatake. Situated at a high elevation, the area is extremely cold in winter but blissfully cool in summer. 'It's so high that there aren't even mosquitoes,' comments the architect. The setting was ideal for the client, who wanted to use the house during the warm months only – a common scenario in Japan where the vacation home is a relatively new concept, spreading in tandem with the country's economic growth.

The client's other hope was for a house with a large terrace. The architect's response was a house that essentially is a terrace. A platform of plain pine, the floor barely distinguishes inside from out. Though there are neighbouring houses, there was simply no need for walls since dense forest surrounds the site. Instead, privacy is protected by isolating personal areas within the boxes. Naturally, the absence of walls all but eliminates the need for windows, aside from the occasional square opening in the larger boxes. 'We made the windows as small as possible,' explains Yamamoto. During the off-season, the boxes become the perfect place to stow furniture and possessions, while the platform in between shelters the local fauna until the warm weather returns.

1

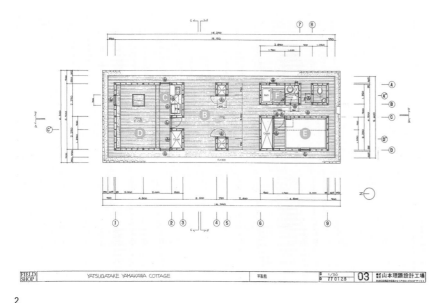

1 Symbolic as well as functional, the hefty roof unifies the house while providing protection from the elements.

3

4

2 Plan: (B) living, (C) kitchen, (D) dining, (E) sleeping, (F) bath.

3 Within the house, the communal space can be used freely.

4 On its long elevations, the house is completely open, providing shelter to animals in the off season.

5 Deck chairs are the perfect spot from which to enjoy the autumn foliage.

5

1

Maki House
Fumihiko Maki
Tokyo
1978

2

The Pritzker Prize laureate Fumihiko Maki has built urban developments, cultural facilities, academic buildings and places of worship all over the world. But even in this comparatively modest structure – the first house designed by his firm – signatures of Maki's architectural approach are embodied. Articulated with a rich material palette and a generous use of daylight, the home's fluid modernist space has the timeless elegance characteristic of his opus.

A two-generation home for the architect's family, the building is located in central Tokyo amidst a quiet residential enclave populated with single-family dwellings and low-scale apartment blocks. The house abuts the street

with a stepped entrance, where a warm wooden door welcomes. It leads into a central hall with stairs bathed with soft daylight from above, graciously connecting the home's two floors. The lower level holds bedrooms and a second kitchen. The upper level contains the combined living and dining room – a sweeping space whose ceiling soars 3.6 metres (11 feet 10 inches) over the seating area – as well as the main kitchen and the master bedroom with an adjoining study. In lieu of corridors, every room has more than one doorway, enabling each space to connect seamlessly to the next. 'My favourite part of the house is the circulation, or rather the continuity of circulation,' says Maki. 'There are no "dead ends".'

The introduction of daylight throughout the house is another way that continuity is achieved. Unrestrained by the Western convention of positioning windows to offer eye-level views, glass is also placed up high and down low. This strategy illuminates the interior with ever-changing natural light without compromising privacy or reducing the availability of wall space for displaying art. Unified by a steel crossbar, a series of windows opens the home's south side to the garden, while an enclosed courtyard on the north side looks skywards, admitting daylight at both levels.

Neutral white walls predominate inside, creating the ideal backdrop for the play of light and shadow. But the house's exterior is a collage of textured materials, plus those sleek modernist staples: glass and steel. Extending up from a tile-clad base, the concrete walls are articulated by horizontal banding with a wood-grain imprint created by the formwork used during construction. As if acknowledging Japan's wet climate, the durable surface wears well, rain or shine.

1 The skylit stair hall leads up from the entry foyer.

2 A steel crossbar unifies the south elevation facing the garden.

1

GROUND FLOOR

FIRST FLOOR

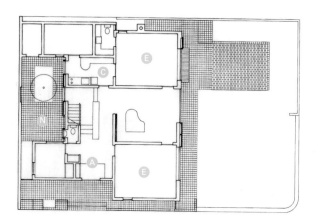

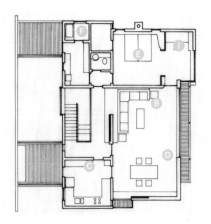

2

1 High windows in the living room admit light from above.

2 Plans: (A) entrance, (B) living, (C) kitchen, (D) dining, (E) sleeping, (F) bath, (I) study, (N) courtyard.

At Home
Maki House

Fumihiko Maki and Naomi Kobayashi

I was born in 1928 and turned ninety-five in 2023. Endowed with relatively good health, I am still active in my architectural design practice.

My first encounter with a modern house came when I was a few years old. My mother took me to the opening ceremony of my aunt's home in the Den-en Chofu district, west of Tokyo. It was very 'Corbusian', though I did not realize it at the time. During my youth, I often enjoyed visiting that house, but my aunt (my father's younger sister) did not like bright sun coming through its large glass windows, and always closed the curtains. Contemporary critics of modernist architecture would have been delighted to hear of her antipathy to those windows! But I, naturally, enjoyed running in, out, and around their house.

It turns out that this house was the second architectural design by Yoshiro Taniguchi (the father of Yoshio Taniguchi, another prominent Japanese architect), built in 1933. Even when he was a young student at Tokyo University, Yoshiro Taniguchi was a frequent visitor to my grandfather's house, because my grandfather lived near the campus. How did Taniguchi get the commission? According to my relatives, the owner, Shigeo Sasaki, and Taniguchi were both young faculty members at the Tokyo Institute of Technology. Sasaki asked Taniguchi to design a house for him and his wife. Of course, he was delighted by the commission. And I hear that the house was used quite often as a movie set in those days.

When I was young, my parents would often take me to Yokohama when a large passenger ship arrived in that port town. The zigzag organization of the ship interiors was another early introduction to modern architecture. Anyway, we first moved to the site of the Maki House when I was a few years old. It is in a quiet residential district, on a hill 20 metres (66 feet) or so above Gotanda's railway station along Tokyo's Yamanote Line. At that time, you could still hear the trains running below quite clearly. Not anymore. You could also enjoy a view of Mount Fuji from the first-floor windows of the house. Not anymore, of course. In those early years, Gotanda Station was occupied in the mornings only by people working in the centre of Tokyo, around 10 kilometres (6 miles) away. Today, the station is crowded all day long, and not just with commuters.

The old house lasted almost fifty years. It was a quasi-modern house, designed and built by my younger uncle. Except for a few *tatami* rooms, the interior was mostly contemporary. I remember my parents enjoying dance parties there with their close friends. In retrospect, I feel quite lucky to have been brought up in a modern, upper-middle-class family.

I built the present Maki House in 1978 to my own designs. It had become increasingly difficult for my mother (above left, pictured with me and my wife) to manage her residence alone (though she was quite healthy and active for her age). I decided that she should live on the ground floor, and my wife Misao and I would live on the first floor, with our daughters downstairs. My mother occupied the lower floor happily, which had a bedroom, a living room, and her own bathroom and storage, as well as an additional small cubicle. But there were no more dance parties. She passed away peacefully at the age of ninety-seven. Misao and I had our own set of rooms, equipped in a standard Western manner.

My second daughter, Naomi Kobayashi, is an architect like her husband, Hiroto Kobayashi, a professor at Keio University's Fujisawa campus. They took Hiroto's sabbatical year at the University of California, Berkeley, and after returning to Tokyo in 2014 briefly lived in their own place. But soon they decided to join Misao and me in Gotanda, and to use their house in Daikanyama as guest quarters. So, we redesigned the living quarters in the Maki House accordingly. They moved in just a few months later, and we continue to live together happily today.

As I wrote earlier, when I was young the noise of the Yamanote Line could be heard clearly in our house. Now, somehow, it is much quieter. The area around Gotanda Station – before only used by daily commuters – now consists of high-rise office buildings full of shops and restaurants. So that has become much louder! I have observed so many changes occurring around my house. I hope that it continues to survive for future generations, who can write their own stories of how the house became a part of their own lives.
FUMIHIKO MAKI

As with many buildings designed by architects, this house was designed to satisfy our family's immediate needs, but with some flexibility for future changes. One of the new elements of the house was the ground-floor quarters for my grandmother. She was supposed to move in when she had finished taking care of her aged mother nearby, so the main dining and living spaces went upstairs, along with my parents' master bedroom.

As an elementary-school student then, I was too young to be involved in the design, but I earnestly wished for my own private room, though that dream didn't come true. I was quite disappointed to find a children's room to be shared with my sister instead! However, when I started studying architecture, I came to understand that the family room between our room and my grandmother's room on the ground floor plays a very important role. Having a semi-public room in the middle takes sunlight from the south into the hallway, and creates both effective ventilation and a sense of transparency between the major garden on the south and the courtyard on the north. I am now convinced that my father's decision as an architect – that this layout would be more meaningful than assigning private rooms for his two daughters, who would probably be leaving the house soon – was correct.

As expected, my sister and I got married and left home in the 1990s. After my grandmother passed away in 2005, my parents lived by themselves for almost ten years until I returned with my husband and daughter in 2014. My parents originally considered moving out to a flat as they grew old, but changing their living environment in their eighties was not easy, so they preferred the idea of having us move in. Fortunately, our family was a good fit for the house. Our daughter was an only child, and she always wanted to live in a house with stairs, and also longed to be part of a large family. The original kitchen and bathroom for my grandmother worked perfectly – we only did some minor remodelling of the bathroom before moving in.

Returning to the house this time has given me a different perspective, and not just one resulting from the chemistry created by three generations living together. Now that I am responsible for doing what my mother used to do over a long period, I feel strongly that this house has been a collaboration between my father and mother (opposite page left, shown companionably together). The bright, spacious, modern architecture that everyone admires is undeniably due to my father (below, with a priest at the ground-breaking ceremony),

but it also owes a great deal to my mother for maintaining it over forty years. In addition to simple cleaning, she used to cover the handles on furniture to prevent them from getting dirty during use, and to clean even exterior louvres on wooden shutters one by one, using chopsticks and a cloth – the house is a testament to my mother's daily efforts and dedication (opposite page right). Now I tell myself every day that I should feel grateful to be so close to this treasure created by my parents.

NAOMI KOBAYASHI

1

Our House
Masako and
Shoji Hayashi
Tokyo
1978

After almost twenty-five years, Our House needed an upgrade but, unlike most, they chose to refresh and enlarge, not scrap and rebuild. Shoji was no stranger to renovation. As a child, his parents' home, which once stood on the property next door, had undergone a major addition, but was then destroyed during World War II. Following this precedent, the architects realized an ambitious renovation of their own. At the time, Masako, who specialized in residential design, had opened an office with two other female architects, while Shoji was on staff at Nikken Sekkei, a growing practice producing large-scale projects. But he also had a desk in his wife's studio, where the couple spent evenings updating Our House. 'Masako did the design, but Shoji did one hundred per cent of the drawings,' comments architect Koichi Yasuda, who is the current owner of Our House.

Their scheme kept the original rectangular volume, but expanded it in different directions, including a triangular extension for new kitchen and dining areas, and a second floor with a pitched roof. Incorporating a study overlooking the garden, a music-listening room, a spa-style bathing suite and a small kitchenette, the new upper level was intended as the architects' retreat. 'They were so busy they didn't have time to go to a weekend house,' explains Yasuda, who acquired and renovated Our House in 2013. Although worn-out parts had to be replaced and surfaces refinished, Yasuda and his family prioritized preservation throughout the renovation. In such features as Masako's distinctive red-stained walls and Shoji's long, low desk, the artistry and elegance of the Hayashis' architecture remain alive and well today.

2

By the 1970s, many first-generation post-war houses were deemed ripe for replacement. But Masako and Shoji Hayashi were ahead of their time. The architect couple had originally built Our House way back in 1955, shortly after completing their studies and getting married. Like My Home I (see page 64), built by their academic advisor Kiyoshi Seike the previous year, the Hayashis' modest flat-roofed building centred on a combined kitchen-dining-living room. They flanked this with sleeping and study areas plus a *tatami*-mat room for Shoji's mother.

❶ The angled entry creates a sense of arrival.

❷ The house opens to a spacious garden out back.

1

① The music-listening room flows into the study with its long, low built-in desk.

② The circular bath on the second floor was designed for relaxation.

③ Sliding *shoji* screens compliment the architects' collection of modernist furnishings in the living room.

④ Plans: (A) entrance, (B) living, (C) kitchen, (D) dining, (E) sleeping, (F) bath, (I) study, (M) terrace.

2

3

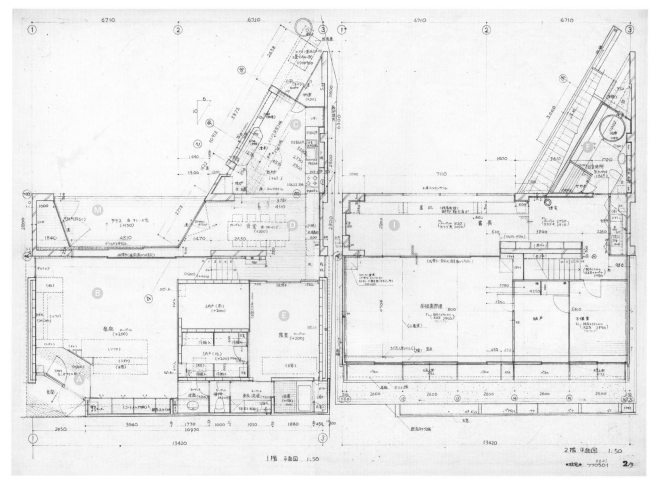

4

Toy Block House I
Takefumi Aida
Yamaguchi Prefecture
1979

The first of ten 'Toy Block House' projects, this commission came from a dentist who wished to build a combined residence and clinic. The resulting building consists of two layers, or floor levels, each one composed of a symmetrical arrangement of blocks. Four rectangular volumes comprise the ground-floor clinic. Perpendicular to these is the mixture of rectangles and roof-shaped triangles that makes up the first-floor residence.

Functionally, the two levels are completely independent. Expressed with stepped walls, stairs ascending from opposite sides culminate at the home's entrance. For patient privacy, the clinic is entered from a different direction and its wall openings are carefully controlled. Appropriately, glass blocks admit light from outside into the waiting, treatment and staff areas that encircle the skylit indoor plaza in the middle. Upstairs, the skylight's concrete enclosure is the centrepiece of the patio. 'The glass top is so strong, it becomes a table during family barbecues,' jokes Aida. Wrapping the courtyard, a corridor leads to the bedrooms on one side and the communal spaces on the other. Like a house within a house, a pitched-roof mini room made of cork contains the dining area. 'This makes the space more intimate,' explains Aida. Not to mention more fun for parents and children alike.

1

When Takefumi Aida was an architecture student, modernism was the name of the game. But shortly after launching his practice, the Tokyo architect began searching for ways to expand his design approach, a quest that led him to the notion of play. 'Pleasure as the goal of play is an important issue related to a basic aspect of human life,' he explains.[6] In toy blocks, Aida found a medium for connecting this idea to architecture. When using them to build his projects in miniature, the tiny cylinders, rectangles and triangles were not only fun, they could also be a tool for architectural composition – precisely the new direction that Aida was hungering after. Once he'd made that connection, adopting toy blocks as a design device was just a hop, skip and jump.

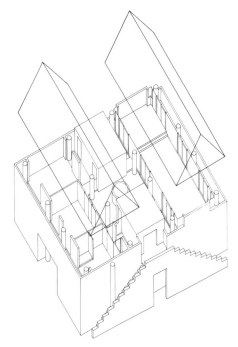

2

1 The symmetrical facade with stairs from either side leading to the residence.

2 An axonometric rendering of the building, with the home on top and the clinic below.

3 The glass-covered skylight channels daylight through to the ground-floor clinic and also serves as a table on the home's terrace.

4 The pitched-roof house-within-a-house contains the dining room.

5 Glass blocks arranged in stepped formation wash the room with soft light.

3

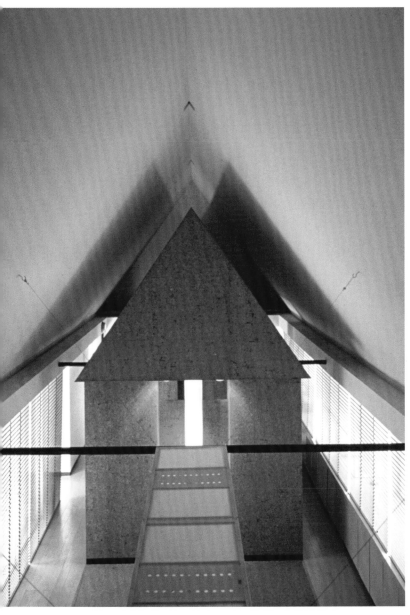

4

5

Spotlight

Walls and Doors

Typically, walls in Western-style homes protect and partition. In the historic Japanese house, where divisions were less explicit, their role was somewhat different. Frequently, movable panels were used to create walls that doubled as doors, doors that behaved like windows, and an ambiguity between inside and out (opposite page). These homes were built not to subdue, but to coexist with, the sun, wind and rain. Naturally, the absence of air-tight closure had comfort implications. Even today, Japanese homes can be draughty or downright cold. But, for most, this remains a welcome trade-off for living in harmony with the environment.

The wall's ambiguous role was made possible by the building's support system. Separating skeleton and skin, traditional post-and-beam construction freed walls from the heavy lifting. They could be made of a variety of materials – wood, rammed earth and paper were all fair game – and placed freely within the column grid. The homes of commoners, such as *minka* farmhouses or *machiya* townhouses, tended to have solid external walls. For the homes of the aristocracy, however, the balance shifted. Their grounds were usually encircled with walls, while the building itself was enclosed mainly with sliding screens, which could open an entire room or side of the house to the garden.

In many cases, interiors were divided with lightweight, movable panels. While opaque *fusuma* separated the rooms, their perimeters were lined with translucent *shoji* screens, along with the *amado* wood shutters that protected their delicate surfaces. Light enough to open with one finger, sliding panels also served as doors. This wall mobility enabled remarkable flexibility, an appealing feature that is still well-suited to contemporary Japanese lifestyles.

Unsurprisingly, walls in Japan have evolved over time. As the country recovered from World War II, durable materials, such as steel and concrete, grew in popularity but, as in traditional wood construction, were often minimally finished. Due to rampant urban development, blank facades became common, mitigating unpredictable and rapidly changing conditions outside. Subsequently, some architects rejected this strategy by embracing the surroundings with porous walls and plenty of glass. This acceptance yielded a more spacious atmosphere, not to mention closer relations with the neighbours.

Today, regardless of their exposure, homes are considered the owners' private domain, as defined by exterior walls and entry foyer – the place where outsiders are greeted and street shoes are shed. Once across the threshold, however, boundaries are often more fluid and, as in historical Japanese houses, the use of walls sparing. Fewer divisions are thought to maximize space – where walls are needed, sliding panels made of paper, polycarbonate or even punched metal often suffice.

1980—1989

1980s
The Go-Go Era

The decade was unquestionably dominated by the rapid expansion of Japan's economy, which took off in the mid-1980s. As the stock market boomed and real-estate values soared, the bubble economy grew at a ferocious clip, turning Tokyo into a global financial centre.[1] At its peak, the grounds of the Imperial Palace in central Tokyo were rumoured to be worth as much as the entire state of California.

It was a heady time for Japanese consumers, who now had increasing discretionary income and leisure time. Luxury fashion brands were all the rage. Porsches and Ferraris populated city streets. And overseas holidays became de rigueur. Just hailing a taxi on a Saturday night in Tokyo's notorious Roppongi district was nearly impossible. So was scoring an entrance pass for the newly opened Tokyo Disneyland, the entertainment conglomerate's first theme park outside the US. Though conspicuous consumption was rampant, the sky-high land values priced some potential homeowners out of the market. But for many commercial entities, as well as government agencies, this period of wealth was a chance to launch ambitious development projects.

Practically overnight, Japan became the go-to destination for lucrative building commissions, drawing architects both foreign and local. While flashy projects, such as Philippe Starck's Asahi Super Dry Hall (opposite page), popped up on the shore of Tokyo's Sumida River, everything from public housing to park furniture took shape on the island of Kyushu under the aegis of the Artpolis programme. Spearheaded by Arata Isozaki and bankrolled by Kumamoto Prefecture, this initiative turned an agricultural backwater into an architectural mecca.

But this spending spree on the part of Japanese investors was not limited to their own country. The world looked on with a modicum of disbelief as prominent international assets were snapped up, from Manhattan's Rockefeller Center to Hollywood's Columbia Pictures studio and the legendary Pebble Beach golf resort. Not to mention Vincent van Gogh's masterpiece, *Sunflowers*, which sold at auction to the Yasuda Fire and Marine Insurance Co. in 1987 for a whopping $39.9 million.[2] In part, these acquisitions were enabled by the appreciation of the Japanese yen after the Plaza Accord, an international agreement signed in 1985, which was intended to reduce the American trade deficit by adjusting the US dollar exchange rate.

Taking a stand against the glitz and glamour, the Seibu Saison Group opened the first MUJI store in 1983, ironically just around the corner from Omotesando, the epicentre of Tokyo's burgeoning fashion world. The MUJI concept of 'All Value No Frills' was positioned as an antidote to the waste and excess of the era.[3] This ethos was also prescient, given the belt-tightening that followed the bursting of the economic bubble in the 1990s.

The decade closed with the death of Emperor Hirohito in 1989. This event brought an end to the Showa era, a sixty-two-year span coloured by both war and recovery. But it also ushered in the reign of Emperor Akihito and the start of the Heisei era.

1

House in Kuwahara
Itsuko Hasegawa
Ehime Prefecture
1980

Unsurprisingly, this two-storey house was commissioned by a manufacturer of architectural metals and his wife. Located on the outskirts of Matsuyama City on the island of Shikoku, their property was ringed by rice paddies on three sides. 'It was a very bright and refreshing place with rice stalks fluttering and mountains in the distance,' recalls Hasegawa. Naturally, the architect aimed to connect her building to these surroundings. Aluminium's shiny surface was one way to do so. 'Unlike other metals, aluminium does not reflect shapes,' says the architect. But its colour is constantly changing, reflecting the sun's movement, weather's variability and other organic phenomena.

Facing south, a combination of perforated screens and solid panels fronts the house. While the latter conceals the private areas – a *tatami*-mat room on the ground floor and bedrooms upstairs – the former defines the patio extending out from the living and dining areas. 'Punched aluminium wasn't on the market yet, so I asked the client to make aluminium plate with the openings I wanted,' explains Hasegawa. The apertures she chose balanced enclosure and exposure, yielding a space with the indoor–outdoor ambiguity of an *engawa*-style porch. Behind the screen, X-shaped steel bracing adds another layer of visual interest.

Inside, the gleaming metal is complemented by glossy marble floors and ceiling-suspended curtains of fine stainless-steel mesh – an existing product that Hasegawa spotted in the client's warehouse – which partitions functional areas within the flowing communal space. 'Growing up near the beach, I've always been attracted to the shimmery spectacle of the sea,' explains Hasegawa. Here she duplicates it in machined metal.

2

A homage to the qualities of aluminium panels, both plain and perforated, this house makes a case for metal. At the time of its design, steel was a common choice for structural frames, but punched metal had yet to be adopted as a construction material. Mass-produced and easy to assemble, these lightweight panels could streamline the building process. But equally important was their aesthetic potential. While the panels' thinness conveyed delicacy, their openings fostered translucency, an effect akin to *shoji* paper screens. Here was a material that connected to the past and pointed the way towards the future. Punched metal went on to become a staple not just of Itsuko Hasegawa's works, but of 1980s architecture.

1 Similar to *shoji* paper, punched metal lets light filter into the patio.

2 A mixture of perforated and plain metal screens form the house's south side.

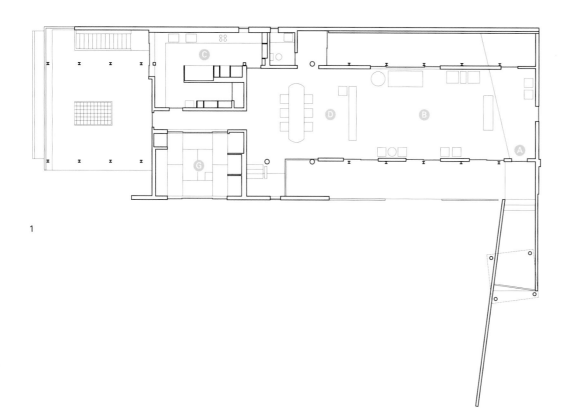

1

2

3

① Plans: (A) entrance, (B) living, (C) kitchen,
(D) dining, (E) sleeping, (F) bath,
(G) *tatami*.

② Metal and marble accent the dining room.

③ The nighttime view through the patio to
the living room.

④ Unsurprisingly, metal was used down
to the details.

4

ROIB
Minoru Takeyama
Sapporo
1980

In Tokyo, commercial buildings vie for attention, and few truly stand out. But Minoru Takeyama had a knack for making statements. Loaded with tiny bars and nightclubs, his Niban-kan complex in Shinjuku, designed in 1970, was adorned with eye-popping supergraphics. Nine years later, Shibuya 109 emerged, a metallic temple to trendy retail anchoring one of the city's busiest intersections. The polar opposite of all that glitz and gleam, ROIB is an elegant home for a dentist and his family in the Hokkaido city of Sapporo.

ROIB – a name derived from the words 'residence of' plus the client's initials – was built amidst a newly developed housing subdivision where an apple orchard once stood. 'When I visited the site for the first time, it overlapped with the landscape of my childhood memories,' wrote Takeyama, who was born in Sapporo.[1] Initially, the clients wanted one-storey living, but Takeyama countered with a three-storey structure that left plenty of room for a garden.

Inside, the house is laid out in a traditional *tanoji* plan. Named after the Japanese *kanji* character for 'rice field', this square formation is divided into four equal parts. At ROIB, each of these quadrants holds a distinct functional component. On the ground floor, one contains the kitchen and dining room, another the double-height terrace, and the remaining two are filled with the living room, half of which is also double-height. On the first floor, two squares hold void spaces, and two contain *tatami*-floored rooms. On the second floor, the master bedroom occupies one square, the two children's bedrooms another, the bathroom and walk-in closet one more, and the last one is a terrace accessible from the bedrooms.

Squares also dominate the exterior, relating the various apertures geometrically. Like nesting blocks, they articulate the concrete walls, outlining windows and screening devices and holding panels of square glass blocks. The exterior stairs running up two sides of the house provide another riff on the theme. Both functional and ornamental, their square treads lead up to the roof while hinting at the interior stairs concealed underneath.

Integrating outdoor and indoor space may seem counterintuitive given the local climate. But it yields a light-filled, airy and mainly white interior. 'It was not a formal space at all,' recalls the architect's wife Rumi. 'Rather than modern and cool, it was warm and relaxing.'

1

1 Squares of several sizes articulate ROIB's concrete exterior.

3

GROUND FLOOR   SECOND FLOOR

BASEMENT   FIRST FLOOR

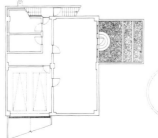

2

❷ The covered terrace abutting the double-height
living room (right) and kitchen (left) at night.

❸ The double-height living room adjoins the
covered terrace with window-walls.

❹ Plans and sections: (A) entrance, (B) living,
(C) kitchen, (D) dining, (E) sleeping, (F) bath,
(G) *tatami*, (L) void, (M) terrace.

4

Stainless-Steel House with Light Lattice
Shoei Yoh
Nagasaki Prefecture
1980

1

Typically, steel construction reads as a framework of slender metal surrounding large glass panes. In this house, however, a grid of glass outlines stainless-steel wall panels instead. Composed of thin transparent strips, this grid infuses the house with natural light during the day. But, after the sun goes down, the panels recede into darkness and the glass turns into a glowing lattice.

'Shoei Yoh was very interested in the expression of natural phenomena,' explains Masaaki Iwamoto, assistant professor of design at Kyushu University, Fukuoka. 'The Pantheon in Rome was very inspirational.'

Evoking the interior of that sanctuary, an ever-changing influx of daylight activates Yoh's eye-catching house in Nagasaki Prefecture, changing its character throughout the day. The architect achieved this result with industrial materials – at first glance, the lines of light appear to magically support the opaque-panelled walls and roof, but the heavy lifting is done by a matrix of hidden steel channels. Between pairs of these C-shaped bars, the glass strips are secured by silicone, creating a waterproof and, in the event of an earthquake, seismically responsive seal. In select spots, the opaque panels are swapped out for hinged sheets of smoky glass that act like windows, opening the interior to provide views and ventilation. Shiny and sharp-edged, the house gives off a futuristic vibe that carries over inside.

Designed for a physician and his wife, the single-storey structure employs a symmetrical butterfly-shaped plan, with public areas, such as the living room and a *tatami*-floored guest room, on one side, and the private areas, which include the bedroom, the kitchen and a dining area, on the other. Between the two stands an entrance hall made entirely of glass. Connecting inside and out, square white tiles lead from the street to the transparent front door and then continue as flooring, repeating the grid motif at a smaller scale. Adding a touch of dynamism, a giant stair cuts across the static plan. Extending from the street, through the house and then out the other side, the broad treads adjust the floor level to the naturally sloping site. Where the stairs pass through the living room, a hearth is built directly into the treads. Hovering above it is a black cylindrical fireplace flue, as if pinning the house in place.

1 Gridded tile walkways lead from the street to the glass-enclosed entrance hall.

2

❷ Suspended from above, the black fireplace cover hovers over the broad stairs in the living room.

❸ Plan: (A) entrance, (B) living, (C) kitchen, (D) dining, (E) sleeping, (F) bath, (G) *tatami*.

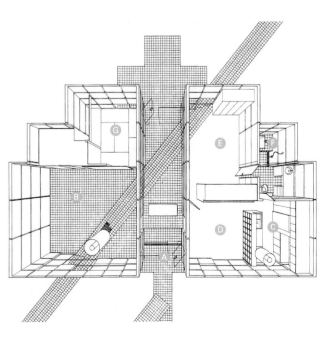

3

House Under
High-Voltage Lines
Kazuo Shinohara
Tokyo
1981

forms. Boldly expressed, the main structural elements are two beefy round columns painted robust shades of green, yellow and blue on consecutive floors. These support equally massive beams holding up cantilevered slabs with scalloped undersides. The motif appears again in both the spiral stair and the exterior wall panels made of glass blocks – each block is a square with a circle inscribed.

Topped with a one-sided swooping roof, this house is a paean of sorts to Tokyo's above-ground utility lines. Unlike many countries, where power cables are increasingly buried, Japan stubbornly holds onto its ubiquitous concrete poles and black cables. Like convenience stores and police boxes, they are simply part of the cityscape. For Kazuo Shinohara, they were also a source of design inspiration.

Created at a time when the chaotic conditions of the city were impacting Shinohara's work, this dwelling does not possess the geometric purity of his earlier schemes. In fact, its overall form is all but hidden from view, since the property is hemmed in by buildings (except where a narrow accessway connects to the street). As well as these surroundings, there were code restrictions to consider – sunshine protection laws limited one side of the property, and the overhead utility lines, which required a radius of clearance, the other.[2]

Using that radius as his guide, Shinohara carved two curves out of the roof, which yielded the building's unique profile. Naturally, this move reverberated inside. While the lower two floors could remain clean rectangles, the top floor angles obliquely where the roof cuts in. Communal areas are on the ground level, the master bedroom and study above that, and additional sleeping quarters on the top floor. As if occupying an attic garret, one of those bedrooms is tucked beneath the roof's convex form.

Throughout the house, the roof's round indentations are echoed by repeated circular

1 The above-ground utility lines inspired the roof's scalloped profile.

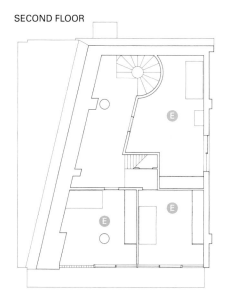

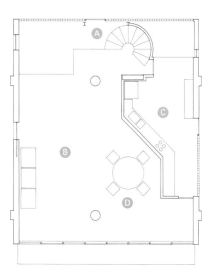

GROUND FLOOR

FIRST FLOOR

SECOND FLOOR

3

❶ Painted blue, structural underpinnings support the convex roof on the second floor.

❷ The yellow column in the first-floor stair hall.

❸ Plans: (A) entrance, (B) living, (C) kitchen, (D) dining, (E) sleeping, (F) bath, (G) *tatami*.

❹ Square glass blocks with circular indentations fill in the concrete structural frame.

Koshino House
Tadao Ando
Hyogo Prefecture
1981, 1984, 2006

courtyard separates the two rectangular components that comprised the house when first built, while an underground passageway tied the two blocks together. Lowest on the hill but longest in dimension, the single-storey block held the children's bedrooms and the *tatami*-mat guest rooms, while a shorter two-storey block contained the double-height living room and dining-kitchen areas, with the master bedroom and study upstairs.

The curved component housing the client's atelier, completed in 1984, is more than a straightforward addition – rather, it is a logical, geometric extension of the existing building. Though open at one end, its arched outer wall implicitly aligns with the adjacent block. It also shelters the sloping lawn wedged between the two building parts.

Twenty years after the atelier was added, the house underwent a second major change, the children having grown and gone. Instead of introducing an additional structure, Ando replaced the single-storey bedroom wing with a two-storey guest house, which includes a reception room and gallery. While the new construction stands in the footprint of the old, it is as tall as the adjacent block.

Inside all three parts, the connection to nature is palpable. Though solid concrete walls create an explicit divide, slit-like skylights and windows admit slivers of daylight and offer well-considered views. There is no need for more. In lieu of ornament, the sublime play of light and shadow on the textured walls changes throughout the day.

2

A trio of geometric forms, this house is as much an abstract sculpture as an elegant work of architecture. The flat-roofed building consists of two parallel rectangular volumes, plus a curved element added four years later. Each of these discrete components is fashioned from concrete and glass only. But it is their interaction with nature that completes Tadao Ando's composition and brings his building to life.

Created for a well-known fashion designer and her family, the house occupies a generous property in Ashiya, an exclusive suburb of both Kobe and Osaka. Taking advantage of the land's natural assets, the building is angled in relation to the street – a strategy that preserved existing trees – and is embedded in the sloping topography. Like an outdoor room, the stepped

1 Angled in relation to the street, the home consists of three concrete components.

2 The dining and living areas.

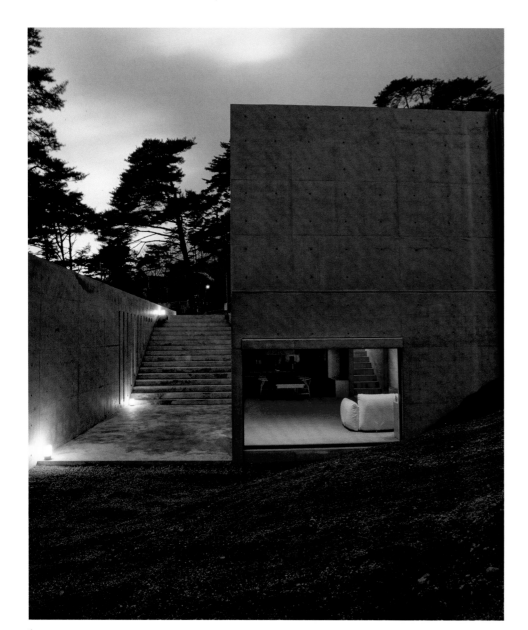

1

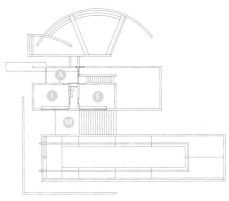

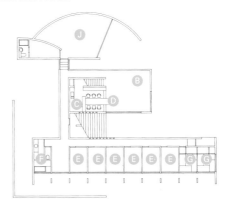

2

3

194

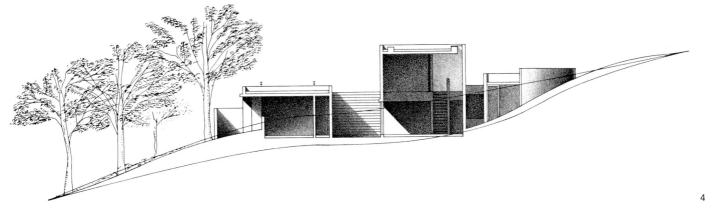

4

❶ Sandwiched between Koshino House's two rectangular volumes, the stepped terrace is like an outdoor room.

❷ Plans: (A) entrance, (B) living, (C) kitchen, (D) dining, (E) sleeping, (F) bath, (G) *tatami*, (I) study, (J) studio, (M) terrace.

❸ Natural views complement the hall in the guest quarters that replaced the children's rooms.

❹ A cross-section shows the building nestled into its sloping site.

❺ Admitted by a skylight, daylight illuminates the atelier's curved wall.

5

House in Yokohama
Kazuo Shinohara
Kanagawa Prefecture
1984

A collage of three-dimensional forms, this house is a far cry from the pure squares, rectangles and pyramids favoured by Kazuo Shinohara at the start of his career. Fittingly, it exemplifies a point when the chaotic conditions of the city were having an impact on the architect's work, and his attention was shifting to public or institutional commissions. Instead of shutting out the urban cacophony,

Shinohara seemed to derive inspiration from its energy. 'There is currently a delight in Tokyo's landscape of chaos, or in activities enabled by such a landscape, completely unrelated as it is to the well-ordered streetscape and planned-city aesthetic anticipated by modernism,' he wrote in 1988.[3] Small but mighty, this house is a case in point.

The project began as an addition to a wooden house that Shinohara had moved to the site in the 1960s, according to Professor Shin-ichi Okuyama of the Tokyo Institute of Technology. After retiring from the same university, Shinohara turned the old house into his studio, and built this new residence next door. Among his chief concerns were preserving the trees that dotted the steeply sloping site, and maintaining sunlight access for the existing house.

Abutting the old building, the new structure consisted of a tubular space shaped like a quarter cylinder, with the communal functions upstairs and private areas nestled up against the hillside below. Extending out from this metal-clad volume were a full cylinder used for storage; a stepped volume containing a two-mat *tatami* room; and angled bay windows that directed the eye up towards the sky or out into the landscape.

Shinohara's bold geometry also dominated the two-dimensional surfaces, both inside and out. Made of corrugated aluminium, the highly textured exterior skin was perforated by a variety of rectangular, triangular, circular and square windows. Within the house, these shapes repeated as internal doors and window treatments, as well as Shinohara-designed tables and chairs. Against the pure white walls and floors, the strong colours used for doors and window covers, along with the furniture's exaggerated shapes, complemented the building's complex form.

1

❶ Bold geometric forms characterized the house exterior.

❷ The galley kitchen and dining area with Shinohara-designed furnishings.

❸ Plans: (A) entrance, (B) living, (C) kitchen, (D) dining, (E) sleeping, (F) bath, (G) *tatami*.

2

LOWER LEVEL

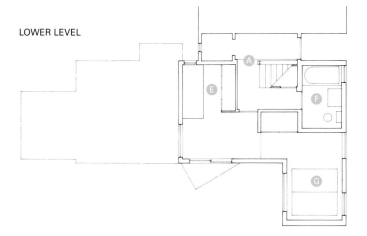

UPPER LEVEL

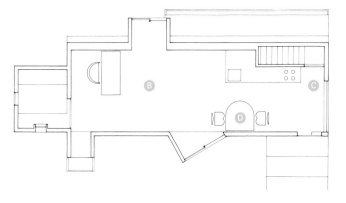

3

Silver Hut
Toyo Ito
Tokyo
1984

A family affair on multiple counts, the house replaced a modest wooden dwelling where Ito had grown up from the age of sixteen, and originally abutted White U, the home he designed for his older sister in 1976 (see page 156). Despite their proximity, the two Ito-designed houses bore little resemblance. Unlike its introverted concrete neighbour, Silver Hut was light, airy and open to the natural surroundings. It was entered through a square courtyard wrapped on three sides by the various programmatic sections. Uniting indoors and out, the courtyard was paved with *kawara* tiles, which continued into the kitchen, dining and living areas at its rear. Flanking the courtyard on one side was a study and a *tatami*-floored room. On the other stood two stacked bedrooms (the only part of the house that was two storeys), plus the bathroom.

Like houses within the house, the different functional zones were articulated by individual vaults, which rested on a grid of concrete columns. This structural strategy enabled the architect to place internal walls freely, creating a sense of enclosure in some places and fluidity elsewhere. The vaults themselves were composed of triangulated units that held perforated metal panels or skylights. But above the largest 'room' of all, the courtyard, the arched truss served as the scaffolding for a movable tent-like cover. It provided shelter on rainy days, but could be moved aside on clear ones, filling the entire house with fresh air and sunlight. 'It was overflowing with light,' recalls Ito.

As with many nomadic dwellings, the time came for Ito to pull up stakes. And in 2010, he elected to take down the building but give it a permanent home on Omishima Island, where it was resurrected as a workshop space at the Toyo Ito Museum of Architecture, Imabari, overlooking the Seto Inland Sea.

1

Aptly named, Silver Hut combined high-tech metallic materials with one of the most elemental types of shelter. Built in central Tokyo by the architect for his family, Silver Hut was topped with seven vaults, each one corresponding to a different functional component. Barely contained by a metal-mesh fence, the dynamic form evoked a primitive village. 'In the past, people gathered and built their houses clustered together,' explains Toyo Ito. Yet its steel space-frame support system exemplified 1980s construction.

2

GROUND LEVEL

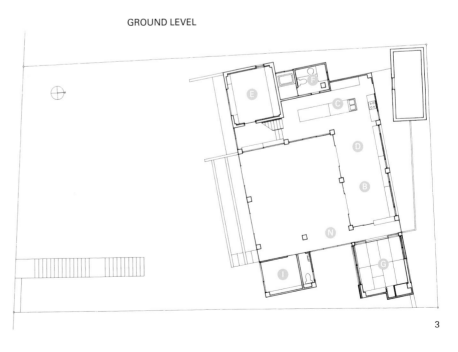

3

❶ Seven metal vaults formed the roof of
the house.

❷ The courtyard at night.

❸ Plan: (B) living, (C) kitchen, (D) dining,
(E) sleeping, (F) bath, (G) *tatami*, (I) study,
(N) courtyard.

Farmer's House
Osamu Ishiyama
Nagano Prefecture
1986

at his practice. 'He imagined the construction process in his brain.' With that in mind, the architect posted weekly letters to the farmer, outlining sequential directions for the building process. There were no working drawings or formal construction documents, just Ishiyama's handwritten instructions and cartoon-like sketches. His idea utilized readily available prefabricated materials, which the farmer and his accomplices could easily fashion with the tools and techniques at hand. But the final assembly was anything but conventional.

For the building exterior, steel sheets normally used for civil engineering works were bolted together into a squat cylinder. Since there is no basement or foundation, the cylinder's splayed base stabilizes the house while its overall shell-like form behaves as a self-supporting monocoque structure. The steel floor helps the bottom keep its flattened shape. 'It's almost like a brace,' says Watanabe. The building's ends were filled in with a combination of concrete blocks and brick-shaped glass bands supported by a steel framework.

Inside, the fireplace and chimney were among the first components to be completed. Situated in the middle of a womb-like, warming room, they are critical for creature comfort, since the mountain property is subject to harsh winters. Another accommodation to the climate was the recessed entrance, where a zigzag glass screen lets light in but keeps the cold out. While partitions were erected to designate rooms, most can be moved or removed.

Unsurprisingly, more than ten years passed before the house was deemed done. But truth be told, it will never be finished. Like a living entity, it continues to grow and evolve as the needs of the farmer and his family change.

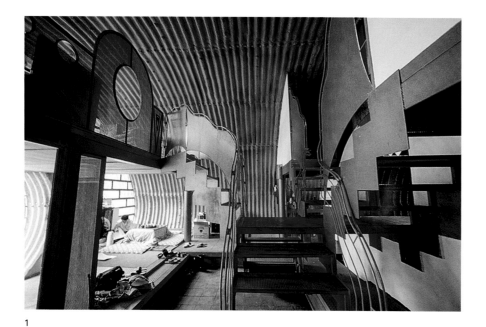

1

A tube of corrugated steel sitting out in the landscape, this building looks more like a farm machine than a farmhouse. But, contained within its metal casing, is a home for a family of four. The house arose out of a collaboration between an architect knowledgeable about the self-build process, and a client eager to give it a go. Bypassing the usual sequence of design and construction, the scheme was envisioned by the architect but realized by the farmer. Having grown up in rural Japan, the latter was no stranger to metalwork or machinery. This was his chance to try his hand at housebuilding.

'Basically, Osamu Ishiyama designed the building methodology rather than its shape,' explains Professor Taishi Watanabe, a former Ishiyama student and staff member

2

GROUND FLOOR   FIRST FLOOR

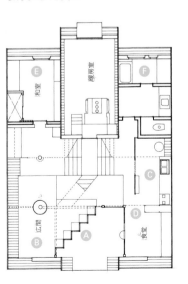 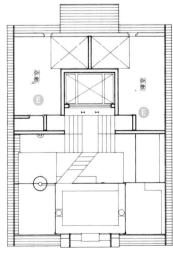

❶ Inside the cave-like interior, with the living
room on the left.

❷ Steel framework on the end elevations
holds glass panels and props up the
corrugated metal exterior.

❸ Plans: (A) entrance, (B) living, (C) kitchen,
(D) dining, (E) sleeping, (F) bath.

3

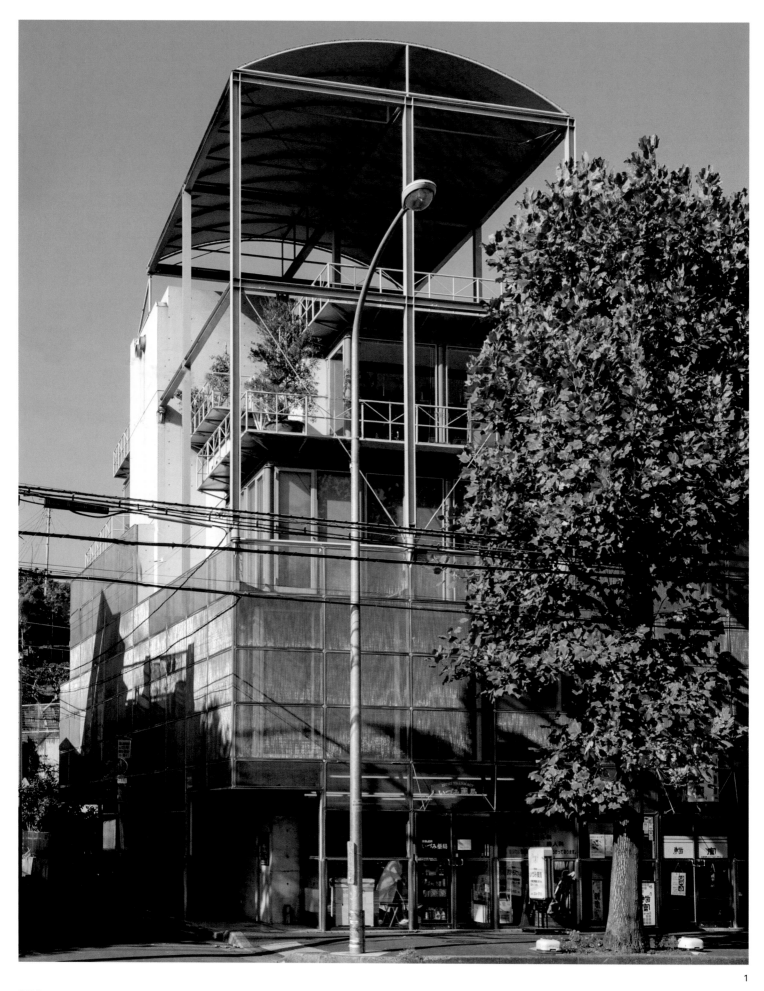

1

GAZEBO
Riken Yamamoto
Kanagawa Prefecture
1986

2

GAZEBO is a fresh take on the small mixed-use buildings called *zakkyo biru* that can be found all over Japan. At the time of completion in 1986, it held a pharmacy and café at street level, followed by a floor of offices directly above, then a floor of rental apartments, and finally the architect's home on top. Encased with glass, the architect's abode gazes out over Yokohama like a penthouse apartment. But it has the intimacy and independence of a private house.

The origin of the project can be traced back to 1955, when the narrow street in front of the site was transformed into a four-lane thoroughfare as part of a national push to promote urban development and improve transportation networks. Prior to its expansion, the street had been lined with small shops where locals bought their daily groceries and exchanged chit-chat. 'Making roads wider destroyed the sense of community in that area,' laments Riken Yamamoto, whose parents' pharmacy was a neighbourhood fixture. After three decades had passed, the decision was finally made to replace their store with this multi-storey building, the miscellaneous contents of which mirrored the mixed composition of the wider city in miniature.

The heart of the home is its wood-decked courtyard. 'It's like an extension of the living room,' explains Yamamoto. This multipurpose outdoor space proved equally suitable for children's play as for grown-up dinner parties. Around it, Yamamoto placed an eat-in kitchen, a bathroom and a bedroom, with additional sleeping quarters at the back and a *tatami*-mat room embedded in the rental units below. Inwardly focused and self-contained, the dwelling is completely removed from the tenant spaces on the lower floors.

Taking advantage of this isolation, Yamamoto embraced transparency. Full-height glass windows and doors open the interior to balconies overlooking the street and to the courtyard. Instead of compromising privacy, see-through walls foster familial closeness while filling the rooms with daylight, breezes and skyward views. Similarly, a large operable panel above the cooking area in the kitchen flips open to let in soft light and fresh air.

But there can be too much of a good thing. Mitigating the sun is a series of sail-like awnings. The most impressive of all is the arch-shaped canopy crowning the very top. Visible from afar, it implicitly unifies GAZEBO's various parts and gives it an urban presence. 'It's a symbol of the building,' remarks Yamamoto.

① From the street, GAZEBO reads as a conventional mixed-use building.

② The kitchen (left) opens onto the courtyard.

THIRD FLOOR

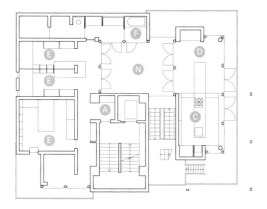

SECOND FLOOR

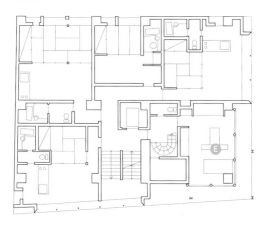

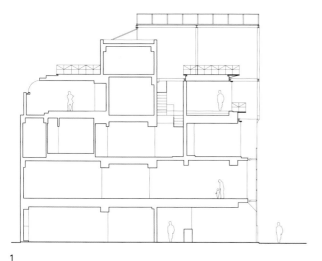

1

1 Plans: (A) entrance, (C) kitchen, (D) dining,
(E) sleeping, (F) bath, (N) courtyard.

2 Sail-like sunshades shield the courtyard.

2

1

House in Kohan
Yoko Kinoshita and Makoto Shin Watanabe
Tokyo
1987

2

A fresh take on Classical villas in Europe, the House in Kohan has a symmetrical plan, vaulted roof and an upper floor like a *piano nobile*. But this home for a couple and their dogs is rendered in steel and glass and located on the edge of Tokyo. The corner property had been purchased by the clients in the late 1960s, and sits within a residential area, with houses on three sides and a municipal nature preserve in front. After some twenty years, the existing prefabricated building was tired, and the clients' needs had changed. To design a

replacement, they commissioned their architect daughter, Yoko Kinoshita, who had just launched her own practice, ADH Architects, with Makoto Shin Watanabe.

In addition to heeding her parents' request for a comfortable house where they could co-exist amiably with their frisky Labrador, the architects wanted to maximize the visual connection to the protected public land. With support spaces below and the main living area above, the prototypical Western villa was the perfect model for the cross-shaped, two-storey house.

Straddling the building's north–south axis, the patio doubles as the home's entrance. It adjoins the dining room, around which Kinoshita placed the stairs, kitchen, utility room and two extra bedrooms. But the real pièce de résistance is the living room upstairs. Here the ceiling arches up, sunlight streams in, and a panorama of lush greenery is revealed. 'I wanted to erase the road in front,' explains Kinoshita. Elevating the room not only concealed the cars, it also offered an unimpeded view of the nature preserve. Framed for the most part by fixed glass, this scene is primarily for the eyes, but the terrace behind the bathroom at the back opens to the elements.

The integration of outdoor space on both levels contributes to the home's relaxed, easy atmosphere. On the ground floor, it also benefited the dogs, who could roam freely out to the fenced yard. The soft soil of the property, once an irrigated rice paddy, was tackled by placing the house on a concrete platform.

A short run of stairs leads up from ground level to a covered patio reminiscent of a traditional *doma* – an earth-floored transitional space. While continuous *mokurenga* wood-block pavers and sliding glass doors fuse the terrace with the dining area, angled steel supports – the home's signature visual element – branch out to support the living room overhead.

❶ Clad with *mokurenga* wood-block pavers, the elevated terrace leads the way inside.

❷ In lieu of a foyer, the home is entered from the terrace, which connects to the dining room.

1

2

GROUND FLOOR

FIRST FLOOR

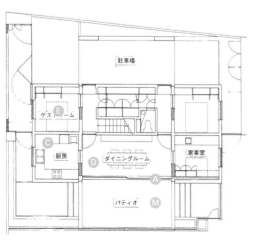

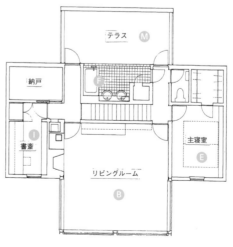

❶ Raising the height of the custom-built dining-room table discourages the family dogs from sampling food.

❷ Topped by a vaulted ceiling, the living room looks out at the nature preserve.

❸ Plans: (A) entrance, (B) living, (C) kitchen, (E) sleeping, (F) bath, (I) study, (M) terrace.

3

At Home House in Kohan

Makoto Shin Watanabe and Yoko Kinoshita

The literal translation of Kohan, the area where this house was built, is 'lakeside'. Lake Tama and Lake Sayama – two large reservoirs completed in 1927 to supply water for metropolitan Tokyo – are in the neighbourhood. The district was developed during the 1960s and 1970s as a suburban residential neighbourhood, and it was here that Yoko's father purchased a lot and built a PanaHome prefabricated house. Constructed from lightweight steel, this factory-made house was for me a symbol of post-war modernization. Every material used, for instance the melamine countertop, seemed to represent the rapidly developing industrialization of post-war Japan. In the 1980s, though the prefab was not in bad shape, Yoko's father decided to build the House in Kohan, designed by his daughter.

Yoko went to New York in 1963 at the age of six with her family, as her father was working for the Bank of Tokyo in Manhattan. Life in New York was like a dream – you could eat bananas and use hot water at any time. In Japan, bananas were quite expensive, and I remember my mother boiling water for her children to wash their faces every morning during wintertime.

Initially, Yoko's family lived in Queens, but then moved to Scarsdale, a suburb of New York City. Kohan is not Scarsdale, but the House in Kohan reflects the suburban life that the Kinoshita family encountered in America. Its site area is much smaller than those of comparable American houses, yet the House in Kohan has a clear, T-shaped floor plan. Its rigorous symmetry reminds me of Palladian villas, but at a 'transistorized' Japanese scale.

Pets and gardening are essential parts of suburban life. In the House in Kohan, life with dogs had an impact on the design, for instance in the dining room, where the high table prevents the dogs from reaching dishes. In most Japanese houses, shoes are not worn inside, but here the wooden-block floor connecting the dining area and the covered patio is like the traditional earthen-floored *doma*, an area where shoes are kept on. It also suited the dogs.

The dishwasher in the kitchen and the under-counter washer dryer in the utility room were very rare in Tokyo when this house was built. A bathroom with a jacuzzi tub has become more common, but a bathroom without a separate washing area has not. The fireplace in the living room is another reflection of American life, while the gas central heating system and the underfloor heating provided comfort not only for human beings but also for pet animals. These things were accepted naturally by the Kinoshita family because of their American experience.

A house is the container of the family that lives there, and becomes a receptacle for family memories. But, in the House in Kohan, there is another force driving the design – a desire to supersede the industrial modernization that Japan had tried to achieve during the 1960s and 1970s, when Sony's transistor radios and steel prefabricated houses were first introduced. In the field of architecture, overcoming pure functionalism was a big issue in the 1980s. By blending the clean geometry of the Palladian villa with the memory of suburban American life, this small house was a step in the right direction.

MAKOTO SHIN WATANABE

After living abroad for many years, my parents returned to Japan for good and wanted a permanent home where they could live with their beloved dogs, so they gave their novice architect daughter her first design commission.

My father gave me these encouraging words during our early conversations regarding the house: 'Design to your heart's content.' While this seemed to give me a lot of liberty, I felt a great pressure and responsibility to live up to my parents' expectations. The topping-out ceremony (left and below), a celebration when the last beam is placed atop a structure, gave me confidence in executing the architectural work. That aside, I kept questioning whether my parents would appreciate the space I was designing, or whether they would be able to use the house as I intended. Despite these worries, my parents lived happily together there for over thirty years.

The House in Kohan supports an informal lifestyle – my father also envisioned it as a weekend retreat for my and my brother's families. It does not have the formal *genkan* entrance that is common to most Japanese homes. Instead, one enters the house from the patio, without even recognizing that one has crossed the threshold. The ground level has a

doma earthen floor, where both humans and dogs can move around freely. A healthy if well-padded Labrador, weighing in at over 50 kilograms (110 pounds), used to assist my mother with her daily cooking chores by consuming, and thus reducing, biodegradable waste. The dining room and the patio could be fully connected by opening the sliding glass doors. My parents regarded these areas as a home not only for them but also for their dogs.

In contrast to the ground floor, the upper level is entirely for humans. The Italian term *piano nobile*, which refers to the principal floor containing a house's main space and bedrooms, is a pertinent one. In the prefabricated house that was previously on the site, where I had lived as a teenager, my room was on the upper level, commanding the fabulous view of the nature preserve. So when it was my turn to design, I knew exactly where the major space of the house ought to be – looking out over the preserve.

Aside from spatial comforts, I wanted my parents to enjoy the environmental comforts that they had very much appreciated when living in America. The conductive heating system and the underfloor heating in the House in Kohan seem to have been effective. My father commented on the luxury of sitting in the *piano nobile* and watching the white snow blanketing the nature preserve. Another reason for his glad acceptance of these extra energy costs was the presence of the self-invited neighbouring cat, who also appreciated the warmth from the floor. These environmental comforts, together with a staircase that kept my parents healthy as they climbed up and down between the two storeys, were features of the house that enhanced my parents' lives until they finally decided to move to an easier-to-manage one-storey home for the elderly in 2019.

YOKO KINOSHITA

1

House F
Kazunari Sakamoto
Tokyo
1988

A refreshing departure from convention, this house has neither pitched roof nor formal entry. There are barely even floor levels. The heart of the house is its airy communal area, where the folded ceiling floats delicately above the living, dining and kitchen spaces. From here, separate stairways go off in different directions as they ascend or descend to the private quarters: three bedrooms, two studies and a *tatami*-floored tearoom at the very top. This is a place where spaces segue organically. 'It has the casualness and good fit of a T-shirt,' observes the client.

The commission grew out of a collegial friendship between Kazunari Sakamoto and the client, both professors of architecture at the Tokyo Institute of Technology. 'I frequently visited his office, where there was a table full of small house models,' recalls the client. In addition to their asymmetrical composition, the models' walls, floors and roofs were only loosely connected – qualities that caught his attention.

Bringing these studies to life, the walls and roof at House F don't even touch. 'I had the image of the roof being as light as a tent,' reveals Sakamoto. Making this point crystal clear, a band of glass separates the roof and walls while admitting light and views from all directions – a subtle but effective means of connecting inside and out. 'We can even see the moon from the living room,' notes the client. Creased all over like origami paper, the roof is supported by angled steel pipes anchored to a grid of steel columns. Ranging in length, the pipes extend up and outwards, resembling tree branches. 'Normally, the roof dictates

the ceiling height,' explains Sakamoto. 'But a floating roof can be used to create spaces with different heights.' Though the roof and ceiling were fabricated from rigid materials, Tokyo's merciless sun is screened out by a flexible membrane above the stepped courtyard that connects the street-level garage to the entrance upstairs.

The house sits on a quiet street amidst a residential area developed in the 1920s, but these surroundings are bound to change eventually. Like many architects, Sakamoto could have dealt with this uncertainty by focusing House F inwards. Instead, he adopted a more accepting stance by loosening connections and relaxing the rigid divide between the interior spaces and the outside world.

1 The covered courtyard connecting the ground and first floors.

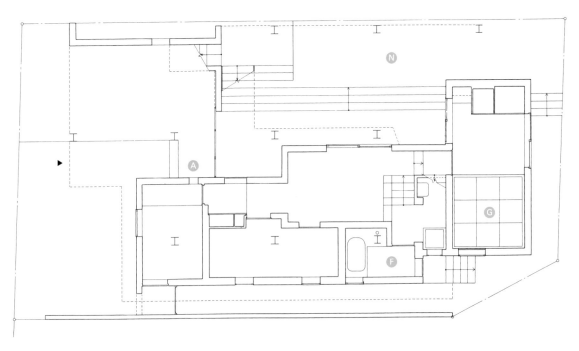

1

GROUND FLOOR

2

3

FIRST FLOOR

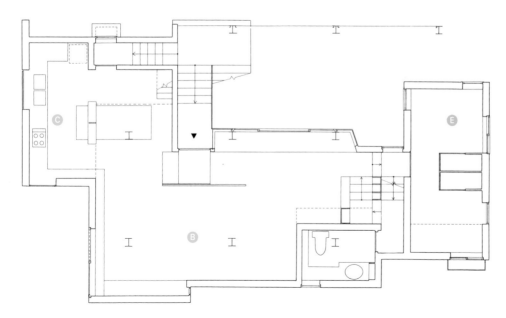

1 The view from the street.

2 Plans: (A) entrance, (B) living, (C) kitchen, (E) sleeping, (F) bath, (G) *tatami*, (N) courtyard.

3 Creased like origami paper, the tent-like roof is supported by white steel pipes.

Spotlight

The Window

In Japan, the matter of the window is not black and white. The muted grey light imparted through traditional *shoji* screens was famously celebrated in Jun'ichiro Tanizaki's 1933 masterpiece, *In Praise of Shadows*. Sufficient for reading and writing, the filtered rays were easy on the eyes, while the semi-darkness soothed the spirit. These window-walls of translucent rice paper and delicate wood lattice remain one of the most distinctive features of Japanese architecture.

In some ways, the movable screen is the root of Japanese windows. As historian Atsushi Ueda explains, the word for window, *mado*, is composed of two *kanji* characters meaning 'a space between two posts' and 'door'.[1] He identifies the 'upward-swinging lattice shutter', which straddled the line between window and door, as 'the earliest form of Japanese window'.[2] The most enduring of these window-walls, however, is the *shoji* screen and its kin. Over time, its wood and paper have often been swapped out for aluminium sash windows, glass panels, and other mass-produced materials, yet the feel and function of these contemporary versions still evoke the traditional.

The remarkable exposure enabled by sliding panels was complemented by small openings, mainly for fresh air. In *minka* farmhouses, for example, simple holes in solid walls crossed with wood or bamboo laths served this purpose (opposite page). Unlike Western-style windows, which provide view, ventilation and daylight all in one, these functions could instead be distributed among different sorts of openings. For many contemporary designers, divide and conquer remains the way to go.

Another consideration is placement. Western-style windows are often situated at eye level for those seated on chairs. But in Japan, a country with a long-standing habit of floor-sitting, windows can be located up high as well as down low. Even in rooms with upholstered furnishings, window positions are calculated to edit the view without severing the connection to the outdoors.

But some architects favour the opposite approach when it comes to the surroundings. Says Ryue Nishizawa, 'The city environment is inherently what gives our city life richness. You shouldn't build closed houses just because there may be shabby or undesirable aspects to urban life.'[3] Amiable coexistence with the sights and sounds of the street, as well as sunshine and fresh air, has been a welcome change for many. And the bigger the window, the more possible this becomes.

1990——1999

1990s
The Bust after
the Boom

The peaking of the Japanese stock market in late 1989 brought an end to the wild speculation of the bubble era, triggering a collapse of asset values as land prices plummeted, non-performing loans proliferated, and consumer belt-tightening became the norm. These losses did not bottom out till 1992, and even after that recovery proved slow-going.

Due to the burst bubble, many construction projects were put on hold or cancelled altogether. Yet there was no absence of cranes on the Tokyo skyline in the early 1990s, as ambitious projects conceived in the 1980s arose one after another. Among the most conspicuous were Kenzo Tange's Tokyo Metropolitan Government Building, whose twin towers dwarfed Shinjuku's famous skyscrapers, and Rafael Viñoly's Tokyo International Forum. Ironically, the latter – a combined cultural hub and convention hall – replaced Tange's original city hall built in 1957. In the coming years, however, architectural commissions moved to the hinterlands.

In 1994, to help rekindle the economy, the central government committed to spending 630 trillion yen on public works.[1] This provided support for the countrywide construction of new museums, libraries, community centres, police stations, and more. Replacing the developers with deep pockets of the 1980s, municipal and prefectural agencies became leading patrons of architecture. Though many bubble-era buildings were criticized as slapdash and shoddily built, their unique expression underscored the possibilities offered by design. And that had a positive impact on all building sectors moving forward. '[T]hroughout Japan, public architecture began to depart from simple functionalism whose aim was to be neutral and easy to use,' observed architect Fumihiko Maki.[2]

The discomfort and unease caused by the economic downturn were compounded in 1995 by the Great Hanshin Earthquake in Hyogo Prefecture and the sarin gas attack that befell Tokyo a couple of months later. The natural disaster caused more than 6,000 deaths and more than $100 billion in damages,[3] while the terrorist emergency left thirteen dead and thousands of others injured following the release of the lethal gas on three of Tokyo's central subway lines during rush hour.[4] Both events shook the Japanese psyche and tested national confidence. The Paper Church (opposite page), defined by 58 paper tubes and a tent-like roof, was built in Kobe by Shigeru Ban for survivors of the Great Hanshin Earthquake.

On the upside, the decade also witnessed Japan's growing globalization. While the rapidly expanding internet facilitated an unprecedented global exchange of information, international events, such as the 1998 Winter Olympics held in Nagano Prefecture and the 'Visions of Japan' exhibition at London's Victoria and Albert Museum in 1991, brought foreign audiences face to face with Japan. As the country's profile increased worldwide, it shed its association with antiquated notions of 'the exotic Orient' once and for all. As Maki points out, '[G]lobalization means not simply internationalization, but the incorporation of Japan itself into a worldwide network.'[5]

House in Ajina
Toru Murakami
Hiroshima
Prefecture
1990

2

A bare minimum of a building, this house is an assemblage of the thinnest of walls, the slenderest of columns and the lightest of roofs. Together they form a C-shaped structure embracing an outdoor terrace. Unsurprisingly, the house was commissioned by a young couple with a taste for simple design and monotone space. In hiring Toru Murakami, they found their match.

For Murakami, house design begins with a careful inventory of the site. Though the picturesque island of Miyajima is visible from the road running in front of the property, the

immediate area is a sea of conventional two-storey houses. For the clients – the son and heir apparent of a high-end traditional Japanese inn owned by his father, and his wife – privacy was paramount. They also wanted an interior garden. Instead of the traditional *nakaniwa* composed of greenery, rocks and water, Murakami answered with 'a garden without plants'. Every room opens to this expansive outdoor space – the heart of the house. In the cooler months, it functions as a terrace. But when the weather warms up, a layer of water turns its paved floor into a shallow pool. Surrounded by floor-to-ceiling glass, this 'garden' bathes the interior with sunlight and skyward views year-round. By contrast, windowless walls shield the house from the street outside.

Approached through the garage, the interior is divided into two blocks, with the garden in between. Separated by half levels, the floors within the blocks are linked by enclosed ramps criss-crossing the edge of the outdoor space. 'Gradual ramps are more fun and more interesting than stairs,' comments Murakami. Nonetheless, he did provide a spiral stair to minimize the distance between the bath and bedrooms located on the first and second floors. Unifying the house, vaulted roofs soar overhead, like sails catching the wind.

Instead of canvas cloth, however, the roof segments are made of steel, supported by concrete walls and columns laid out on a 3.6-metre (11 foot 10 inch) grid. '[The module] comes from the *minka* [farmhouse] tradition,' explains Murakami. While delicate pin joints connect the structural framing elements, slit-like openings separate the walls. Though rendered with contemporary materials, the articulated post-and-beam construction also recalls historic houses. 'It's not *wafu* [Japanese style], but it has the feeling of *wafu*,' observes Murakami.

❶ Gentle ramps connect one side of the house to the other.

❷ The house is entered through the garage.

FIRST FLOOR

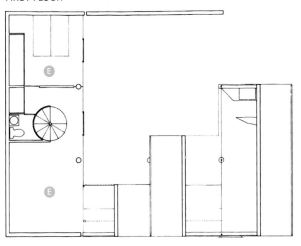

GROUND FLOOR

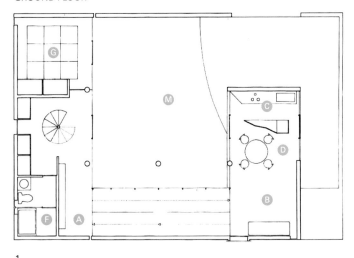

1

1 Plans: (A) entrance, (B) living, (C) kitchen, (D) dining, (E) sleeping, (F) bath, (G) *tatami*, (M) terrace.

2 During the warm months, the terrace is covered with a thin layer of water, turning it into a shallow pool.

2

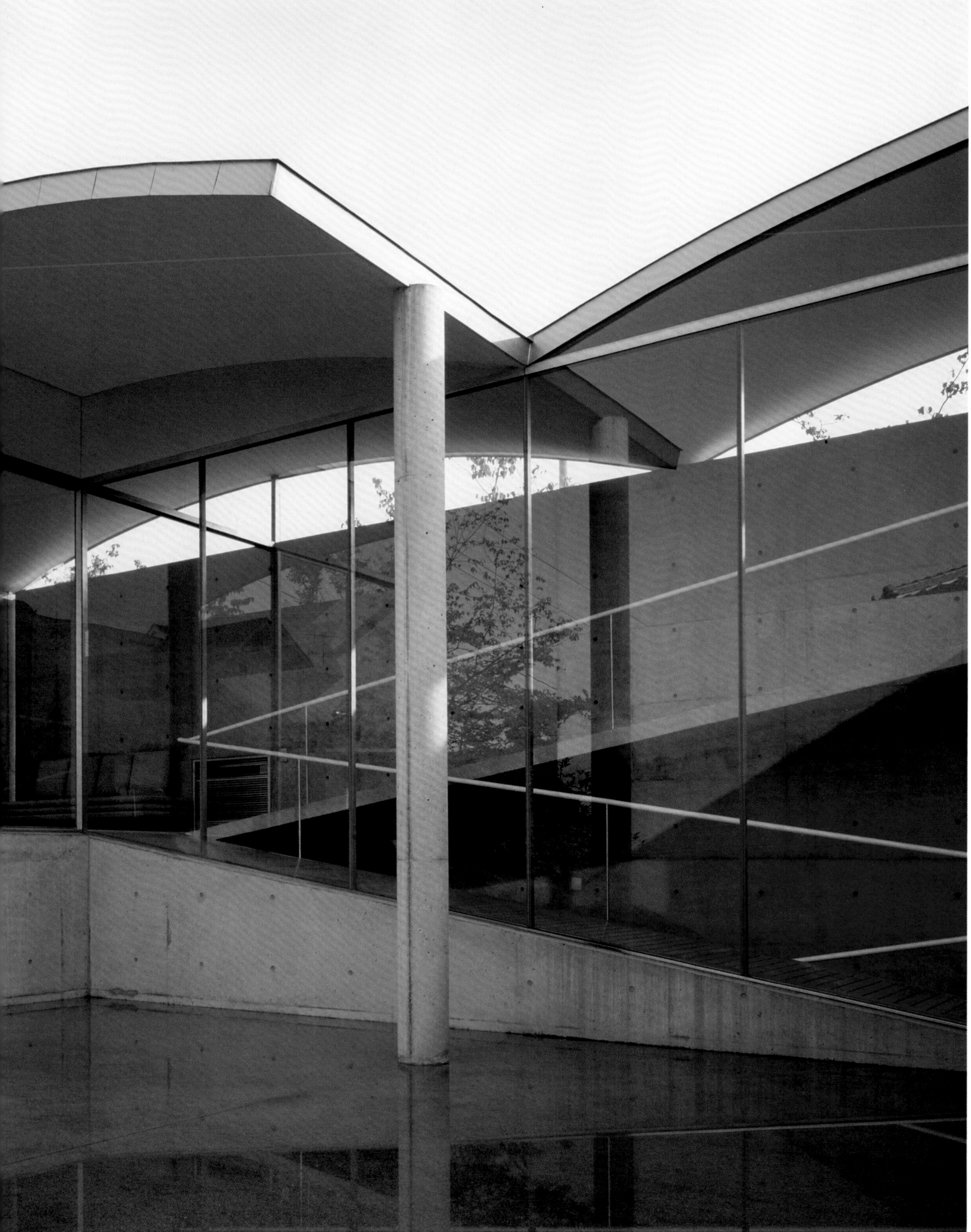

House in Ajina

1

House in
Nipponbashi
Waro Kishi
Osaka
1992

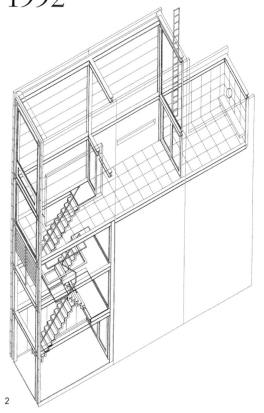

2

A busy commercial district, Osaka's Nipponbashi isn't exactly a place to call home. But Waro Kishi's clients, an older couple who ran a small store in the neighbourhood, couldn't imagine living anywhere else. Instead, they tasked Kishi with turning a super-skinny site – it measures a mere 2.7 by 13.5 metres (8 feet 10 inches by 44 feet 3 inches) – into their dream house.

While the site's oblong shape posed challenges, its location was exempt from sunshine protection laws and height restrictions that normally govern residential zones. To maximize his clients' property, Kishi was keen to build as tall as possible, but going too high would compromise the

home's structural integrity. Striking the perfect balance, the house is stabilized by a hefty 3-metre (10-foot) deep block of concrete embedded underground. This supports the slender white structural-steel frame, which in turn elegantly outlines the four-storey building. Bound by a semi-open stair at the front, the house contains a rental office space at street level, with the clients' home above, consisting of a *tatami*-floored room and bathroom on the first floor; the bedroom and storage on the second; and the combined kitchen-dining-living room, plus an outdoor terrace, on top.

Crowning the building with the home's communal space may seem counterintuitive. But this strategy minimized the site's deficits, maximized its assets, and enabled Kishi to recreate what he calls the 'image of living in the sky', an idea that came to him while visiting a friend's Hong Kong penthouse. Hoping to evoke a similar atmosphere, he stuck to the conventional 2.3-metre (7 foot 7 inch) ceiling height downstairs. Upstairs, however, it jumps to a staggering 6 metres (19 feet 8 inches), creating a sense of hierarchy and compensating for the narrowness. Though barely wide enough for a dining table (Kishi had to design one himself to fit), the communal space is enclosed with full-height glass at either end. Replaced by daylight and skyward views, the hustle and bustle of the city below simply melt away, allowing the house to connect to nature despite its densely packed surroundings.

Ease of construction was an unexpected consequence of the property's odd size. Because bringing big machinery on site was not an option, Kishi favoured factory-made industrial materials that could be easily assembled. Even the facade arrived in two ready-made pieces that were simply stacked and welded together. Made of glass, steel and pre-cast concrete panels, the building connects to the city, but its sense of enclosure creates a sense of home.

❶ At night, the house glows like an *andon* paper lantern.

❷ An axonometric drawing reveals how the floors stack up.

1

2

GROUND FLOOR

機械室

オフィス

Ⓐ

FIRST FLOOR

Ⓕ

Ⓖ

和室

SECOND FLOOR

納戸

Ⓔ

寝室

THIRD FLOOR

Ⓜ

テラス

Ⓑ Ⓓ

ダイニング
ルーム

Ⓒ

❶ Facing the street, the double-height living
area with the kitchen beyond.

❷ Looking out from the custom, Kishi-designed
dining table towards the terrace.

❸ Plans: (A) entrance, (B) living, (C) kitchen,
(D) dining, (E) sleeping, (F) bath, (G) *tatami*,
(M) terrace.

❹ Metal-grate stairs and landings allow light to
filter down at the front of the building.

3

Soft and Hairy House Ushida Findlay Partnership Ibaraki Prefecture 1993

Located amidst a residential development in a Tokyo 'exurb' – a planned community beyond the city's suburbs – the house is nestled into the site's sloping ground plane. Fittingly, it is capped by a shaggy grass-covered roof speckled with wildflowers. The entire building is never revealed – it looks like a continuation of the surrounding open landscape. Inside is a fluid sequence of curvaceous spaces wrapping a central courtyard. Instead of internal partitions, subtle level changes, fabric-bedecked ceilings and built-in furnishings, including a sofa made of concentric leather tubes, distinguish each area. As Findlay has observed, 'In Japan, architecture isn't just about what something looks like, but about all the senses: smells, sounds, textures.'[3]

The only enclosed room is the bath. One of the home's most eye-popping elements, this egg-shaped volume bulges out into the courtyard, straddling inside and out. Contrasting with the home's beige masonry, its blue outer shell is dotted with small circular windows, while its interior, including the floor, walls, ceiling and bathtub surround, is completely tile-covered. This self-contained mini room is ideal for steeping the body in hot water – a favourite Japanese pastime.

Today, complicated architectural geometries are a given. But this house was way ahead of the curve: its luscious forms were conceived just as digitally aided design was arriving. Constructed from hand-drawn documents, creating the Soft and Hairy House was surely a labour of love.

1

Some sixty years prior to the completion of this house, the artist Salvador Dalí penned an essay stating that the 'future of architecture will be soft and hairy'. It was the Spanish Surrealist's response to Le Corbusier's brand of modernism, with its geometric purity and plain concrete surfaces.[1] Named after these attention-grabbing words, this voluptuous little building gives one pause. But straight-up shock value was not its architects' only intention. 'I loved the idea of combining something poetic with something practical,' commented one of its creators, Kathryn Findlay, a founder of the former Tokyo-based architectural practice Ushida Findlay Partnership.[2]

❶ The shaggy, grass-covered roof overlooks the sunken courtyard where the blue bathroom bulges out.

❷ Steps and subtle level changes differentiate functional areas.

❸ Plan: (A) entrance, (B) living, (C) kitchen, (E) sleeping, (F) bath, (N) courtyard.

❹ While dots of light punctuate the bathroom walls and ceiling, a porthole-like window looks out at the courtyard.

2

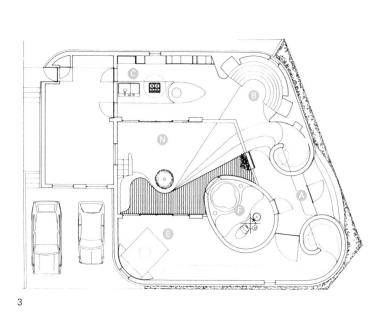

3

4

1

Villa in the Forest
Kazuyo Sejima
Nagano Prefecture
1994

The building's strong geometry was elicited by the land. Unlike many second-home properties, this one had neither a view nor a southern exposure to dictate the shape or orientation of the new house. It only had trees. And more trees. The absence of a well-defined axis or dominant landscape feature was liberating. 'I wanted to make the house free from direction,' explains Kazuyo Sejima. A building with an obvious front and sides simply did not suit the site. But a continuous round wall was in the spirit of the forest's meandering terrain.

This sense of wandering carries over inside, where functional areas segue from one to the next (but can be divided by movable partitions). Hugged by warm wood walls, the living, dining and kitchen zones occupy the ground floor. Hierarchy among them was created by the studio's eccentric placement in relation to the home's circular plan, with wider areas for gathering and narrower ones for circulation. Two bedrooms, plus the bathroom, fill the partial upper level tucked beneath the tilted roof. In contrast to the domestic portion, the double-height studio is a pure white round room – a neutral backdrop for making art. 'I imagined the atelier as a semi-exterior interior space,' says Sejima. The two components are pinned together by doors and openings in the studio wall.

Similarly, protuberances extending from the building's exterior – the entrance vestibule, storage room, outdoor terrace and bathroom – conceptually anchor the house in its setting. Due to the site's sloped topography, the bathroom is entered from the first floor but hovers just above the ground plane. Aimed at the woods, this wedge-shaped room widens steadily, culminating in the bathtub at the end. 'I wanted to make one space free from the curved movement,' explains Sejima. Enclosed with a picture window, it truly is a room with a view.

2

Bold and basic, this cylinder-shaped vacation home was designed for a pair of scientists with an appreciation for art. It consists of two concentric circles and two separate functions: the outer ring houses the clients' living area, and the inner one a studio for visiting painters. With windows gazing out all around, the residence reaches out to the woody environment. But the focus of the studio is inwards. Its only connection to the outdoors is the soft daylight filtering down from the skylight above.

1 The house's white cylindrical form stands out from the forested site.

2 Select openings in the inner and outer walls admit daylight.

233

1

2

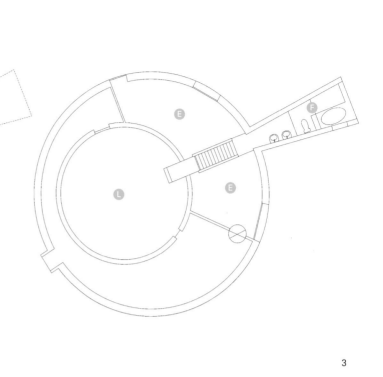

3

❶ The arc-shaped kitchen counter with the range hood suspended overhead.

❷ Illuminated by soft daylight, the white-walled studio is the perfect setting for visiting artists.

❸ Plans: (A) entrance, (B) living, (C) kitchen, (D) dining, (E) sleeping, (F) bath, (J) studio, (L) void.

❹ The view into the bathroom where floor-to-ceiling glass looks out at the forest.

4

1

Curtain Wall House
Shigeru Ban
Tokyo
1995

In architectural parlance, the term 'curtain wall' generally refers to the thin glass surfaces within metal frames that wrap around many building exteriors. But this house gives new meaning to the words. As much a play on the traditional *shoji* screen as on this archetypal modernist motif, the two-storey drapery not only gives the house its name, but is also its defining element. Fashioned from a washable polyester cloth used for awnings, the billowy white fabric is suspended from above but unattached below, dramatically enclosing and forming the thinnest of barriers on the dwelling's south and east sides. When pulled shut, the giant curtains provide privacy while admitting muted light and sound from outside. But when pushed aside, they open the interior completely to fresh air and sunshine – as well as to the neighbours.

Occupying a corner site amidst a quiet residential enclave in Tokyo, Curtain Wall House looks out at narrow streets densely lined with small houses and low-scale apartment buildings. Made of glass, steel and, of course, cloth, the home's appearance contrasts sharply with these conventional surroundings. Yet conceptually it is rooted in the clients' traditional house, which stood on the property previously. A couple with two children, the owners appreciated their home, but it was too small, worn out after years of use, and ready for replacement. 'When I visited the clients, they were enjoying the *engawa* veranda opening onto a small garden,' recalls Ban. Sharing their admiration for historic Japanese architecture, Ban turned this idea of a covered indoor–outdoor space into a key component of his design. But instead of locating it at grade, he placed the deck on the first floor – the main level of the new three-storey house – where its acutely angled shape resolves the friction between the site's irregularities and the home's rectangular floor plan.

Ban achieved this by elevating the primary living spaces with columns that hold up the floor and roof slabs. This created room for street-level parking below, with the husband's photo studio filling a bean-shaped volume at the back. Stairs lead up to the free-flowing space designated for living, dining and kitchen areas on the first floor, followed by the bathroom and three bedrooms on the second floor. Both upper levels are enclosed by the curtains, as well as by sliding glass doors, providing sufficient protection from the winter cold but allowing the space to flow out onto the deck during the warm months.

1 Billowing curtain 'walls' completely open two sides of the house to the street.

1

GROUND FLOOR

FIRST FLOOR

SECOND FLOOR

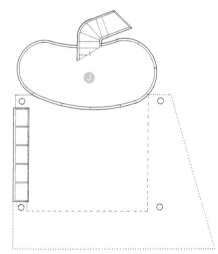

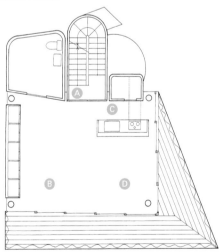

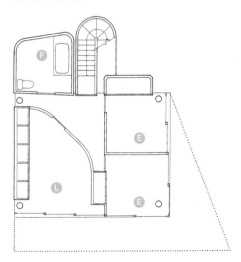

2

❶ The first-floor deck is reminiscent of the *engawa* porch in the clients' previous home.

❷ Plans: (A) entrance, (B) living, (C) kitchen, (D) dining, (E) sleeping, (F) bath, (J) studio, (L) void.

❸ At night, the curtains create a sense of enclosure even when the sliding doors remain open.

Paper House
Shigeru Ban
Yamanashi
Prefecture
1995

Located near Lake Yamanaka on a wooded site just ninety minutes from central Tokyo, Paper House has all the trappings of an easy country getaway. But the architect who owns the house, Shigeru Ban, is more likely to spend weekends jetting off to his offices in Paris or New York than jumping in his car and heading for the hills. Despite the benign neglect that it has since experienced, the house was an important professional milestone. As Ban's first building supported exclusively by paper tubes, Paper House turned a simple industrial product into a signature of his architecture.

Ban's affection for the cylinders began with his design for an Alvar Aalto exhibition in 1986. He wanted wood for the installation, but the budget would only stretch to paper. A series of temporary paper-tube buildings followed. However, when Ban wanted to use paper as the structure for a permanent work, the Japanese government required a careful study first. And what better way to prove his point than by building a paper-tube house of his own?

Sandwiched between a 10-metre (33 foot 10 inch) square floor plate and a flat roof, the house's defining feature is its sinuous S-shaped wall composed of 110 tubes. This encircles a large, flexible space for living, dining and sleeping, and a smaller one enclosing the bath plus a small patio. For privacy, sliding doors and movable closets for *futon* mattresses can subdivide the communal space. Aside from the built-in kitchen counter, the only furnishings are Ban's own Carta Chairs and Table – both made with paper tubes. 'Even the toilet is inside a paper tube,' jokes Ban. The fixture is housed in a beefy tube that marks one corner, while a slender solo column subtly indicates the house's main entrance. Yet when the sliding glass panels encasing its four sides are opened, the tube-studded interior practically fuses with the tree-studded exterior.

Though built with mass-produced, factory-made components, Paper House is redolent with traditional Japanese spirit. In addition to Ban's reinterpretation of the *engawa* porch, *ofuro* bath and sliding screens, the presence of paper evokes the past. Set off by the neutral white of the floor and ceiling, the paper tubes are the only natural-coloured element. '[Their surface] has a very warm, brown colour,' notes Ban. 'You might even think it is plywood.' Composed of laminated layers of recycled paper, the sturdy tubes turn inherent weakness into strength, a quality historically understood in Japan and underscored by Ban's visionary design.

1 A solo paper tube marks the home's entrance.

1

1

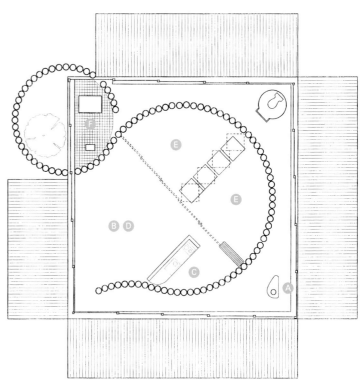

1 Sandwiched between the floor and flat roof, a sinuous wall of paper tubes encloses the habitable space.

2 Plan: (A) entrance, (B) living, (C) kitchen, (D) dining, (E) sleeping, (F) bath.

3 The section shows the interior flowing out to exterior porches on either side.

4 The house is appropriately furnished with the paper-tube Carta Table and Chairs designed by Ban.

2

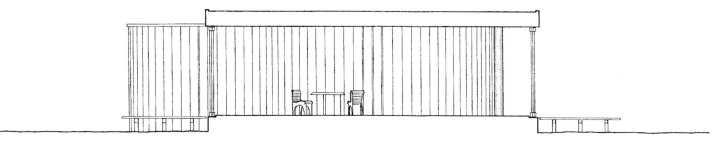

3

4

1

House Surgery
Katsuhiro
Miyamoto
Hyogo Prefecture
1997

considered its publicly funded demolition. 'Because of this government initiative, houses which don't need to be destroyed are taken down anyway,' remarks the architect. For Miyamoto, accepting the government's offer entailed losing the building as well as the memories it holds – a trade-off he was unwilling to make. Instead, he resuscitated his antique timber home by bandaging it with a brawny white steel frame.

Located in the suburban city of Takarazuka, the remodelled house – which Miyamoto named Zenkai, meaning 'completely destroyed', in Japanese, and House Surgery in English – announces itself with an off-centre X-shaped brace, securing the facade and poking through the roof. Inside, the ground floor, which functions as the architect's studio, originally held a reception room for guests, a traditional *chanoma* living room, and a skylit void space separating the kitchen at the back. The three *tatami*-mat rooms upstairs were intended for sleeping. It was here that Miyamoto, his wife and their daughter were jolted awake by the earthquake. 'I remember a big bookshelf dancing up and down which broke the ceiling,' recalls Miyamoto.

Instead of altering individual rooms, the architect maintained the old building and simply inserted the steel scaffolding on top of or around it, carefully positioning the new beams and columns to reinforce the structure without scarring the interior unnecessarily. Contrasting strongly with the dark wood walls, mullioned windows and *tatami* floors, the white elements run the width and length of the building, with zigzagging trusses to bolster the especially vulnerable gap in the middle of the house. A visual as well as structural intervention, the new skeleton infuses the tired bones with a fresh, exuberant energy that Miyamoto hopes will keep the house standing for another hundred years.

2

When it comes to old houses, Japan can be surprisingly unsentimental. In addition to the country's robust appetite for the new, land is generally valued more than architecture, especially when stringent structural codes render renovation more costly than reconstruction. But, as Katsuhiro Miyamoto knows, destroying old houses is not without its repercussions. After the Great Hanshin Earthquake of 1995 severely damaged the architect's home – a modest, two-storey rowhouse that belonged to his parents and his grandparents before that – Miyamoto

❶ The facade reveals the white steel frame bandaging the building.

❷ View from the studio into the *tatami*-floored *chanoma* sitting room.

FIRST FLOOR

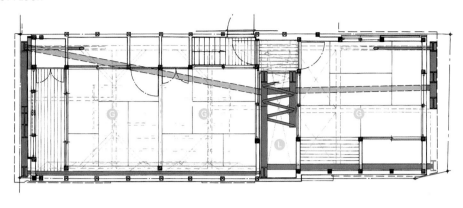

STRUCTURAL PLAN

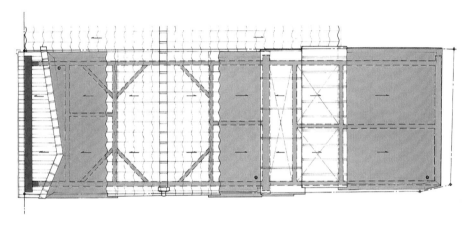

GROUND FLOOR

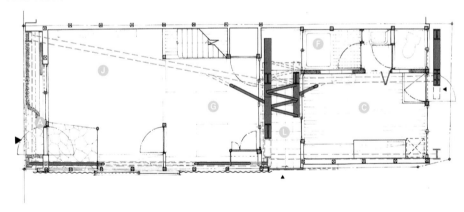

1

1 Plans: (A) entrance, (C) kitchen, (F) bath,
(G) *tatami*, (J) studio, (L) void.

2 New steel supports slice through the
traditional *chanoma* sitting room without
impairing room function.

2

Yomiuri Media Miyagi House
Hitoshi Abe
Miyagi Prefecture
1997

Located near Mount Zao, this house was commissioned by an advertising executive for use by his family as well as his company. He wanted a weekend getaway where he could forage for wild mushrooms, but also host business-related seminars and employee gatherings. Blending the professional and the personal in this way may be uncommon in the West, but in Japan second homes often have a dual purpose.

The client's property sits amidst a typical vacation-home development, with a road in the front and neighbours on either side. However, it backs onto a ravine where the trees are dense and the daylight shadowy. It was here that Hitoshi Abe found his inspiration. 'I thought maybe there's a way to connect with the dark browns of nature,' says the architect. This made the orientation of the house obvious, but how to position it required careful study.

Abe began by making boxy cardboard study models, which he moved around his site model. When none of these forms fitted with the hilly topography, the architect grabbed a precision knife and began cutting. Breaking down the models' conventional house shapes resulted in ribbon-like walls, which he manipulated every which way. By the time he had arrived at a final design, there was hardly a right angle left, but Abe had hit upon a house form that sat comfortably in the landscape. Pinned by pointy corners, the external wall loops around to define its perimeter, and then once more to envelop the double-height space at its centre. This dynamic, spiralling movement is visible in the slanted walls and tilted roof planes.

Approached from the road above, one of those angled walls directs the eye to the entrance. 'I like the experience of coming into the compressed, dark foyer and then the space opens up,' comments Abe. Oriented inwards, the communal area centres on a fireplace but flows into the dining room, with the kitchen and bathroom off to the sides. French doors open the dining area to the covered porch. Reminiscent of the traditional *engawa*, it is the ideal place for appreciating the woods. Upstairs, the balcony leads to the clients' bedroom plus a *tatami*-mat room that sleeps twenty.

With its traditional touches and dark wood walls, the house evokes the atmosphere of a historic *minka* farmhouse, similar to the one where the client grew up. But the materials and muted daylight also relate to the ravine. Says Abe, 'It is not a house for looking at the forest but a house for being a part of the forest.'

❶ The heart of the house is the double-height living room with its fireplace.

❷ Dark-brown wood cladding unites house and forest.

2

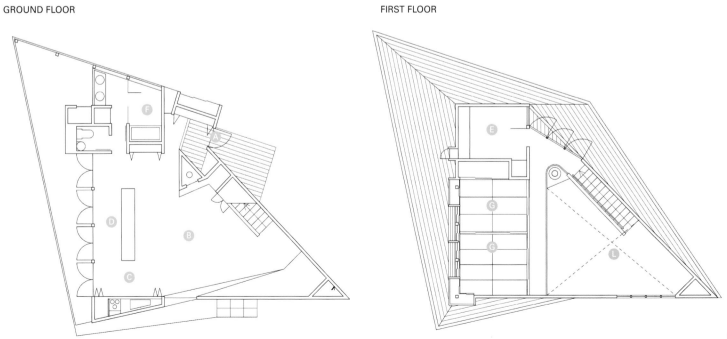

1

GROUND FLOOR

FIRST FLOOR

2

1 An indoor–outdoor space, the covered porch overlooks the shadowy ravine.

2 Plans: (A) entrance, (B) living, (C) kitchen, (D) dining, (E) sleeping, (F) bath, (G) *tatami*, (L) void.

3 This sharply angled wall points the way to the front door.

4 A thin skylight brings daylight into the windowless living room.

3

4

1

Ani House and
Haha House
Atelier Bow-Wow
Kanagawa Prefecture
1998, 2021

2

In designing experimental houses, it always helps if family members are willing to take the plunge – *ani* and *haha* mean 'older brother' and 'mum' respectively. The first of these two houses began with a phone call from the brother of architect Yoshiharu Tsukamoto who, together with Momoyo Kaijima, heads up Atelier Bow-Wow. Tsukamoto's *ani* was keen to build a new house and wanted advice about a property in the Tokyo suburb where the brothers grew up. 'I hadn't been back to the neighbourhood in over twenty years,' recalls Tsukamoto. Sadly, the empty lot where

he played baseball was gone, as was the field where neighbours dried *shirasu* (whitebait). In their place were soulless homes with small gardens. 'I felt that the character had been lost,' laments Tsukamoto. But in this absence, the two architects found inspiration.

'I was looking for a way to build a better environment by building a house,' explains Tsukamoto. Typically in Japan, houses occupy the north end of their sites, with the garden on the south and slot-like spaces on either side. Cramped and closed off, these arrangements turn a cold shoulder to neighbours. By contrast, Ani House sits in the middle of its plot, bounded all around by open land. Used by the clients for off-street parking, exterior stairs and plantings, this space allows light and air to circulate between buildings – a simple gesture that prioritizes the public over the personal.

The same attitude is present within the house, where big windows enable the owners to survey activity outside, and allow passers-by to peek in. The three-storey home holds the parents' quarters in the half-basement, the children's domain on top, and the gathering spaces in between, with the kitchen and the bathing area poking out from the boxy volume.

Some years after completing Ani House, Tsukamoto received another phone call from his brother. This time it concerned the property next door. Reasoning that this would be the ideal spot for their ageing mother, an amateur puppeteer, the land was purchased, and architectural plans were drawn up. Consisting of one big room plus tiny ones for sleeping, bathing and storage, Haha House is the perfect place for solo living. But it is equally welcoming of her fellow puppeteers. 'They use the house like their community centre,' says Tsukamoto. 'There are always lots of "grandma bikes" in front.'

❶ The post box marks the path leading to the entrance of Haha House.

❷ Ani House (left) and Haha House (right) stand side by side with a shared garden in between.

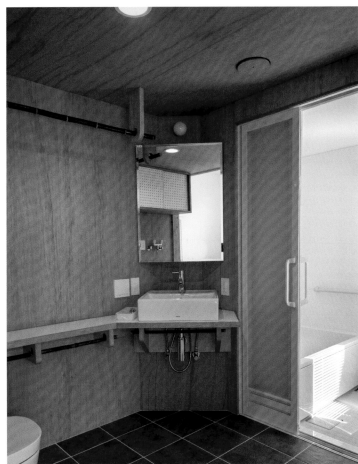

1

2

3

❶ Haha House consists mainly of one high-ceilinged room where the client and her friends share their love of puppetry.

❷ Typical of Japanese homes, the lavatory and bath in Haha House occupy separate spaces.

❸ Sectional perspective drawings reveal the internal alignment of the two houses.

❹ The kitchen and dining area on the first floor of Ani House.

❺ Ani House's communal first floor also holds a study and a picture window open to the street.

4

5

House O-ta
Taira Nishizawa
Tokyo
1998

1

The location of House O-ta has a complex history and, like many parts of urban Japan, faces an unpredictable future. Located near Ring Road 7 – one of eight multi-lane

thoroughfares encircling central Tokyo – the area was underwater until the Edo period (1603–1868), when it was turned into a landfill site. Another major change occurred after 1945 when the network of narrow canals, once used to transport goods, was converted into a web of tiny streets. Typical of Tokyo's outlying neighbourhoods, the area today contains a mix of factories, medium-size commercial buildings, small shops and low-scale houses. But how it will evolve moving forward is anyone's guess – an uncertainty that weighed on architect Taira Nishizawa as well as his clients.

Doing their bit for revitalization, the clients – a couple plus her father – commissioned Nishizawa to design a replacement for their existing house, which had been built shortly after World War II. Nishizawa responded with a long, skinny building whose windowless metallic facade coexists amiably with the industrial buildings in the vicinity. Though the house measures less than 3 metres (10 feet) across, Nishizawa compensated for this narrowness by building upwards. 'I tried to design by height,' he reveals.

Organized vertically, the house consists of four double-height rooms: the combined kitchen-dining room and a *tatami*-mat guest room downstairs, and two bedrooms upstairs. The four rooms are stacked, two in the front and two at the back, with four floors of support spaces squeezed in between. This includes the entrance and stairs plus a bath, toilets and a small study for the husband at the top. Adjacent to the house is a covered carport whose roof doubles as a flower deck, where the father nurtures chrysanthemums – both his own and those of the neighbours.

Dividing the plan as little as possible makes the most of the tight situation. But maximizing verticality with soaring ceilings makes the interior feel positively spacious. Playing with proportions, each room is considerably taller than it is wide. Capitalizing on this, high windows frame skyward views and fill the rooms with daylight. 'The bottom part is just building, but the upper part is architecture,' explains Nishizawa.

2

① Making the most of the home's proportions, high windows open a second-floor bedroom to light and view.

② The roof of the free-standing carport is the ideal place for the client's father to nurture chrysanthemums.

③ Plans: (A) entrance, (C) kitchen, (D) dining, (E) sleeping, (F) bath, (G) *tatami*, (I) study, (L) void.

FIRST FLOOR

2.5 FLOOR

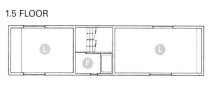

0.5 FLOOR

SECOND FLOOR

GROUND FLOOR

1.5 FLOOR

3

Spotlight

Stairs and Corridors

As with many aspects of residential design in Japan, the circulatory system of the contemporary home is not exactly congruent with its Western counterparts. Hallways are frequently absent altogether, and stairs often function as more than straight-up connective tissue. On tight sites, where the only direction to build is up, stairways may act as corridors linking vertical stacks of rooms. Elsewhere, they may serve as built-in seating. Or even storage, thanks to room-facing cupboards and drawers (opposite page), or lift-up treads. Their landings can sometimes be room-sized, and outfitted with chairs or other furniture. Or their treads so broad that each one becomes a functional space, usurping bona fide floor levels altogether.

But in the past, stairways in Japan were not considered showpieces or decorative elements. Instead, they simply fulfilled utilitarian roles. While sprawling, single-storey estates may have had no need for stairways, ladders and the like were often favoured in *minka* farmhouses to provide access to secondary spaces nestled in their rafters. But in closely built urban homes, such as *machiya*, the two-storey dwellings for merchants and artisans, stairs were integral. Typically, these city homes held commercial space open to the street, with family quarters behind, then possibly a workshop or warehouse at the rear. Located in the middle of the building, stairs led up to storage or workers' rooms. Acting as both furniture and architecture, their narrow, steep treads were rarely accompanied by a handrail, and they were often composed of stepped boxes containing a variety of cabinetry. 'As a child growing up in a townhouse in Hikone in Shiga Prefecture, climbing the stairs meant steadying myself on the stair ahead with one hand and tightly gripping a candle in the other,' recalls the architect and author Atsushi Ueda.[1]

Central to *machiya* and other traditional housing types, internal corridors facilitated movement between rooms, as did narrow *engawa* porches along the building's perimeter. But where sliding *fusuma* wall panels partitioned spaces, rooms could join directly. This strategy laid the groundwork for new floor plans that emerged following World War II. Reminiscent of the informal *chanoma* multipurpose space, which was the centre of family life in many historic homes, the combined kitchen-dining-living room became the focus of many dwellings built during the post-war period and since. With access at multiple points, it eliminated the need for space-consuming circulation conduits – an especially important consideration when dealing with tight urban sites.

2000—2009

2000s
Upward Mobility

The 2000s saw a profusion of high-visibility buildings around Japan. In Tokyo, these took several forms. All along the elegant, tree-lined boulevard of Omotesando – often referred to as the city's Champs-Élysées – flagship stores for fashion brands began popping up, each one more attention-grabbing than the next. Jun Aoki's Louis Vuitton resembled an artfully arranged pile of luggage. Kazuyo Sejima's Dior store was draped with shimmery bands of glass. And, perhaps most dazzling of all, Herzog and de Meuron's Prada Aoyama was clad top to toe with lozenge-shaped windows.

The decade also witnessed the emergence of large-scale, mixed-use developments in central Tokyo. These included Roppongi Hills, whose towers replaced some four hundred individual parcels,[1] and Tokyo Midtown, which converted a 6.9-hectare (17-acre) property previously occupied by the Japanese Defense Agency into a trendy shopping destination with offices and a luxury hotel on top.[2] Making their mark on the skyline, these mega-projects may have invigorated quiet neighbourhoods, but at the expense of the intimate, pedestrian-focused cityscape.

Yet the decade's new construction projects were not exclusively temples to commerce. Up in the city of Sendai, Toyo Ito's Mediatheque, a public library and gallery all in one, broke new conceptual ground with its wavy woven-steel columns and see-through skin. And down on Naoshima, the so-called art island launched in the 1990s, Tadao Ando's Chichu Art Museum welcomed visitors with its sublime submerged building, home to permanent installations of works by Claude Monet, James Turrell and Walter De Maria.

Another architectural, as well as athletic, achievement was the 2002 FIFA World Cup, which Japan co-hosted with South Korea. In preparation, Japan readied venues up and down the archipelago. This process included the construction of Hitoshi Abe's Miyagi Stadium, designed to merge with the surrounding park in Sendai, and Hiroshi Hara's horseshoe-shaped Sapporo Dome with its retractable roof.

In other arenas, the decade birthed the first novel composed entirely on the keyboard of a mobile phone – *Deep Love*, written by a former teacher under the pen-name of Yoshi – as well as Sayaka Murata's *Convenience Store Woman*, which turned the ubiquitous 7-Eleven into a literary locale. The 2000s also witnessed the continued rise of animator and movie director Hayao Miyazaki, whose *Spirited Away* received the Academy Award for Best Animated Feature in 2003. And AKB48, the all-female pop group initially boasting forty-eight members, burst onto the scene in 2005 (opposite page).

Roof House
Tezuka Architects
Kanagawa
Prefecture
2001

Turning a protective cover into a platform for daily life, this house takes the concept of the roof to new heights. The architects, Takaharu and Yui Tezuka, achieved this feat by capping this home for a family of four with a sloping plane of wood decking. Equipped with outdoor furniture, not to mention copious floor seating, this more than doubles the clients' living space. The concept of a habitable roof grew out of a casual comment from the clients describing their practice of eating lunch on the small roof attached to their then home. Expanding on that theme, the architects proposed a modest house topped by a huge roof with a gentle 1:10 pitch, plus a panoramic view of the valley below and Mount Kobo beyond. Located 50 kilometres (31 miles) from Tokyo, the site may be within commuting distance of the metropolis, yet it feels worlds away.

The architects furnished this outdoor room with kitchen-style counters, a dining table and even an open-air shower. To accommodate the slanting floor plane, the heights of the table's legs had to be adjusted accordingly. 'The adults sit on the lower side, the kids on the upper,' jokes Takaharu. A low wall provides the clients with some privacy and, thanks to Japan's forgiving climate, they can use their roof year-round. But in summer, if the heat becomes too intense, they take cover downstairs instead.

Loosely divided by hollow plywood panels reminiscent of traditional sliding *fusuma* screens, the ground level holds two bedrooms – one *tatami*-floored for the parents and the other Western style for the children – as well as a shared study, bathroom, kitchen and combined dining and living room. The latter is accented with a custom-made, free-standing wood stove – a signature of Tezuka-designed homes. During the day, the partitions are pushed aside, compromising personal space but enabling family members to sense each other's presence. 'Inconvenience is important for family communication,' explains Takaharu.

Illuminating the heart of the house are eight operable skylights distributed among the interior rooms. Thanks to two movable wooden ladders, these hatch-like openings double as roof access points. Behaving like chimneys, they also draw up the fresh air entering the lower level through windows on the north and south sides. Bowing politely to tradition, full-height sliding glass walls open the living room to an *engawa* porch, where deep eaves shield the interior from excess sun and the eyes of passers-by.

1 An outdoor room with a view, the gently sloping roof doubles the home's habitable space.

2 In the living room, activity centres on the suspended, wood-burning fireplace – a signature of the architects.

1

2

1

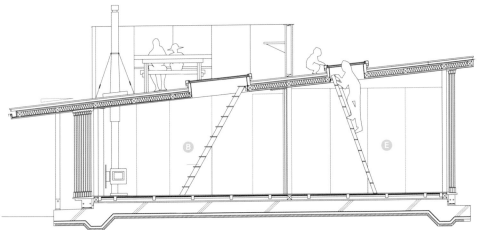

1 Skylights distributed around the house double as access points for moveable ladders ascending to the roof.

2 Section showing the connection between the main floor and the roof; (B) living, (E) sleeping.

2

At Home Roof House

Takaharu Tezuka and Yui Tezuka

Two decades on, we got the chance to catch up with our clients – a family of four – about their experiences at Roof House, giving us an enlightening insight into its practicalities, its challenges and its pleasures. Here is what they had to tell us:

'I think it was right to make it a flexible space from the start. It was really just an empty box with big windows enabling good cross-ventilation. We have added things here and there in this house, but there was no significant alteration. When you get a house, there are always some parts you want to work on. Sometimes it is very tiring, but I wouldn't call it an inconvenience – it's fun. This house is demanding. We added some shelves in the walk-in closet. It doesn't change the meaning of the house. We don't need to go on vacations as it is so much fun to spend time here. Inconvenience is not a bad thing. Overcoming obstacles is all part of being human.

'There is a wood-burning stove in the centre of the house, and it requires attention. We have to find a way to get firewood. I chop a lot of wood! It's not as convenient as modern heating systems, but we like the stove – life plays out around it. We roast fish. We make stew. We boil water in a big kettle for the bathtub. We believe the water boiled with the wood-burning stove is softer than the water from a boiler. There is no replacement for a wood-burning stove. It's real. Real takes energy. It makes us smile.

'Some people say there is no privacy in our house. Yes, it is true from a normal point of view, but our definition of privacy is different. For us, privacy doesn't mean being alone. Privacy means spending time with someone we like. Privacy is not about individuality. It's comfortable to be with somebody else. I need to feel that life is being lived around me, even when there is no reason to talk. It's about being together but apart. I remember Takaharu used to talk about how lovers sit a little way apart on the slope along the river bank. Couples will sit down at the same distance from each other along the riverside, just as birds do. The same thing happens on our roof. On the rooftop (left), we can choose to keep a comfortable distance from each other. This house is a place to work together. We can see each other all the time. We do housework together. We help each other in this house.

'Even during the Covid-19 pandemic, we never had any trouble. Nothing was different. It is easy to keep social distancing in this house. But I think the pandemic revealed something crucial about human beings. We need to be connected with society. Human beings are not designed to be alone. My elder daughter says, "I can be alone in both good and bad ways. There are only three ways to get some real privacy here: in the toilet, up on the roof and out in the garden." This house has been teaching us how to live together. Maybe it's not about how much we do together, it's about how we have helped each other. That's what brings our family together. There has been so much to learn through living here. If the Roof House didn't exist, we would be different. We think that the house has truly formed our family.'

1

Natural Ellipse
Masaki Endoh
and Masahiro Ikeda
Tokyo
2002

An alien white object, Natural Ellipse looks as if it has dropped out of the sky and landed in the heart of Shibuya. Dotted with clubs, bars and love hotels, the area, one of Tokyo's most vibrant entertainment districts, is hardly homey. But against the backdrop of garish neon, pulsating music and fashionistas clad in attention-grabbing garb, Natural Ellipse blends right in.

The project began when the client, then a twenty-something student with an active nightlife and an appetite for eye-popping architecture, held a mini competition for the design of his house. In addition to its small size, his corner plot was saddled with rigid legal restrictions governing fire prevention and sunshine preservation. But visually, the conditions were a free-for-all. Capitalizing on this, Masaki Endoh and Masahiro Ikeda won

the commission with an egg-shaped scheme that barely looked like a building, let alone a house.

Their scheme consisted of four floors wrapped with a taut white skin of fibreglass-reinforced plastic, with the bottom two storeys acting as a rental apartment and the upper two (plus the basement) as a home for the owner and his future wife. For the interior, the client's priority was floor area – as much of it as possible. Coupling this request with the city's code constraints led to the building's unique form. Organized around a skylit spiral stair, it expands in the middle like a balloon, where the main living spaces were located, and tapers at the top and bottom.

To maximize open space at each level, the stair stands off-centre, with kitchens and toilets concentrated nearby. Though white surfaces, absent corners and minimal furniture engendered a sense of capaciousness, precious space could not be squandered on partitions. Not even around the toilets. 'We simply couldn't fit everything in,' explains Endoh.

But prior to the early 2000s, the architects might not have tried. Thanks to the proliferation of laptops and engineering software, new shapes became a possibility and daring structural feats a reality. These tools resulted in the sprouting of tiny houses – often to the detriment of the then prevalent nLDK system. Predicated on a combined living-dining-kitchen plus a number of bedrooms, this planning format, which first appeared in the 1950s, does not always fit well with Tokyo's increasingly small sites. Nor does it suit the desired lifestyle of many clients, or mesh with the complicated geometries enabled by computer-aided design. 'Technology became a really important design factor and helped create new ways of living,' explains Endoh.

GROUND FLOOR

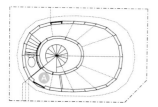

SECOND FLOOR

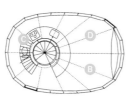

ROOF

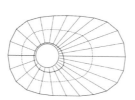

BASEMENT

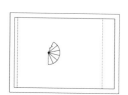

FIRST FLOOR

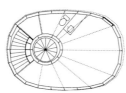

THIRD FLOOR

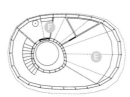

1 Clad with white, fiberglass reinforced plastic, the house barely looked like a building – let alone a house.

2 Plans: (A) entrance, (B) living, (C) kitchen, (D) dining, (E) sleeping, (F) bath.

2

1

❶ The kitchen counter wrapped around
the skylight stair core.

❷ A ladder connected the living area
and the sleeping loft.

Picture Window House
Shigeru Ban
Shizuoka Prefecture
2002

The home's double-height entrance, plus a bathroom, occupies one of these end blocks, while the other contains a two-storey ceramics studio, the ideal workplace for the original owner, a retiree-turned-amateur potter. In contrast to these compact rooms, the flexible open space in between serves as the living, dining and kitchen areas, the latter defined by counter-height cabinetry – there is nothing at eye level to detract from the scenery. Similarly, free-floating stairs ascend to the four bedrooms upstairs, each one accessed through the bathroom, which, amazingly, doubles as a corridor. A fittingly long, narrow slot of space, it contains five sinks and two toilets. 'I took two places that are only used occasionally and combined them into one,' says Ban of this unusual, yet highly efficient, functional pairing. While curtains can be used to partition individual fixtures, sheets of floor-to-ceiling glass are all that separate the bathroom from the outside, completely opening it up to the greenery behind the house.

Though this high degree of exposure may sound daring, Picture Window House sits above and beyond the sight lines of the neighbouring houses that dot the hillside further down – an unusually isolated condition for the Izu Peninsula, where many Tokyoites have second homes. But permeability of this extreme sort required various devices to maintain comfort year-round, an important consideration as the house was intended as a full-time residence. In addition to insect-blocking screens, slatted Venetian blinds and curtains, a substantial roof overhang extending from the house's south side cuts the summer heat while admitting the winter sun. These interventions subtly modify Ban's exquisitely pure concept. Yet they enable a free-form lifestyle and an interior that is as much an exterior.

1

Most houses have windows. But, as its name attests, this house is a window. Perched on a steep slope overlooking the Pacific Ocean, the oblong building opens completely on both sides, framing spectacular unimpeded views and allowing unlimited access to fresh air and daylight. Shigeru Ban, who has a penchant for components that move, achieved this feat with 20 metres (66 feet) of operable glass wall – his fresh take on the traditional sliding screen – enclosing the two-storey building's lower level. Eliminating the need for columns below, the first floor is fashioned like a giant structural truss, with its white diagonal bracing anchored in the two-storey volumes at either end of the house.

1   The living and dining areas segue effortlessly out to the deck, with long views to the ocean.

2   Massive structural steel elements made the 20-metre opening onto the deck possible.

3   Plans: (A) entrance, (B) living, (C) kitchen, (D) dining, (E) sleeping, (F) bath, (J) studio.

4   When the sliding glass doors are open, light, air and breeze move freely from one side of the house to the other.

2

FIRST FLOOR

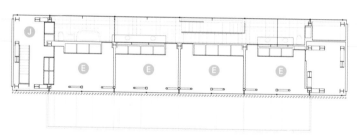

GROUND FLOOR

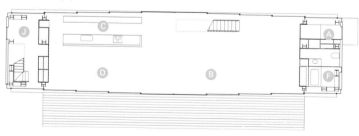

3

4

1

4 × 4 House
Tadao Ando
Hyogo Prefecture
2003

The architect's response was a concrete mini tower with a 4-metre (13-foot) square cube on top. Also measuring a mere 4 by 4 metres (13 by 13 feet) in plan, the lower three floors are just big enough for stairs and a single room. Entered from either the street or the beach, the ground floor contains the entrance and bathroom, with the bedroom on the first and the study on the second respectively. Above that, the cube holds the combined kitchen-living-dining room. Placing the communal space on the third floor was unquestionably unconventional, perhaps even inconvenient. But it also separates the room from the roadway and maximizes its access to the picturesque scenery. Constituting the entire sea-facing wall, floor-to-ceiling glass frames the bridge and the shimmery blue water extending out as far as the eye can see. 'In Ando's scheme, one did not so much enjoy a view of the sea as live at one with the sea,' explains the client.[1]

In many respects, it is Ando's concrete that makes this possible. Coupled with well-placed windows, the masonry forms a thick barrier that edits the unsightly surroundings. It is also able to withstand the spray of salt water and seaweed when the surf gets rough. Inside, the rugged material is silky smooth to the touch. 'When I was young, exposed concrete tended to be used in places no one looked at, such as the insides of warehouses and parking garages,' says the client.[2] Created with exacting precision and exquisite craft, Ando's version takes on a completely different cast.

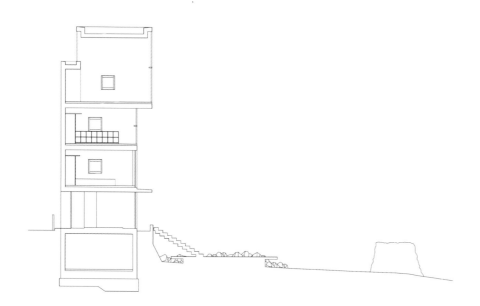

2

In 2001, *Brutus*, a trendy men's magazine in Japan, offered readers a chance to build a starchitect-designed house. All they had to do was send in a tear-out postcard describing their dream house and, if chosen, provide land and budget for the project. The winning entry came from a construction-company executive who had his sights set on Tadao Ando, and owned a coastal property near Kobe. Confined by a multi-lane highway on one side and a seawall on the other, his parcel was tiny. But it commanded an expansive view of the Seto Inland Sea and the Akashi Kaikyo Bridge, connecting to Awaji Island in the distance. Such unusual conditions might cause some to think outside the box. Ando did just the opposite.

❶ Maximizing the view, the combined living-dining-kitchen area occupies a double-height, offset cube crowning the house.

❷ The section shows the progression from roadside (left) to waterside (right).

THIRD FLOOR

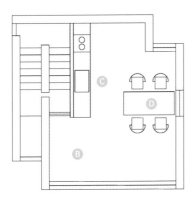

SECOND FLOOR

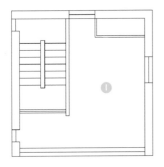

FIRST FLOOR

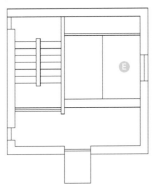

GROUND FLOOR

1

❶ Plans: (A) entrance, (B) living, (C) kitchen, (D) dining, (E) sleeping, (F) bath, (I) study.

❷ The full-height window-wall frames a spectacular view of the Akashi Kaikyo Bridge and the shimmery Seto Inland Sea.

2

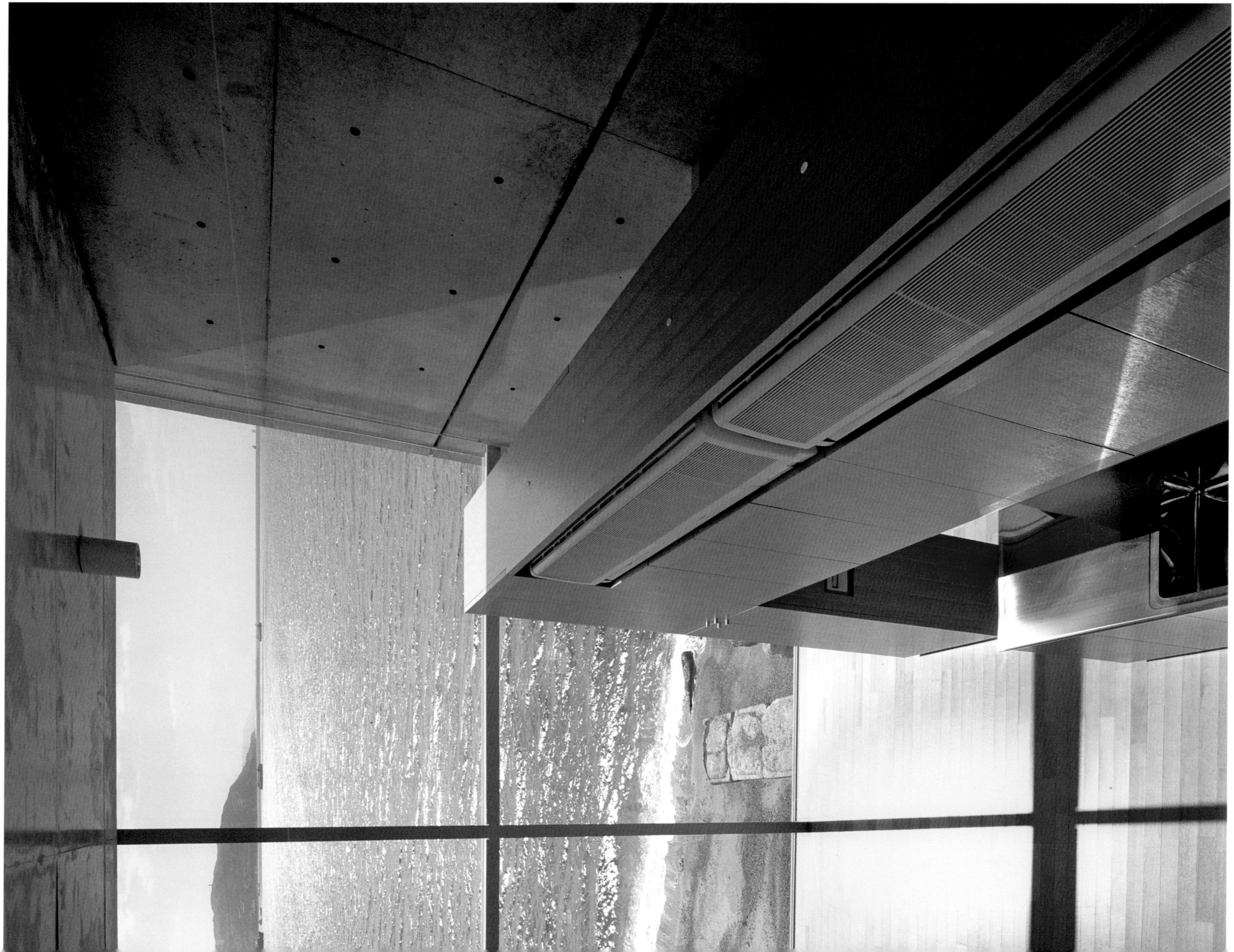

House in a
Plum Grove
Kazuyo Sejima
Tokyo
2003

Situated on a corner lot adjacent to a playground, House in a Plum Grove reads as a plain white box. But behind its poker-faced wrapping lies an intricate arrangement of tiny rooms that fit together like a three-dimensional puzzle. Some are short and skinny, others small and tall. Each one is barely bigger than the piece of furniture it holds.

'Before designing this house, I thought I should use the maximum footprint in Tokyo,' says Kazuyo Sejima. After meeting with the clients, a working couple with two children plus a live-in grandmother, she thought otherwise. Since they wanted to keep the existing plum trees, Sejima cinched in the footprint and set aside land in front for the

trees (which were removed before construction and replanted afterwards). Fitting a home for five on the now even smaller plot, however, upped the ante.

Typically, a small Japanese house will hold only bedrooms and shared essentials. But even that minimal approach was too big for this site, so Sejima broke the rooms down into functional components and assigned them size-appropriate spaces. The result is a collection of mini rooms scaled to furniture dimensions – bedrooms no wider than beds, studies no bigger than desks, and a dining room just right for a table and five chairs. This innovative strategy provided the necessary places to sleep, eat and bathe, along with a few welcome extras, such as a double-height library and a two-person sitting room abutting the roof terrace.

Despite their diminutive sizes, the rooms do not seem small. Soaring ceilings help compensate for the small floor areas. And openings – each room has at least one – relieve the sense of confinement. Well-placed windows frame the ever-changing street scene or a swathe of blue sky, while wall openings inside connect rooms to rooms and levels to levels. Creating a chain of linked spaces, these openings enable light, air and sound to move freely about the house. They also make it easy for family members to communicate yet preserve a modicum of privacy.

Unsurprisingly, building tiny rooms called for super-thin walls. 'I couldn't use normal construction methods,' comments Sejima. Instead, the architect used 16-millimetre (⅝-inch) thick steel plates, which function as both partitions and structure, while their white-tinged surfaces provide a neutral backdrop for all elements of daily life.

1 Like an outdoor room, the roof terrace is partially enclosed by walls.

2 Occupying a corner site, the house reads as a plain, white box from the street.

3 Plans: (A) entrance, (C) kitchen, (D) dining, (E) sleeping, (F) bath, (G) *tatami*, (I) study, (L) void, (M) terrace.

1

2

GROUND FLOOR

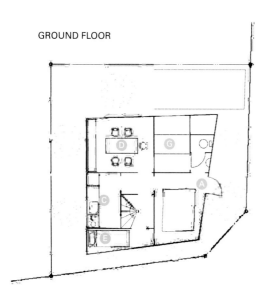

FIRST FLOOR   SECOND FLOOR

3

1 A window-like wall opening connects the *tatami* room on the second floor to the first floor.

2 The ground-floor child's bedroom is the width of the bed but has a double-height ceiling.

1

2

Sloping North House
Hiroshi Sambuichi
Yamaguchi
Prefecture
2003

1

In Japan, fashioning a home on a north-oriented site can be a challenge. Such properties frequently lack direct sunlight in winter, and the buildings they accommodate tend to be dark and cold. But, when Hiroshi Sambuichi viewed a north-facing, steeply sloped site in Yamaguchi Prefecture, he saw the value of this land and advised his clients, a university professor and family, to go through with its purchase.

'Basically, it's a house like a climbing pottery kiln,' explains the architect, who encountered this traditional device at the home of a famous ceramicist. Composed of discrete but connected chambers stepping up a hill, the 300-year-old *noborigama* oven used the rising of hot air to distribute heat along its

length. Similarly, this angled two-storey home has operable windows at the top and bottom, enabling cool breezes from the forest to enter from below, while the hot air exits at the top. 'The airflow and shape are united,' explains Sambuichi. The slanted roof is aligned with the sun's lowest point during the year, cutting the summer sunshine while admitting winter's warm rays. Though equipped with underfloor heating, the semi-underground house leans heavily on geothermal energy for climate comfort. Instead of trying to conquer nature, Sambuichi prioritizes it.

Working with the topography, stairs connecting the road above to the entrance tunnel down through the earth. Inside, the foyer leads to the dining area in the front and a sequence of small rooms off to the side: the pass-through kitchen, the bathroom and a laundry. By contrast, the dining area is an expansive platform-like space barely contained by pipe railings – except where it abuts the drawing room, it is completely open to the rooms downstairs. Two sets of steps descend to the lower level, one to the client's study and the other to the double-height living room and adjacent tearoom. Backed by the earth, the bedrooms are tucked in between. 'They're really just for sleeping,' comments Sambuichi. Thanks to sliding doors, these quarters open to the children's study space with its counter-like desk and strips of windows.

Despite being partially embedded in the ground – even the concrete roof is planted – the house is remarkably light and airy due to Sambuichi's generous use of glass. The entire interior is enhanced by forest views on three sides, while the dining area's picture window frames the Chugoku Mountains in the distance.

❶ A free-standing wall separates the study from the adjacent bedroom.

❷ Mirroring the sloping ground plane, the monolithic roof hovers protectively over the house.

❸ Plans and section: (A) entrance, (B) living, (C) kitchen, (D) dining, (E) sleeping, (F) bath, (I) study.

2

UPPER LEVEL

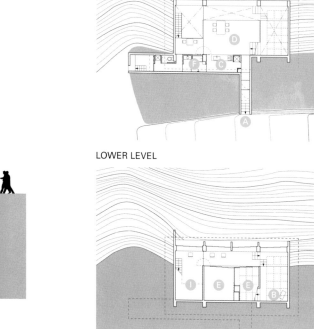

LOWER LEVEL

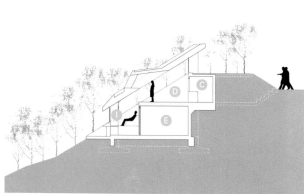

3

1

HP
Akira Yoneda and Masahiro Ikeda
Tokyo
2004

A small house with a big twist, HP takes its name from the hyperbolic paraboloid of its outer wall. This uniquely shaped building was designed for a couple with a young child and a tiny property in central Tokyo. In hiring architect Akira Yoneda and engineer Masahiro Ikeda, they got the structural know-how and design aesthetics needed to make the most of their property.

'The early 2000s was an interesting time for architects making small houses,' recalls Yoneda. During the previous decades, when Japan was in the throes of its bubble era, only the very rich could stomach Tokyo's stratospheric land prices. After the bubble burst and values dropped slightly, people of more modest means could afford to buy and build on small or odd properties. 'This was a bit of a tough situation, which many architects tried to resolve through innovative thinking,' comments Yoneda. For Yoneda and Ikeda, maths was that solution.

Hugged by mid-sized buildings on three sides and a two-lane street to the north, their clients' property was challenging. 'It wasn't so good for daylight,' says Yoneda. Plus they had to squeeze in off-street parking. This generated the house's sophisticated geometry: bending the bottom of the exterior wall inwards yielded a tiny triangular plot. 'They still had to trade their big car for a small one,' jokes Yoneda. At the top, the wall curves back out again to accommodate the required living space.

Divided vertically, the house has a split personality. One half holds three storeys of compact rooms; the other is a soaring triple-height void crowned with a skylight. This illuminates the interior from top to bottom and holds two staircases, one straight and the other a twist of super-thin steel. The curving steps are a dynamic sculptural element that culminates at the second floor, a tube of space bracketed by windows at either end. Finishing with a bang, this entire top level is coated with automotive-grade reflective red paint.

2

❶ A large skylight coupled with the triple-height stair hall allows light to filter down to the ground floor.

❷ Twisting the side elevation enabled off-street parking while maximizing the size of the house.

❸ Plans: (A) entrance, (B) living, (C) kitchen, (D) dining, (E) sleeping, (F) bath, (I) study, (M) terrace.

GROUND FLOOR   FIRST FLOOR   SECOND FLOOR   THIRD FLOOR

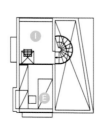
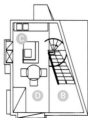

3

1

House and Atelier Bow-Wow
Atelier Bow-Wow
Tokyo
2005

Combining architectural practice with academic positions can be a real juggling act. It requires daily movement between campus, office and home, with each venue clamouring for attention. 'Maintaining three different places really is quite difficult,' explains Yoshiharu Tsukamoto, who founded Atelier Bow-Wow with his wife, Momoyo Kaijima. For these two, who also teach at separate universities, it was clear that something had to give. Mixing home and university was a no-go, but blending home and office had potential. They initially toyed with renovating an existing building, but when a cheap, centrally located lot came their way, they jumped on it. Except for a narrow alley connecting it to the street, the flag-shaped property was surrounded by

buildings – conditions that would scare off some, but proved attractive to Tsukamoto and Kaijima.

Nearly invisible from the street, the four-storey building leans inwards on one side due to code restrictions. At first, the architects considered independent office and home components, but space constraints led them to stack the two instead, with the studio on the bottom two floors, their private quarters on the top floor, and a shared space in between. This contains the kitchen and dining area, which doubles as a conference room. The levels are linked by short stairways that are interspersed with room-size landings large enough for bookshelves or even a chair.

Living close to their workspace is a plus for the architects. 'Having our office downstairs is really convenient,' remarks Tsukamoto. It is also very efficient, cutting their commuting time and – given that the building is rarely empty – keeping the environment consistently warm in winter and cool in summer. Even when their bosses are away, the staff keep the proverbial home fires burning. 'It really is a twenty-four-hour building,' comments Tsukamoto.

Naturally, this mix-and-match strategy also redefines the meaning of privacy. In addition to sharing much of their interior with employees, the architects opened their home to the neighbours with abundant glass and outdoor space. While a loggia off the dining area overlooks the back of the site, a roof terrace gazes out at the front. Most homes are designed to shut out their surroundings as much as possible, but here the textured walls of neighbouring houses behave like wallpaper, and ever-changing light animates every room. 'We never get bored,' laughs Tsukamoto.

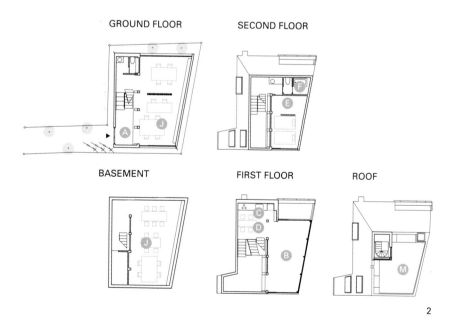

GROUND FLOOR

SECOND FLOOR

BASEMENT

FIRST FLOOR

ROOF

1 A narrow walkway connects the entrance shared by the home and atelier to the street.

2 Plans: (A) entrance, (B) living, (C) kitchen, (D) dining, (E) sleeping, (F) bath, (J) studio, (M) terrace.

2

1

1 Stacked vertically, the studio and the home are connected by open stairs.

2 The roof terrace enjoys expansive city views.

3 Room-size stair landings double as model storage and drawing display.

2

3

1

Lotus House
Kengo Kuma
Eastern Japan
2005

2

Both open to nature and encased in Italian travertine, Lotus House is an architectural oxymoron of sorts. But Kengo Kuma has a talent for finding unexpected potential in materials. Even stone. The idea of using travertine came from the client, a businessman who had admired the material in Mies van der Rohe's Barcelona Pavilion. It was up to Kuma to figure out how to integrate this porous limestone. 'When I heard that request, I was a little shocked,' recalls the architect. 'The challenge for me was to use stone to create a different feeling.' Though usually chosen for its heaviness and solidity, in the Lotus House the travertine is infused with lightness and transparency.

Located in a secluded valley amidst a large property, this private oasis is a linear string of solids and voids centred on a cavernous shaded terrace. The house is approached by stairs leading up from the garage to a covered walkway that overlooks a rooftop reflecting pool. This upper floor also contains a sauna and steam room, as well as indoor and outdoor baths. A second run of stairs descends to the ground-level terrace, which on one side abuts a kitchen, with two bedrooms beyond; and on the other borders the double-height living room, which features a built-in niche holding an antique Buddha statue.

The cadence of solid and void is repeated in the chequerboard walls defining the building's back and sides. Composed of thin slices of travertine, they screen the interior without severing ties to the surrounding environment – an indoor–outdoor ambiguity present in traditional Japanese architecture. 'This conversation with nature was very important to the client,' explains Kuma. Though the stone panels are suspended by nearly invisible stainless-steel supports, they appear to float. In many places, they don't even touch the ground.

By contrast, the front of the building is largely enclosed with floor-to-ceiling glass. Though the window walls in the living room are fixed, elsewhere they can be pushed aside completely, opening other rooms to the lotus pond, which Kuma placed parallel to the house. Situated between the building and a small river beyond, the pond mediates between the architecture and the unspoiled landscape. While the body is engaged by the rectangular stepping stones leading to a viewing platform in the middle of the pond, the spirit is engaged by clusters of sumptuous pink lotus blossoms, a flower often associated with Buddhism.

❶ A Kuma-designed lotus pond sits parallel to the house.

❷ The travertine chequerboard screen enclosing the terrace imparts lightness and transparency.

1

❶ The covered terrace spans the dining (left) and living rooms (right).

❷ Plans: (A) entrance, (B) living, (C) kitchen, (D) dining, (E) sleeping, (F) bath, (M) terrace.

❸ With glass walls on three sides, the living room is immersed in nature.

GROUND FLOOR

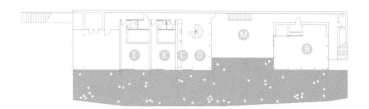

FIRST FLOOR

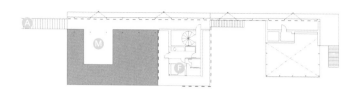

2

3

Rooftecture S
Shuhei Endo
Hyogo Prefecture
2005

1

Extreme sites often call for extreme solutions.
Like Rooftecture S. Perched precipitously
on the side of a steep slope with train tracks
directly below, this sliver of a house is defined
by a single sheet of steel. Folded diagonally like
a piece of origami paper, it forms the roof and
south-facing exterior wall – no doubt to the
delight of commuters who whip past daily
on their way to work.

The project began with a commission
from a retired couple in their sixties. They
had been living in what is known in Japan as
a 'mansion' apartment, but wanted a house
with a view for their next chapter. Despite its
drawbacks, this terraced parcel, which had

previously been used for growing crops,
fitted their criteria. Among other things, it
was budget-friendly and offered a distant
view of the Seto Inland Sea.

Measuring 20 metres (66 feet) in length
and 1.5 to 4 metres (5 to 13 feet) in width, the
triangular property is approached from a road
that runs 3 metres (10 feet) above the house.
From here, stairs lead down to a covered deck
that runs the length of the house. Entered in the
middle, the upper floor is essentially one room,
with the kitchen at the narrow end, the sleeping
area at the wide end, and the living-dining area
in between. Downstairs are the bathroom
and a multipurpose space modelled after the
traditional *doma* dirt-floored work area, along
with an open court. Although there was no
wiggle-room plan-wise, the architect, Shuhei
Endo, manipulated height to relieve the
geometry and differentiate functional zones.
While the ceiling soars to 3.5 metres (11 feet
6 inches) in the kitchen, it drops to just 2 metres
(6 feet 7 inches) in the sleeping area.

Another way that Endo made the space
feel bigger was by enclosing much of the upper
level with sliding glass doors on one side. When
open, the deck becomes an extension of the
interior. When closed, the lozenge-shaped
stones of the retaining wall, which supports the
hill behind, act like patterned wallpaper. By
contrast, the steel wall is selectively punctured
with a row of small windows, resembling the
train cars beneath. 'There is no need for big
windows to enjoy the view,' explains Endo.
Carefully placed, they deftly edit unwanted
sights and sounds from below. 'It's noisy but
not intolerable inside,' remarks the architect.
Though just 1.2 millimetres (¹⁄₁₆ inch) thick, the
steel looks and acts like a protective covering.
Commonly used in Japan for agricultural and
industrial buildings, the ribbed metal is a
signature of Endo's architecture.

1 Sited on a sliver of land above the railway
tracks, the house is partly clad with steel –
reminiscent of the train cars trundling
past below.

2 The full-height window beyond the kitchen
and dining area turns the train lines below
into a picturesque view.

3 Plans: (A) entrance, (B) living, (C) kitchen,
(D) dining, (E) sleeping, (F) bath.

2

GROUND FLOOR

FIRST FLOOR

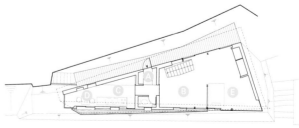

3

Stone House
Hiroshi Sambuichi
Shimane Prefecture
2005

It's not every day that architects get to design houses for farmers (see page 200). But when they do, the results can be striking. Rising from lush green rice fields, Stone House appears as an angled glass roof hovering over a mound of river rocks. Like Sloping North House (see page 282), it exists partially below ground, but Sambuichi chose to realize this home in wood. Combined with well-placed glass panes and wood walls, its bold canopy shelters the roomy interior from harsh winters and damp summers.

Unlike urban sites saddled with code restrictions, rural properties answer to different considerations. At Stone House, both the unchanged landscape – rice paddies that the client's family has cultivated for generations – and the local climate offered design footholds. On one of the rectangular fields, the client envisioned building a new home for his immediate family, plus separate guest quarters.

Because of the area's strong winds and heavy snowfalls, Sambuichi limited exposed surfaces by stacking the two parts to create a two-storey structure, reasoning that a level change would provide sufficient privacy. The family spaces on the ground floor are entered through a covered patio, which doubles as indoor parking. Upstairs are the guest rooms, a study and also an outdoor area overlooking the patio. Shielded by the transparent roof, this first-storey terrace is ideal for drying clothes, even in the rainy season, and has the feel of a solarium in winter.

Supported by a slender wood frame, the glass roof slants to the south, enabling the low winter sun to wash the interior and snow to slide off onto the stone base wrapping the bottom of the building. Where needed, metal mesh contains the rocks to form walls, entryways and even stairs. But it is the spaces between stones – and the air they hold – that create creature comfort inside. For Sambuichi, air itself is an important construction material.[3] In summer, the gaps foster the natural circulation of a cool breeze throughout the house, entering below and exiting through openings upstairs. In addition, chilled air gathers in the rocks when the sun vaporizes the moisture caused by daily drizzles and irrigated rice fields. In winter, the openings fill with snow – the area gets 40 centimetres (16 inches) each year – blanketing the home with igloo-style insulation.

1

1 The dining and *tatami*-floored areas on the ground floor look towards the covered patio.

2 Snow acts as an insulator for the wood house, settling on its glass roof.

3 Plans: (A) entrance, (B) living, (C) kitchen, (D) dining, (E) sleeping, (F) bath, (G) *tatami*, (I) study, (L) void.

2

GROUND FLOOR

FIRST FLOOR

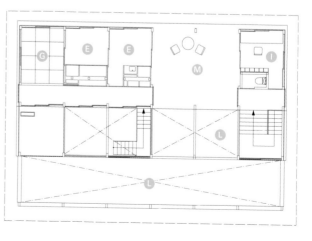

3

House in Gotanda
Go Hasegawa
Tokyo
2006

Normally, houses are embedded in the city. This time the city is embedded in the house. Located in central Tokyo, the building consists of two tall, super-skinny volumes sandwiching a void space – the heart of the house. Scaled to match the gaps and glitches integral to Tokyo, it is a continuation of the urban fabric.

For client and architect alike, that urban fabric was the house's starting point. As students under the aegis of their mentors, Yoshiharu Tsukamoto and Momoyo Kaijima

of Atelier Bow-Wow, they had researched Tokyo's 'pet architecture' – the impossibly small buildings scattered across the city, as well as the tiny spaces in between them, such as pocket gardens, pedestrian pathways, and narrow emergency access routes for fires or earthquakes. 'We shared this sense of Tokyo,' comments Go Hasegawa. Although the client swapped advertising for architecture, his affection for the city never waned. And for his own house, he wanted his family to enjoy living in Tokyo. Literally.

Small even by Japanese standards, the property he bought was a 46-square-metre (495-square-foot) corner parcel facing a large parking lot. Fortunately, these conditions relaxed some of Tokyo's strict code regulations, including building height. This enabled Hasegawa to compensate for the small footprint by going tall. Though it meant sacrificing precious floor area, he incorporated a gap space that related the building to the city's network of streets and alleyways, while also serving as the home's entrance. Containing one room per floor, the three-storey south block holds parking at street level, with the living room and bedroom stacked above. The four-storey north block houses an office at the bottom, the study on the first floor, the dining-kitchen area on the second floor, and the bathroom at the top. The two halves are linked by a spiral stair that sits at the back of the void space, offering city views as you ascend. The entire space is topped with a skylight and backed by transparent polycarbonate.

In front is a single steel door 10 metres (32 feet 10 inches) tall by 1.2 metres (3 feet 11 inches) wide, which both shutters the void and opens it completely, inviting passers-by to peer inside. Manufactured by a factory specializing in doors for aeroplane hangars, TV studios and the like, it has continuous hinges along one side, making it easy to manoeuvre, even for one person. 'It creates the sense of living not just inside the plot but within the landscape of Tokyo,' explains Hasegawa.

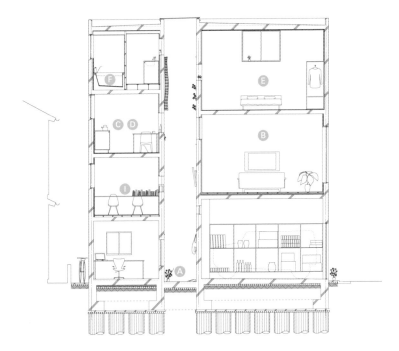

1

1. Revealed in the section, the home's two halves each hold one room per floor: (A) entrance, (B) living, (C) kitchen, (D) dining, (E) sleeping, (F) bath, (I) study.

2. In the gap in the centre of the building stand the spiral stair (left) and the super-tall steel door (right).

3. The height of the building maximizes its small footprint.

2

3

Ring House
TNA Architects
Nagano Prefecture
2006

1

In Japanese, the word *wa* means both 'harmony' and 'ring'. A play on this dual definition, Ring House's original name, *Wa no Ie*, was aptly chosen. Ringed by black bands of wood, this weekend retreat stands at the bottom of a forested valley, where it coexists amiably with the native pine and cherry trees just a stone's throw away.

Though situated amid a second-home development in Karuizawa – historically the place where well-to-do Tokyoites escaped the summer heat – the site did not offer the coveted view of Mount Asama. Instead, its strongest selling point was the abundant and dense foliage, but trees alone were not enough to draw potential buyers. Keen to unload the property, the developer decided to package it with a house and commissioned Makoto Takei and Chie Nabeshima, the founders of Tokyo-based practice TNA Architects, in the hope that they could design him out of his fix. Happily, the home was purchased by a young family before construction even finished.

Turning the land's presumed deficits into assets, the architects positioned the house in relation to the existing trees. 'We only cut down three trees,' comments Takei. This strategy limited the house's footprint but also inspired its verticality. Designed to facilitate the appreciation of greenery from different vantage points, the house consists of three square levels. 'You can see the leaves' undersides from the bottom and deep woods from above,' explains Takei. While there is no dominant facade, there are two entrances. The first is at ground level, leading to the *doma*, a traditional transitional space between exterior and interior, and a *tatami*-floored guest room. Tethered to the slope at the back by an elevated walkway, the other entrance is on the first floor, which contains the combined kitchen, dining and living room. Above that is the family bedroom, from where additional stairs lead to the bathroom – the highest room in the house – followed by the roof deck on top.

Balancing transparency and opacity, alternating strips of traditional *yakisugi* (charred cedar) and clear glass form the house exterior. 'They are like *obi* belts,' explains Takei. Inside, the wooden bands, which vary in height, are painted white, and support all manner of built-ins, including the kitchen sink and wood-burning stove. The placement of the wood keeps the glass free of view-blocking impediments at eye level, whether seated or standing. Upstairs, the height of the glass is positioned in relation to the beds and bath, enabling views in multiple directions without compromising privacy.

❶ Wrapped with alternating ribbons of clear glass and blackened cedar siding, the house has a strong connection to its forested surroundings.

❷ Bands of glass enable unimpeded views in the light, airy dining area.

❸ Plans: (A) entrance, (B) living, (C) kitchen, (D) dining, (E) sleeping, (F) bath, (G) *tatami*.

2

GROUND FLOOR

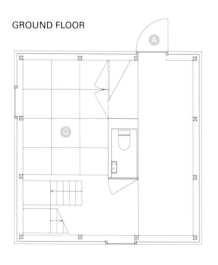

FIRST FLOOR

SECOND FLOOR

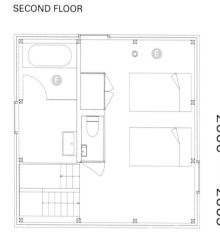

3

n
Jun Aoki
Kanagawa
Prefecture
2007

1

Located in a suburban 'new town' between Tokyo and Yokohama, n is a house with a hidden life. Outside, its pitched roof, brick-flavoured chimney and mullioned windows echo the off-the-shelf 'housemaker' homes lining the streets nearby. Behind that thick facade, however, the interior departs radically from convention. As expected, the bedrooms are upstairs, but the heart of the house is a sunken cube of white space where the clients congregate.

As in most homogeneous pre-planned communities, the plot came with rigid regulations governing what could, and could not, be built. 'It was a very artificial place,' recalls Jun Aoki. It felt more like a playground than a residential neighbourhood. But, as Aoki points out, it is easy to create something unique when the buildings all look alike. While the clients – a commercial photographer and his family – didn't want their home to blend in, they didn't exactly want it to stand out either. In the words of Aoki, the solution was to 'use the same words as the neighbours but with different grammar'.

Another consideration was the limit placed on the property's footprint – more than half of the lot had to be left open. This restriction challenged the clients' request for a large room with living, dining and kitchen zones. Usually, these communal areas are on the ground level, but Aoki placed them underground where they were exempt from the floor-area calculations. This strategy also freed up plenty of open space to accommodate a yard for the dog at the back, and a parking spot for the car in the front.

Elevated on a grey concrete base, the house faces the street with a pure white facade and a quartet of rectangular windows. Inside, the 4.4-metre (14 foot 5 inch) high cube reveals itself immediately from the foyer, where stairs go off in two directions. One run leads up to the parents' first-floor suite, followed by cosy bedrooms for the two daughters tucked beneath the second floor's sloped ceiling. Contained within a sculptural spiral of concrete, the other set descends to the family-sized room, where free-standing partitions and built-in cabinetry define discrete areas for cooking, eating, studying and relaxing. The only fully enclosed space is a *tatami*-floored guest room at the back. Though a room without a view, the cube's white walls, cloth-covered light fixtures, well-placed skylights and giant aquarium enliven the space. Windows may be absent, but they aren't missed.

2

1 The house greets the street with a conventional pitched roof, chimney and mullioned windows.

2 The basement communal area is loosely divided by free-standing partitions, built-in cabinetry and cloth-covered light fixtures.

3 Section and plan: (A) entrance, (B) living, (C) kitchen, (D) dining, (E) sleeping, (G) *tatami*, (M) terrace.

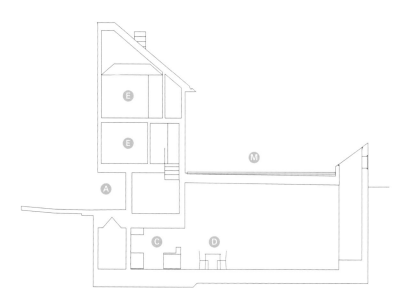

BASEMENT

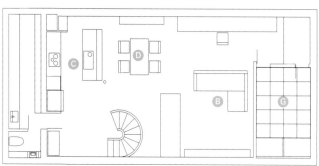

3

Yakisugi House
Terunobu Fujimori
and Keiichi
Kawakami
Nagano Prefecture
2007

Defined by zebra stripes and a slanted roof, Yakisugi House is straight out of a story book. But this one-of-a-kind dwelling is surrounded by suburban Nagano City. Buffered from the sprawl, the house sits amidst a vast property that has been in the client's family for hundreds of years. After retiring from a career in television, he decided to update the family farmhouse where he was living with his wife and child. It had been renovated some fifty years before, but needed another fix. 'It was very big and very dark,' recalls Terunobu Fujimori. Reasoning that he'd be better off starting from scratch, the owner razed the house and cast his lot with Fujimori.

Having grown up nearby, Fujimori, who is both an architect and an architectural historian, possessed a sensitivity to the landscape as well as a sense of history. After spending years looking closely at old buildings, he had shifted his focus to design, often seeking inspiration from the past. This time he turned his gaze to the other side of the Pacific. 'I love American saltbox houses,' he says. Reinterpreting these gable-roofed structures, Fujimori covered the single-storey Yakisugi House with one massive angled plane. It starts at the carport and then rises steadily, sheltering two bedrooms with a bathroom in between; a combined living-dining room and a kitchen; and, finally, a study and a prayer alcove jutting out from the west wall. Capped by its own hipped roof, this niche holds a hand-carved wooden Buddha. Like an exclamation point at the end of a sentence, a tiny tearoom perches at the roof's topmost edge. Accessible only by a handmade ladder, it is the client's preferred spot for afternoon shut-eye.

Carpenters and a local architect, Keiichi Kawakami, saw to the construction, but Fujimori also participated in the making of the building himself. On his parents' property, he felled mulberry wood for the ladder and, with the help of friends, he also charred cedar wood for the exterior cladding. Known as *yakisugi*, the resulting singed wood is a traditional means of controlling vermin and decay. Here, the shimmery black planes are paired with narrow bands of white stucco and playfully punctured by mini mullioned windows. Inside, bits of the treated wood are embedded in the plaster-coated fireplace – a focal point of the spacious living-dining room. Defined by a faceted ceiling, roughly hewn chestnut-wood surfaces and a gaping window wall, this gathering place evokes Fujimori's memory of French cave dwellings.

1. The massive roof culminates in a tiny tearoom, with the prayer alcove jutting out below.

2. Plan: (A) entrance, (B) living, (C) kitchen, (D) dining, (E) sleeping, (F) bath.

3. Inspired by the architect's memory of French cave dwellings, a glass window-wall connects the communal space to the fields outside.

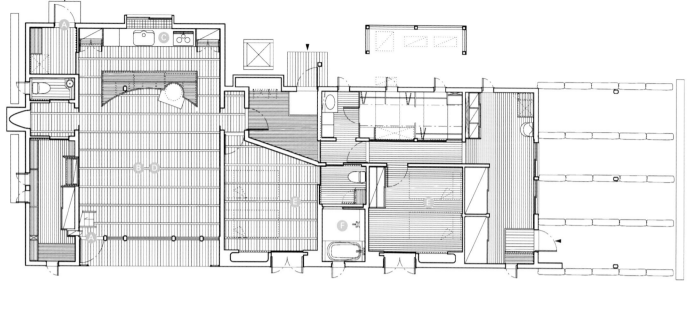

2

3

House N
Sou Fujimoto
Oita Prefecture
2008

Designed for a retired couple living on the southern island of Kyushu, House N consists of three pure white boxes that nest like *matryoshka* dolls. Devoid of the usual windows, walls and roof, the trio gradually step down in size, deftly bridging urban and residential scales.

This idea evolved from Sou Fujimoto's initial plan to enlarge the clients' thirty-year-old home by wrapping it with a porch-like *engawa* space. When they decided to rebuild instead, the scope of the job grew. But the architect kept his original concept of creating an indoor–outdoor space by covering the whole site with a giant porous box, and placing two additional boxes inside, which contain enclosed living space.

Entered from the street, the semi-sheltered outermost box contains an L-shaped yard that holds parking for two cars as well as a wood deck flanked by trees. Transitioning to the interior, the next box houses the entry foyer, followed by the sleeping area on one side and a *tatami*-floored guest area on the other. It also houses, in its middle, the smallest box, which contains the combined living and dining room. At the back of the site, in the space between the external box and these inner boxes, are the kitchen, bath and toilet.

Due to differences in size and position, the character of each box is distinct. Yet the spaces they define are knitted together with openings that range in size but relate proportionally, as all are golden rectangles. More than windows or doors, these openings are simply voids in the solid surfaces forming the walls and roofs. Actual doors and windows with glass panes and wood sash appear only where enclosure is needed for comfort. The result is a loft-like atmosphere where space simply flows between functional zones.

But figuring out how to position the forty-four openings in relation to each other was like a three-dimensional puzzle. In addition to preserving views of Kyushu's brilliant blue sky while mitigating the intense southern sun, Fujimoto had to consider sight lines both into and from the home. 'It's a private house yet it's not completely private,' he says. But by balancing open and closed, he was able to break down the building's bulky mass, forging a meaningful relationship between the people inside and their environment.

1 A set of three white nesting boxes, the building navigates the shift in scale from urban to residential.

1

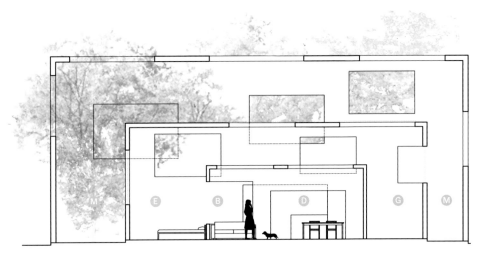

2

1 Punctured with carefully considered openings, the outermost box encloses an indoor–outdoor space reminiscent of a traditional *engawa* porch.

2 Section: (B) living, (D) dining, (E) sleeping, (G) *tatami*, (M) terrace.

3 Wall openings connect the sleeping and living areas.

4 Plan: (A) entrance, (B) living, (C) kitchen, (D) dining, (E) sleeping, (F) bath, (G) *tatami*, (M) terrace.

3

4

1

Rainy/Sunny
Mount Fuji
Architects Studio
Tokyo
2008

The project began when the clients decided to replace their fifteen-year-old developer-built house. Their son had flown the coop, their lifestyle had changed, and their home no longer suited their needs. A bank executive-turned-novelist, the husband wanted a place where he could write fiction, and the couple wanted a secure home that would last a long time.

In response, the architects proposed a two-storey, parallelogram-shaped building – a bold departure from the norm. Neighbouring houses are rectangular in plan, and most hug the site's north side, making room for the largest possible yard on the south side. But Rainy/Sunny cuts diagonally across the property, leaving triangular patches for off-street parking in the front and a private terrace at the back.

Inside, the house is essentially one continuous space containing a mixture of light and dark, as well as tall and low, areas. It begins on the ground floor, which holds the entry foyer, the double-height living-dining room, a semi-enclosed kitchen and, behind that, the bedroom. Separated by stairs and a long walkway, the husband's mezzanine study is open to below, letting him hear activity elsewhere in the house, or catch sight of the cat. The main rooms face the terrace with a two-storey glass window-wall, which admits light without compromising privacy. 'You could walk around in pyjamas,' says Masahiro.

By contrast, the concrete wall provides protective cover. Like the floors and ceiling, its inner surface is clad completely with wood strips arranged in a herringbone pattern reminiscent of a traditional tearoom. Outside, the wall also has a wood-grain texture thanks to the plywood moulds used to construct its zigzag profile. On sunny days, the crisp edges create parallel shadow lines. But on rainy days, they are decorated with water droplets. 'Most houses are prettiest in the sun,' comments Masahiro. 'But this one looks best in the rain.'

2

In Japan, there is a lot of rain and a lot of concrete. But the two are about as compatible as, well, oil and water. Despite concrete's strength, chronic exposure to rain can cause degradation and a streaky appearance, both problematic over time. The long-term implications of this interaction are often ignored by contemporary architects, an oversight lamented by Masahiro Harada, who founded Mount Fuji Architects Studio with his wife Mao. Together, they designed this house to weather well, rain or shine.

❶ Wood strips arranged in a herringbone pattern clad the interior.

❷ On the street side the house is wrapped in textured concrete that looks just as good in the rain as in the sun.

1

1 View towards the kitchen (below) and the study (above).

2 Plans: (A) entrance, (B) living, (C) kitchen, (D) dining, (E) sleeping, (F) bath, (I) study, (L) void, (M) terrace.

3 In contrast to the closed concrete street front, glass completely opens the house's back side.

GROUND FLOOR

MEZZANINE

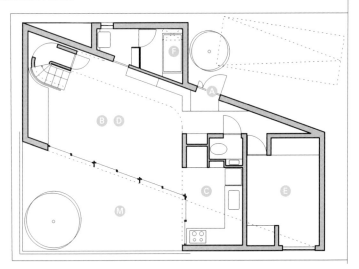
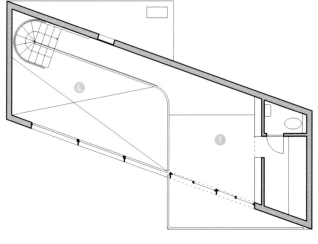

2

Minimalist House
Shinichi Ogawa
Okinawa
2009

1

In Japan, there are minimal houses – and then there is Shinichi Ogawa's Minimalist House. Contained within this simple volume – an unadorned rectangular concrete box – is a sublime interior where furniture designates functional zones and nature shows up in unexpected places.

The starting point for the clients, a working couple without children, was the site. Located on the southern island of Okinawa, the property abuts a busy road. 'The challenge was creating privacy while bringing in nature,' explains Ogawa. For the architect, this meant turning his back on the surroundings and turning his attention to geometry – the foundation of Ogawa's design strategy

throughout his career. This time, that approach took the form of a 3-metre (9 foot 10 inch) grid, which set up a rational relationship between the home's 18-metre (59 foot) length, 9-metre (29 foot 6 inch) width, and 3-metre (9 foot 10 inch) height.

Running parallel to the street, the box is divided into three long strips of open space. The middle (and widest) of these bands holds the sleeping, living and dining areas, their functions differentiated only by a bed, a sofa, and a table and chairs respectively. Buffering this loft-like room from the street is a sliver of enclosed courtyard containing just a shallow pool and two maple trees. These can be appreciated through a window wall made up of fixed panes and operable doors that let in daylight, blue sky and garden views, while the roof eaves curb the Okinawa sun. Consistently minimal, this gesture connects the otherwise closed interior to nature, yet the cars rushing by on the street outside are masked, and a sense of calm and serenity created.

On the other side, the living area is defined by a thick wall containing closets and storage, plus the refrigerator, toilet and shower. Between the plumbing components stands a glassed-in mini courtyard, a surprise opening in the middle of the house. There is, however, no bathtub. Elsewhere in Japan, a daily soak is de rigueur, but Ogawa explains the absence: 'Due to Okinawa's hot climate, people are fine with just a shower.' Behind this functional wall, at the back of the house is the third strip of space – a narrow slot as compact and efficient as an aeroplane cockpit. At one end is the entrance, followed by a single Corian counter running the length of the house. This smooth surface segues effortlessly from kitchen appliances, to a sink for the powder room, then to a long desk at the end. Carefully placed out of sight, small windows beneath this counter provide ventilation, hinting at nature but keeping the outside world at bay.

2

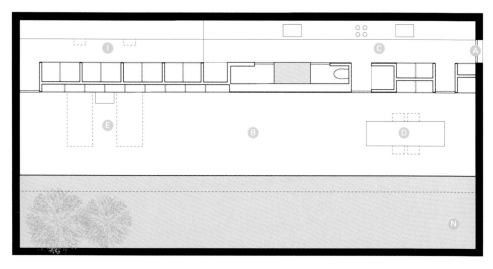

3

❶ The poker-faced facade reveals nothing of the home's inner workings.

❷ The loft-like main room fronts the garden and is divided into functional zones by furniture.

❸ Plan: (A) entrance, (B) living, (C) kitchen, (D) dining, (E) sleeping, (I) study, (N) courtyard.

Spotlight

Kitchens and Bathrooms

Among the most radical changes to the post-war Japanese home were those to the kitchen and bathroom. These modifications were caused mainly by the shift from the extended household to the nuclear family, the separation between spaces for eating and sleeping, and the increased equality for women stipulated by the new constitution. Thanks to the proliferation of utilities, such as gas, electricity and running water, and the emergence of appliances, like the rice cooker, washing machine, refrigerator and flush toilet, convenience, cleanliness and family harmony became increasingly attainable household goals. But these objectives contrasted sharply with what came before.

Historically, the Japanese kitchen was an unappetizing place on the home's north side where women prepared food while seated on the floor (opposite page). Meals were eaten in a separate room that doubled as sleeping quarters. To improve hygiene, cooking became a standing activity during the inter-war period.[1] But eating and sleeping were not divided until after World War II, when the push to modernize triumphed over deeply engrained traditions. The problem was corrected by combining cooking and eating instead, and in the 1950s the Japan Housing Corporation (JHC), which was tasked with creating housing for urban families, adopted the 'dining-kitchen' or 'DK'. Yet sanitary conditions were not achieved overnight – people continued eating on the floor until the JHC provided tables and chairs.[2]

Additional improvements were introduced by Miho Hamaguchi, one of Japan's first female architects and an advocate for improving women's status. As a JHC advisor, she proposed making the kitchen the middle of the home and equipping it with an easy-to-clean stainless-steel sink. Another early kitchen reformer was the architect Kiyoshi Ikebe, who sought to liberate women from the drudgery of housework. A keen observer of movement patterns, Ikebe created several kitchen layouts designed to maximize efficiency and minimize unnecessary actions.[3]

Similarly, bathroom hygiene increased with the inclusion of the flush toilet, shower and gas-heated bath in Japanese homes. But the bathing ritual still remains largely unchanged. Soothing for the soul and body, it entails thorough scrubbing before sliding into the deep tub for a soak. The steaming water is shared sequentially by family members at home, or jointly by patrons of *sento* public baths – relics from the past that are dwindling in number. While Japan's bath culture is steeped in history, its toilets are among the world's most advanced. The Washlet, which debuted in 1980, supplied warm water and air for cleaning, as well as a heated seat, and spawned numerous increasingly sophisticated variations.[4]

2010——2019

2010s
The Dawning
of Cool Japan

At 2:46 p.m. on Friday, 11 March 2011, a magnitude 9.0 earthquake jolted northern Japan. In addition to aftershocks all along the archipelago, it triggered a colossal tidal wave that, in turn, caused catastrophic flooding at the Fukushima Daiichi Nuclear Power Plant. In a matter of hours, buildings collapsed, towns washed away and upwards of 20,000 people lost their lives. Many thousands more were left homeless, and the threat of an unprecedented nuclear meltdown paralysed the nation with fear. Documented with searing images of rushing water, mounds of rubble (opposite page), and tearful survivors combing through their decimated property, the triple disasters came to be known simply as '3.11'.

As the country looked on in horror, aid workers and volunteers rushed to the scene. Among their number were architects including Shigeru Ban, who produced paper-tube partition systems for the cavernous emergency shelters, and members of the newly formed ArchiAid, who came together to take stock of the damage and begin thinking about reconstruction – what, as well as where, to rebuild was going to be complicated. As the recovery efforts progressed, others sought ways to improve the government-issued temporary housing. As an antidote to the cramped quarters, the Home-for-All initiative enlisted architects to create mini community centres. And the eponymous Ishinomaki Laboratory, launched by Keiji Ashizawa, enabled the town to make much-needed furniture for the meagre dwellings.

The allocation of construction resources to the blighted area limited the materials available for other projects throughout Japan, including homes. This strain and the country's sombre mood gave rise to more modest houses, and to homes with a demonstrative respect for nature. Yet, as time passed, the decade became a productive one for Japanese architects – especially overseas, with the completion of several prominent Japanese-designed projects, including the Louvre-Lens by SANAA in 2012, New York's 4 World Trade Center by Maki and Associates the same year, and the Portland Japanese Garden Cultural Village by Kengo Kuma in 2017. And it also witnessed growing international appreciation of the country's architecture, with the award of the Pritzker Architecture Prize to four Japanese practices: SANAA in 2010, Toyo Ito in 2013, Shigeru Ban in 2014, and Arata Isozaki in 2019. These accomplishments indicated that projects reflecting Japan's attention to detail, care for craft and sense of space could be achieved, and their qualities recognized, anywhere.

But design was not the only international arena in which Japan excelled. In 2011, the Japanese women's football team beat the United States to win the World Cup. In 2013, Japan's traditional Washoku cuisine was awarded UNESCO Intangible Cultural Heritage status, and in 2018 the number of foreign visitors to Japan reached a record 31.19 million, a tourism boom that had been encouraged by the Japanese government.[1] Many visitors were attracted by 'Cool Japan', a public–private branding strategy that capitalized on the foreign appeal of Japanese fashion, anime and additional aspects of its pop culture.[2] Others were drawn to the country's rich heritage.

But even Japan's deeply ingrained traditions are not impervious to change. At the conclusion of the decade, Emperor Akihito became the first monarch to abdicate the Chrysanthemum Throne since 1817, making way for Crown Prince Naruhito to assume the mantle in May 2019, and begin the Reiwa era.[3]

1

House in Utsubo Park
Tadao Ando
Osaka
2010

Measuring 5 metres (16 feet 5 inches) across and 27 metres (88 feet 7 inches) in length, the three-storey house is bracketed by courtyards at either end. One buffers the entrance from the street to the north and the other abuts the park to the south. In between, the rooms align like railroad cars, with stairs and service spaces concentrated towards the home's north end, and the main living areas oriented towards the south. The private realm is partitioned from the public land by a high wall – a blurry boundary at best. A contemporary application of the traditional 'borrowed scenery' concept, the ivy covering the courtyard wall belongs visually as much to the park as to the house. In turn, the park's trees naturally act as the house's backdrop.

Inside, nature is the focus at every level. On the ground floor, an operable window-wall draws the environment into the depths of the long house, blending the outdoors with the double-height living room, which is Ando's favourite place to sit. The large opening also enables fresh air, light and the lush view to reach the dining and kitchen areas beyond. Upstairs, where privacy was a consideration, the bedrooms are recessed but open to the south, thanks to a balcony on the second floor and a roof terrace. Filling the second floor, the clients' suite has exposures in both directions, with its sleeping area facing the terrace and its study area cantilevered over the north court.

Underscoring the continuity between indoors and out, Ando's material palette includes his signature exposed-concrete walls, warm wood bedroom floors and tiles of Mikage stone, a local granite, which pave the entire ground floor. Softening this hard surface, a sculptural pair of yellow arches authored by Ando sublimely completes the courtyard.

2

Long, skinny lots – known in Japan as 'eel's nests' – normally breed houses with dark, shadowy interiors. But when a couple with a mid-block property approached Tadao Ando, the architect knew he could do better. Sandwiched between office and apartment buildings, the oblong parcel faced the street, but backed onto Utsubo Park. Formerly a fish market and then a US military airfield, the land had been converted into a public garden in 1955, creating an oasis of greenery in central Osaka. By maximizing the clients' park-side exposure, Ando could fill their home with daylight, breezes and leafy green views.

1 The Utsubo Park greenery blends with Ando's architecture.

2 On the second floor, the sequence of space flows from inside to covered terrace to outside – and then visually to Utsubo Park.

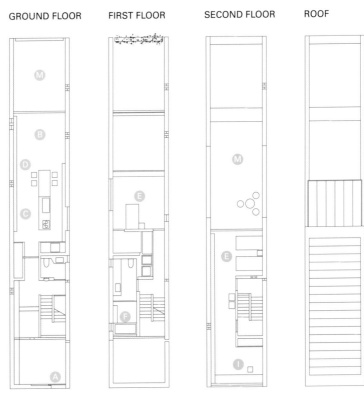

1

2

❶ Folding doors completely open the bedroom to the terrace.

❷ Plans: (A) entrance, (B) living, (C) kitchen, (D) dining, (E) sleeping, (F) bath, (I) study, (M) terrace.

❸ A single continuous space, the dining area flows into the living area and then out to the terrace, which is adorned with sculptural, yellow arches created by Ando.

GROUND FLOOR   FIRST FLOOR   SECOND FLOOR   ROOF

Double Helix House
onishimaki + hyakudayuki architects
Tokyo
2011

Though much of Tokyo was levelled during World War II, many of the wooden houses and temples in its Yanaka neighbourhood survived the conflagration. This quiet area on the city's eastern side remains laced with narrow *roji* walkways and filled with leafy trees, but a recent spate of rebuilding has left those timber homes increasingly few and far between. Clad with cedar, Double Helix House pays homage to this history.

Hemmed in by adjacent buildings, the property is tethered to the street by two narrow pathways only. 'Basically, you cannot see the house from the outside,' remarks its architect,

Maki Onishi. Instead, this neatly packaged home for a couple and three children is experienced as a sequence of spaces, created by wrapping a continuous corridor around a core of stacked rooms.

Tying into the neighbourhood's circulation network, the house can be approached by either path. Both lead to the ground floor containing the kitchen and dining areas, as well as a tiny garden that brightens up the otherwise enclosed space. A stepped corridor leads from the kitchen area to the family bedroom on the first floor, followed by the bathroom, and then the living room on the second floor. Going outside, the stairs continue up to the roof terrace and pergola. Intermittently, the stepped corridor flattens out, becoming more than just a straightforward circulation conduit. At these points, it widens slightly, doubling as a library with a multi-seat communal desk abutting the bedroom; a day bed integrated with the living room; and, adjacent to the bathroom, an outdoor area for clothes drying. 'Lots of houses in Yanaka use the roof to dry laundry,' says Onishi. 'It's a kind of community up there.' As the corridor ascends, windows open to views in every direction, some aligned with wall openings in the core to freshen the heart of the house.

Though private space may be scarce, the house contains a rich array of rooms loaded with nooks and crannies for solitary time. 'It's a small space but the clients use it actively,' comments Onishi. This includes swapping functions around – due to darker conditions on the ground floor, the bed and living rooms started out upstairs. To accommodate growing children, the living room is being converted into another bedroom – a small sacrifice for a good night's sleep.

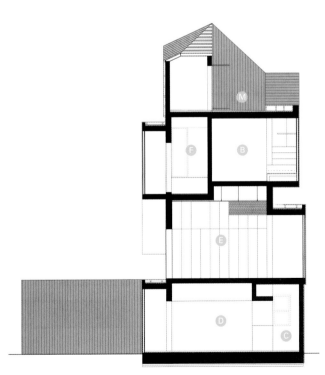

2

1 A wood-clad corridor leads in from the street and wraps the stacked rooms at the building's core.

2 Section: (B) living, (C) kitchen, (D) dining, (E) sleeping, (F) bath, (M) terrace.

1

FIRST FLOOR

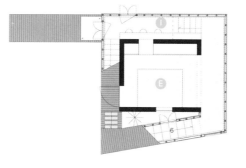

ROOF

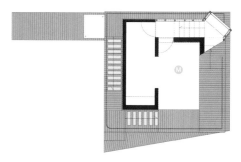

GROUND FLOOR

SECOND FLOOR

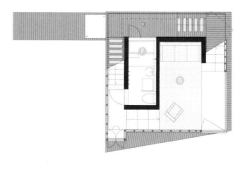

❶ Carefully placed windows forge a connection to the surrounding neighbourhood.

❷ Plans: (A) entrance, (B) living, (C) kitchen, (D) dining, (E) sleeping, (F) bath, (I) study, (M) terrace.

❸ Interior windows enable daylight to flow into the core rooms.

2

1

Garden and House
Ryue Nishizawa
Tokyo
2011

2

Many people in Japan dream of owning a house with a garden – but this house is a garden. In addition to habitable space, each of its five levels holds abundant greenery. Softening the building's hard materials and sharp edges, potted plants and trees screen the interior. As exterior elements, they also loosen the divide between this house and its central Tokyo location, where offices abound and free-standing houses are few. Though an unusual place for a home, the location was just right for two editors with green thumbs.

'[The clients] had an idea to live and work at the centre of the city, where there is history and culture,' says Ryue Nishizawa. But their 4-metre (13-foot) wide oblong parcel was boxed in by 30-metre (98-foot) high buildings and a narrow street, so did not offer much room. For Nishizawa, these conditions ruled out erecting solid walls, which would further reduce the space as well as sunlight access. Instead, he proposed a stack of concrete slabs with glass partitions in between. Since beefy concrete pillars and skinny steel columns do the heavy lifting, the clear walls are independent of the structural system. Their job is to both enclose individual rooms and open them to the adjacent outdoor spaces. Going outside to get to the bathroom or kitchen is a small price to pay for being able to enjoy the open air within the comfort of one's own home.

Set back slightly from the street and shielded by vegetation, the ground floor contains the combined living, dining and kitchen areas. A rounded stair leads up to the first floor, which holds an exterior meeting room at the front and a bedroom towards the back, with exterior space in between. The second floor contains more outdoor space plus separate glass-walled compartments for the stairs and bathroom. The second bedroom and a workspace are on the third floor, along with an additional staircase leading to the roof terrace, where a circular opening enables the plantings below to emerge into the light.

But it takes more than plants to make Garden and House's bare-boned structure hospitable. Like traditional *shoji* screens, curtains can be opened fully or pulled shut for privacy. And, in keeping with Japan's custom of heating or cooling rooms only when in use, each space contains its own air-conditioning unit.

1 Lush plantings provide privacy as well as a connectedness with nature in the centre of the city.

2 The third-floor workspace with its urban view.

1

GROUND FLOOR 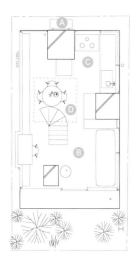 FIRST FLOOR  SECOND FLOOR  THIRD FLOOR 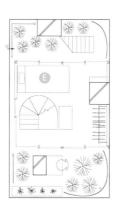 FOURTH FLOOR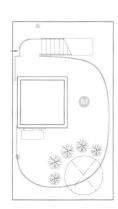

2

❶ The house is hemmed in on either side by tall buildings.

❷ Plans: (A) entrance, (B) living, (C) kitchen, (D) dining, (E) sleeping, (F) bath, (M) terrace.

❸ The third-floor sleeping area abuts the curving steel stairs.

House NA
Sou Fujimoto
Tokyo
2011

2

In Japan, privacy is as much a state of mind as a state of being. But House NA pushes that notion to new limits. Defined by a white steel frame composed of slender square members, the house is enclosed almost completely with clear glass. Not for the faint-hearted, this remarkable transparency fully exposes life inside to passers-by. But it also enriches the interior with a flood of daylight and expansive views – both treasured commodities in Tokyo's tight living conditions.

On the surface, the situation that Sou Fujimoto encountered when embarking on the project was quite conventional. Located amidst a typically dense Tokyo neighbourhood, the site was hugged by houses on three sides and the clients – a 'salaryman' and a pharmacist – had been living in a standard apartment composed of separate rooms for specific functions. But they hoped for a home whose space they could use more freely.

Fujimoto's response was essentially a one-room dwelling, but he articulated it with an astonishing twenty-one floor levels. Alongside the street, the building begins with a carport and a covered entrance. From there, stairs lead down to a guest room and up to the kitchen. The latter connects to areas for dining and living, which abut small platforms that serve both as floors and furniture. Above, the sleeping area segues into the library and sunroom, as well as a dressing area from where stairs ascend to the bathroom topping off the house. While storage and utilities occupy the house's solid rear wall, its glazed front opens to small terraces.

Rather than walls, it is changes in level that loosely separate spaces. Linked together by a variety of steps, staircases and even ladders, many of these surfaces double as tables or seating – a fresh take on the multipurpose *tatami*-mat floor. In addition to a sense of spaciousness, this strategy offers plenty of functional freedom. 'We provided a diversity of spaces which the client can figure out how to use,' explains Fujimoto.

While the owners relished their new-found flexibility, they also had to adapt their lifestyle to the rigour of Fujimoto's scheme. 'From the start, the clients said they wanted openness,' recalls Fujimoto. 'But I didn't know how much.' Though presented with several options, they chose the design with maximum exposure, yet soon discovered that even they had limits. Following the completion of construction, they strategically added curtains, enabling them to partition their space, and to bathe in private too.

1 In lieu of walls, small level changes articulate functional areas.

2 Planted terraces provide a modicum of coverage from the street.

1

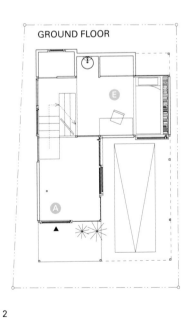

GROUND FLOOR   FIRST FLOOR   SECOND FLOOR   ROOF

2

GL+6,050	GL+5,790	
GL+7,250	GL+6,740	GL+7,040
GL+8,080		GL+8,840
	GL+7,200	

3

① Expansive urban views bring a greater sense of space from the interior.

② Plans: (A) entrance, (B) living, (C) kitchen, (D) dining, (E) sleeping, (F) bath, (M) terrace.

③ Roof plan showing the numerous floor heights in millimetres above ground level (GL).

At Home
House NA

*Naomi
Pollock*

Shortly after its completion, I had the good fortune to visit House NA. As I walked from the subway station, I marvelled at the ordinariness of the neighbourhood: narrow street upon narrow street lined with small apartment buildings and even smaller houses. Abutting the road directly, these buildings were in close proximity to pedestrians and cars, blurring the boundary between inside and out as well as public and private. Out of this conventional scene, Sou Fujimoto's House NA, a most unconventional home, suddenly emerged. Held together by the thinnest of white steel frames, it faced the thoroughfare with nothing but glass (above). No walls, no fences, no window treatments. Inside, as I navigated House NA's many, many level changes, I wondered what it would be like to live here. Curious, I put the question to the husband-and-wife clients.

'My first impression of Fujimoto's proposal', says the husband, 'was that this house was very different from the typical Japanese house.' Undoubtedly, the clients knew that Fujimoto would come up with something unprecedented. What that would look like, however, was anyone's guess.

One of the client's favourite points was the lack of material presence. The floor is thin? How nice, he thought. After construction finished, the couple was surprised by all the attention their novel home garnered – it was a bit overwhelming. But House NA has proved to be a place where friends and family from near and far enjoy gathering.

'I have many good memories,' says the husband. 'One was seeing kids having fun, like my friend's child who danced happily in the bedroom while looking down at us in the living room.' He speculates that, even though the house is small, it has a unique sense of openness that makes people feel comfortable. Especially children. 'They lie or sit in places where adults wouldn't go,' he says. 'They experience this house the right way.'

Adults appreciate Fujimoto's architecture too. Since the interior of House NA is essentially one free-flowing space, it is difficult for the clients to single out a place or room that they like best. Instead, it is distinct characteristics of their home that appeal. 'My favourite part of this house is the way it lets in external noise, such as the sound of rain, wind or cars,' says the wife. 'I dislike enclosed space, so I feel more comfortable being able to sense the outside.'

As the clients adjusted to their new home and as the building settled into its site, changes naturally occurred – some more unexpected than others. Among them was the steady increase of greenery noted by the wife. 'Trees we don't remember planting just took root; maybe birds carried seeds,' she remarks. 'And the trees we planted ten years ago grew bigger than we anticipated, requiring pruning.' No doubt a welcome development, this new growth adds a modicum of cover and enlivens the interior even more with leafy boughs.

But one of the most significant changes of all is a practice adopted by the wife. 'I have a habit of saying *tadaima* [a common greeting meaning 'I am home'] when I enter the house, even when no one else is there,' she says. 'I am not sure why, but I cannot go in without saying it.' Perhaps this expression truly acknowledges how at home she feels in the house that Fujimoto built for her and her husband.

House in Rokko
Yo Shimada
Hyogo Prefecture
2012

Perched on a mountainside plateau overlooking the Seto Inland Sea, the House in Rokko has a split personality. The semi-public ground level is encased entirely in glass, but the private quarters upstairs are clothed in corrugated steel. In a polite bow to neighbours, the house is capped with a conventional pitched roof, but its industrial-strength materials acknowledge the storage facilities and boat sheds in the bay below.

In fact, it was industrial architecture that gave Yo Shimada of Tato Architects his initial cues. At the outset, the client – a graphic designer who had been living in an apartment in central Osaka – tried to find an old warehouse to renovate. But when a suitable

structure did not emerge, he bought this land instead. A thirty-minute train ride from his hometown, the empty plot was big and cheap, plus it offered a splendid view. It was also quite private – in lieu of houses, it backed up against a retaining wall supporting Mount Rokko. 'The neighbours can't really see up and he can't really see down,' explains the architect. The one catch was access. The only way to reach the property was a stepped pedestrian path. Though a temporary ramp aided construction, it was not possible to bring machinery on site. Instead, everything had to be carried by the builders. This constraint meant that only lightweight materials of limited size could be used.

Inside, those materials included painted plywood walls, fibre-cement-board floors and glass partitions. Connected by spindly steel stairs, the ground floor contains the barebones dining, living and kitchen areas. The first floor holds the bedroom, loosely separated from the bathroom at one end and a storage area at the other by glass partitions. 'This is a house where things are not hidden,' explains Shimada. Instead, the wall fronting the storage area is coated with a reflective film, imparting a blue tint on one side and red on the other, which disguises belongings without blocking them from view. 'The objects become part of the house when it is lived in,' comments the architect.

Similarly, the surrounding environment enhances the modest interior. The scenery becomes its visual backdrop, and the local climate helps modulate indoor temperatures. While operable windows enable cross-breezes, a wraparound upper deck blocks the sun below. 'Having simple architecture gives more freedom around how to live,' says Shimada.

1 While the ground floor is encased entirely in glass, the first floor is wrapped with corrugated steel.

2 The ground-floor kitchen (pictured) and the bath on the first floor are the only fixed functional areas.

3 Plans: (C) kitchen, (F) bath.

4 The client's possessions and furnishings activate the space.

2

FIRST FLOOR

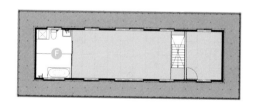

GROUND FLOOR

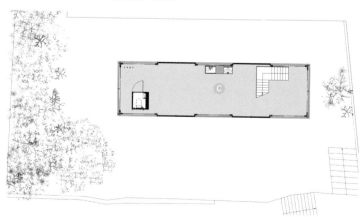

3

4

Optical Glass House
Hiroshi Nakamura
and NAP
Hiroshima
2012

1

Located in the heart of Hiroshima, Optical Glass House faces an eight-lane road filled with cars and trams. But these turbocharged conditions almost disappear once inside. Activated by the play of sunlight and shadow, gentle breezes and carefully tended greenery, the architecture integrates nature, fostering an atmosphere of quietude and calm, while editing out the urban surroundings. 'The idea of tranquillity doesn't just come from silence but from the absence of expected sound,' explains Hiroshi Nakamura.

For convenience, the clients – an obstetrician and his family who had been living in the suburbs – chose this site because of its proximity to the hospital. But when at home, the doctor wanted to leave the antiseptic whiteness and hectic pace of his workplace behind. In response, the architect created a spacious and self-contained three-storey house fronted by a two-storey glass-block wall. The ground floor holds the garage and main entrance, plus a den, spare bedrooms and a small garden beyond. Upstairs, the main floor features a sequence of light and dark spaces, comprising living, dining and kitchen areas, with gardens at both front and back. On the top floor are the bathroom, laundry and, overlooking the gardens below, bedrooms for the couple and their two children.

While the interior is inwardly focused, the presence of nature is felt throughout. Like *shoji* screens, sliding glass panels merge the living room with the terrace. This mixture of trees and smaller plantings is open to the sky but shielded from the street by the wall of 6,000 custom glass blocks. Secured by a well-concealed steel support system, the high-tech glass effectively muffles unwanted noise and visually blurs the movement of cars and people passing by – activity is evident but not intrusive. At the same time, the shimmery, translucent material admits ever-changing daylight, creating countless reflected patterns on the home's walls and floors. The rippling of the living room's metal curtains makes the wind visible, while the terrace's shallow water basin doubles as a skylight for the foyer below, allowing soft light to filter down on sunny days, and creating an intricate pattern of concentric circles when raindrops hit its surface. 'It's a very modern building, but it has a Japanese sensibility in the way that it enables an intimate relationship with nature,' explains Nakamura.

1 In the evening, the glass block facade reveals the planted terrace inside.

2 Plans: (A) entrance, (B) living, (C) kitchen, (D) dining, (E) sleeping, (F) bath, (L) void, (M) terrace.

3 Everchanging daylight streams in through the glass block facade throughout the day.

4 Sliding doors completely merge the living room with the terrace.

SECOND FLOOR

FIRST FLOOR

GROUND FLOOR

2

3

4

Katsutadai House
Yuko Nagayama
Chiba Prefecture
2013

A pâtissier's home and shop rolled into one, Yuko Nagayama's Katsutadai House is a fresh take on Japan's traditional *tempotsukijutaku* – typically a street-facing shop backed by the proprietor's home. Here, the components are layered like a cake, with the shop as the base, the two-storey residence on top, and a wedge-shaped void in between.

The project began after the client took over the family business from his father. At that time, it occupied a 1970s-vintage building sandwiched between a towering apartment complex and a multi-storey medical clinic, with a busy street in front. The change in leadership was a chance to update the architecture – in addition to its outmoded appearance, the building had some functional shortcomings. While visiting the old shop, Nagayama recalls hearing the pitter-patter of toddlers overhead as she eyed the pastries. 'The number one problem was that the public and private areas were too close,' she says.

This time around, the two parts are completely independent. Defined by a low wall bearing its name in small letters, the shop has a small garden in front, which acts as the point of transition between the busy road and the quiet interior. Sliding to the side, a wooden door reveals a built-in case displaying the delicacies that have been created by the owner and his father in the kitchen beyond.

In contrast, the home is accessed by stairs on the side of the building. They lead up to the master bedroom and bathroom on the first floor. The second floor holds the children's room at the back, and the combined kitchen, dining and living room in front. As below, this space is buffered by a small terrace that is open to the sky but closed to the street. Aside from the balcony's glass doors, the communal area has only one window. Embedded in the terrace floor, this looks down into the shop through its glass roof.

Both parts of the building have an angled roof – a signature of Nagayama's architecture. In the home, this is evident in the communal area, where ceiling height differentiates functional zones. Tilting in two directions, it dips to 2 metres (6 feet 7 inches) at its lowest point but soars to 3 metres (9 feet 10 inches) above the living area. Downstairs, the sloped glass roof lightens the shop atmosphere while the concrete hovers protectively above, shielding the creamy cakes from direct sun.

1

1. Layered like a cake, the bakery forms the bottom and the residence the top, with open space in between.

2. The home's kitchen, dining and living areas.

3. A glass roof covers the bakery.

4. Plans and section: (A) entrance, (B) living, (C) kitchen, (D) dining, (E) sleeping, (F) bath, (O) shop.

2

SECOND FLOOR

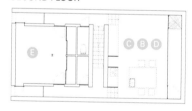

FIRST FLOOR

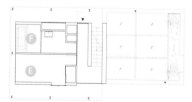

GROUND FLOOR

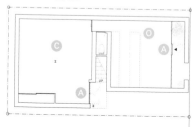

3

4

Window House
Yoshitaka Yoshimura
Kanagawa Prefecture
2013

'It was about the size of a single parking space,' recalls the architect. High tides, especially during typhoon season, posed another challenge. And then there were the neighbours. If Yoshimura proposed a solid structure, the houses across the street would lose their views. These constraints left no choice but to build up. And open.

Anchored by concrete columns, the house's white, sail-shaped volume begins a full floor height above the ground plane, creating a covered patio below. From here, ladder-like triangular treads lead up to the entrance, which opens directly onto the dining and kitchen area (with the shower and toilet concealed beyond). Connected by an open staircase, the living area is one level up, followed by the bedroom above that. Aligned with but separate from the living area, the loft is an additional place for sleeping or sitting, and can only be accessed with its own ladder. In the absence of doors and walls, the entire interior reads like a single, but multi-level, space.

Playing with scale, the jumbo windows contrast sharply with the small footprint. Made of fixed glass panes secured with cross-shaped supports, they maximize the view and relieve the tight interior, making it feel roomier. Small operable windows on one narrow side, plus a skylight above, offer ventilation. But introducing transparency on the wide walls not only benefits the client. It also benefits the neighbours, who can look straight through the building to the waterfront, unless the client is in residence and roller blinds are unfurled for privacy. 'I didn't want to block their views,' explains Yoshimura. 'But whenever the client is not using the house, I asked him to keep the shades up.'

2

Located in the seaside community of Hayama, this weekend retreat is all window. Sandwiched between a pair of oversized mullioned openings, the building consists of a narrow, three-storey-high slot of space that looks out towards Sagami Bay in one direction and mountains in the other.

The project began when the client, a Tokyo-based singleton heading up a fishing-gear company, rented a nearby vacation home designed by Yoshitaka Yoshimura. He enjoyed his stay so much that, having decided to build a home of his own in the vicinity, he turned to Yoshimura. The major snag was the site's tiny area – a mere 3 by 8 metres (10 by 26 feet).

❶ Parallel picture windows preserve the seaside view for neighbouring homes.

❷ Loft-like mini levels expand the house vertically.

SECOND FLOOR

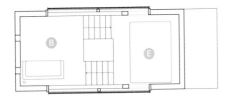

FIRST FLOOR

GROUND FLOOR

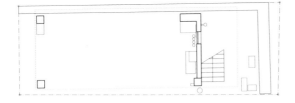

1

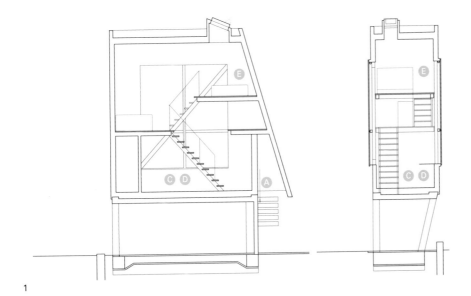

1 Plans and sections: (A) entrance, (B) living,
(C) kitchen, (D) dining, (E) sleeping.

2 Window House and its surroundings as seen
from the water.

1

House on
Yamate Street
Taichi Mitsuya and
Unemori Architects
Tokyo
2014

2

A towering 16-metre (54-foot) high building, the House on Yamate Street hardly looks the part. But concealed behind its anonymous concrete wrapping is a five-storey residence-cum-retail shop belonging to a thirty-something singleton. A leather-accessories designer, he first encountered Taichi Mitsuya when the architect ordered a tote. The bag commission led to the building commission.

'The client had purchased the land but then couldn't find anyone to build on it,' recalls Mitsuya, who designed the house in collaboration with Unemori Architects. The 24-square-metre (258-square-foot) parcel was wedged between a back street barely big enough for a car on one side, and on the other

a six-lane ring road with vehicles racing by constantly. When the road was widened in 2011, a large house was razed, the property was subdivided, and this oddly shaped property was among the resulting lots.

Because of its tiny size, the only direction to go was up, a strategy that dovetailed well with the multi-storey apartment and office buildings nearby. 'Maintaining the facade wall on the street was important as we didn't want the house to stand out,' explains Mitsuya. Instead, the house echoes its neighbours with ten rows of generic rectangular windows that disguise its function yet reflect its inner workings.

Progressing from public to private, the building begins with the client's shop at ground level, followed by the kitchen (a counter with a hob, sink and small fridge) and dining area on the second floor; the bathroom and living room (which are separated by a curtain) on the third floor; the bedroom on the fourth floor; and a roof terrace on top, from where city views fan out in every direction.

While steel stairs connect the levels, ceiling heights differentiate them, reducing from 3.7 metres (12 feet) to 2.1 metres (7 feet) as one ascends the building. Similarly, the windows become shorter and wider. Every floor has two rows of openings but only two operable windows due to ongoing street noise. The road also influenced the choice of concrete – the best material to offset the vibration caused by rushing cars – for the building's structure and exterior. While silvery paint covers the latter, only insulating paint coats the minimal interiors. 'He's a craftsman so he will finish the space,' explains Mitsuya.

1 The building's many windows and silvery exterior disguise its interior.

2 Light-weight steel stairs connect the building's six levels.

SECOND FLOOR

ROOF

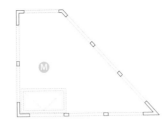

FIRST FLOOR

FOURTH FLOOR

GROUND FLOOR

THIRD FLOOR

1

1 Plans and section: (A) entrance, (B) living,
(C) kitchen, (D) dining, (E) sleeping, (F) bath,
(J) studio, (M) terrace.

2 The section drawing illustrates how the ceiling
heights decrease as the house ascends.

3 Looking down into the client's leatherworking
studio.

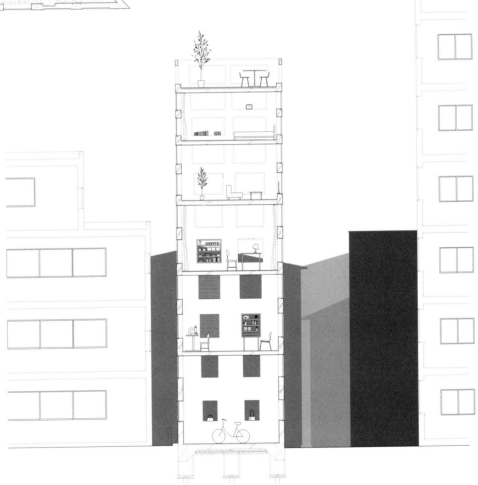

2

A House for Oiso
Dorell.Ghotmeh.
Tane /Architects
Kanagawa Prefecture
2015

Taking the roles of both architect and archaeologist, Tsuyoshi Tane began designing this house by digging into its site – a corner plot in a small rural town on Japan's eastern coast. Situated between the mountains and the sea, Oiso is famed for its inclusion in a series of *ukiyo-e* woodblock prints by Hiroshige, which depict way stations on the Tokaido route connecting Kyoto and Edo (as Tokyo was previously known). But the town has been occupied steadily since ancient times, producing a wide range of dwelling types over the centuries. Drawing on the enduring wisdom and well-worn practices of this architectural heritage, Tane – then of former Paris-based practice Dorell.Ghotmeh.Tane –

designed a house that was not just located in the town, but also created for it. Though a private residence, it is intended to last for at least one hundred years – a responsible public gesture.

The project began when the client, a tea aficionado, decided to leave Tokyo, move her young family to the countryside near her parents' home, and give a friend, Tane, his first residential commission. The architect's concept was to merge elements of the region's early pit dwellings with the elevated sleeping quarters of its later houses. Accordingly, the wedge-shaped building reads as two distinct components: an earthen-walled ground level topped by a pitch-roofed, timber-clad volume. The ground floor contains four boxy rooms – the living area, kitchen, bathroom and *tatami*-floored tearoom – interspersed with five tiny gardens. By contrast, the first floor is one large room. Though envisioned as a traditional *nema* – a communal sleeping quarters – the space is divided with strategically placed furniture, yielding separate areas for the children and their parents, with a sitting area in between.

Climate was another consideration. 'Humidity is a really difficult issue in Japan,' comments Tane. Drawing on soil's natural ability to absorb moisture as well as modulate the temperature extremes of winter and summer, Tane embedded the building base 60 centimetres (24 inches) into the ground, and repurposed the excavated earth as walls, floors and stairs. In the process, ancient Jomon-era pottery shards were discovered, underscoring the house's connection to history. 'When the city removed them, I was a bit sad,' recalls Tane. Likewise, every surface upstairs is wrapped with warm natural wood, which will develop a beautiful patina over time. Linking the memory of place with the medium of architecture, Tane poetically merges past, present and future.

1 The earthen-walled ground floor holds the communal spaces, while the timber-clad first floor contains the family sleeping area.

2 Modelled after the traditional *nema* shared sleeping area, the first floor was designed as a single, spacious room.

3 The view from the living-dining room towards the garden beyond.

4 Plans: (A) entrance, (B) living, (C) kitchen, (D) dining, (E) sleeping, (F) bath, (G) *tatami*.

2

FIRST FLOOR

GROUND FLOOR

3

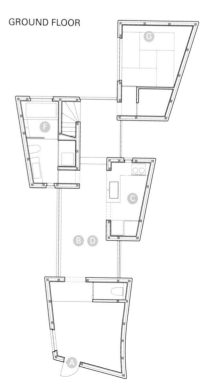

4

Tree-ness House
Akihisa Hirata
Tokyo
2017

Composed of seventeen concrete boxes dotted with potted plantings, Tree-ness House combines the natural and artificial; inside and out; and the two sides of the owner's personality. 'On the one hand, he is very cool,' says Akihisa Hirata. 'On the other hand, he is very wild.' An art enthusiast with a passion for surfing, the client hired Hirata to replace his outmoded house with the home of his dreams. Fronting a busy street in central Tokyo, the new building boasts a ground-level gallery, which is open to the public, and a three-storey penthouse for the client and his family. In

between, there is an independent apartment originally intended for his mother.

The idea behind the building's unique appearance stemmed from a chair conceived by Hirata and produced by the client a few years earlier. As much a sculpture as a seating element, the Csh Chair is a ball of wood ribbons resembling a cluster of coral. This convoluted form gave rise to the folded metal frames inserted at the corners of Tree-ness House's grey concrete boxes. In addition to mollifying the building's hard exterior and breaking down its rigid geometry, the white frames hold window glass and troughs for plantings of various types, enlivening the home.

Inside, fluid functional zones are connected by short runs of stairs and unimpeded sight lines. With every twist or turn of the floor plans, the body is reoriented and new views of city and sky appear. Accessed via semi-enclosed stairs or elevator, the foyer leads to the kitchen and dining areas. From there, a few steps ascend to the living room, which segues into a small study, a leather-clad lounge and a terrace. Additional stairs go up to three bedrooms, with the washroom, bathroom and outdoor spaces above – a terrace for drying clothes and a plant-studded roof garden for relaxation.

In contrast to the residence, the gallery is an abstract, white, windowless cube. 'The only thing the client requested was that he wanted to live in a place very different from the gallery where he works,' comments Hirata. Thanks to the abundance of concrete and glass, walls for hanging art are few and far between in the home, but the entire workspace below is a big blank canvas just waiting for paintings and sculpture.

2

1 Like oversized window boxes, planters enliven the concrete exterior.

2 The hollow core brings daylight into the centre of the building.

1

GROUND FLOOR   FIRST FLOOR   SECOND FLOOR   THIRD FLOOR   FOURTH FLOOR

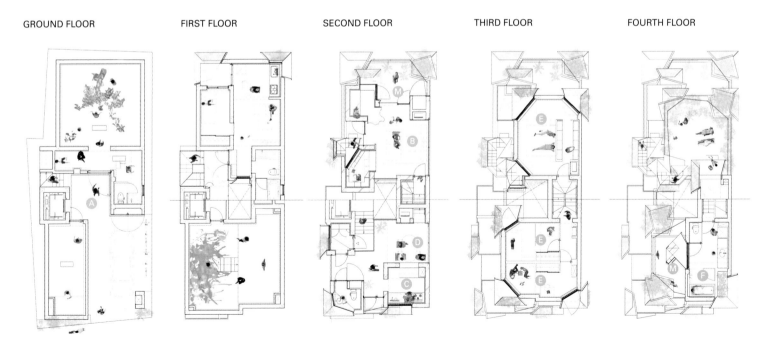

2

1. The building has plenty of nooks and crannies like this study alcove.

2. Plans: (A) entrance, (B) living, (C) kitchen, (D) dining, (E) sleeping, (F) bath, (M) terrace.

3. Completely covered in leather, the lounge is like a room-sized piece of furniture.

3

Todoroki House in Valley
Tsuyoshi Tane
Tokyo
2018

The house consists of three storeys, yet is divided into five levels. It is entered at a balconied mezzanine midway up, from where one set of stairs ascends to the private quarters and roof deck, while the other descends dramatically to the glass-enclosed ground floor. Surrounded by a jungle-like garden, the latter contains the combined living, dining and kitchen areas, as well as a separate study. 'It doesn't look like Tokyo, but it is Tokyo,' says Tane of the dense foliage on display. While greenery is an essential visual component of the ground floor, the wood-walled upper floors are punctuated with individual windows framing distant views of the Tokyo cityscape in one direction and Mount Fuji in another.

In Tane's typically hybrid manner, public and private realms are given distinct expression. Embedded one metre (3 feet 3 inches) in the ground, the common rooms are defined by large windows, low walls and floors made of rammed earth repurposed from the site's excavation. The space's sunken status makes it feel as much a part of the garden as the house – a polite nod to the client's profession. In contrast, the sleeping floors are both sheltered from the elements and shielded from the neighbours thanks to careful window placement. As in many crowded Tokyo districts, controlling visibility from outside was desirable. But inside, walls are few and boundaries are fluid. Instead, niche-like berths hold beds, desks and other furnishings on the upper floors. 'We are not trying to make rooms,' explains Tane. 'We are providing flexible spaces.' In so doing, Tane hopes to avoid a common pitfall – once the children have left home, instead of becoming storage, these spaces can easily be reborn.

1

Sitting amidst a densely populated neighbourhood in a forested valley, this house for a landscape designer and his family is an outgrowth of its site just a short distance from central Tokyo. Thanks to the Tama River nearby, the air at grade is humid, while arid winds course through above. These climatic conditions provided the inspiration for Tsuyoshi Tane, who began the project by studying indigenous buildings built specifically for dry or wet environments, from the vernacular housing of Yemen to stilt-raised dwellings in Vietnam. Merging these diverse responses, he devised a drum-shaped volume and perched it on piloti.

1. Todoroki House consists of a drum-shaped volume perched on slender piloti.

2. The sunken living room is surrounded by dense greenery.

3. In the sleeping areas, curtains and furniture divide the space.

4. Plans: (A) entrance, (B) living, (C) kitchen, (D) dining, (E) sleeping, (F) bath, (I) study, (L) void.

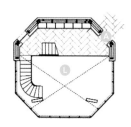

2

3

FIRST FLOOR

THIRD FLOOR

GROUND FLOOR

SECOND FLOOR

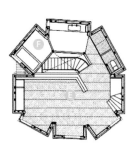

4

stairway house
nendo
Tokyo
2019

Having first met as members of their high-school boating club, the designer and client have known and worked together for some twenty-five years. 'Understanding each other's personalities, lifestyles and favourite things is the reason why building this house went so smoothly,' comments Ito. Another reason was the land itself. Because the Tokyo property has belonged to the family of Ito's wife for generations, there was no question where to build.

Replacing the family home, the house contains separate quarters for Ito's nuclear family and for his wife's parents (plus their eight cats and countless plants). The parents occupy the ground floor; on the first floor are the living, dining and kitchen areas for the young family, with their bedrooms above. Ironically, none of the three levels is directly accessed by the oversized steps. More conceptual than functional, the giant staircase conceals a second flight for going up and down, as well as the main entrance, the parents' bathroom, and additional subsidiary spaces. But its treads, which rise more and more steeply, are ideal spots for both plants and pets to bask in the sun.

Introducing an urban-scaled element and dynamism into the building's boxy form, the stair slices diagonally across the house, and is anchored by the grid of white mullions articulating the south side's window wall. While the full-height glass completely opens the interior to the garden and its historic persimmon tree, the building's north side greets the street with an austere blank white wall.

Though Japan has a long history of multi-generational homes, living with both one's parents and one's children poses challenges. But stairway house deftly balances overlap and independence. 'It is a house where you can feel the comfort of living together while ensuring the privacy of the two families,' observes Ito.

2

Everything created by Oki Sato, the founder of design studio nendo, has its own twist. Be it chopsticks, chocolates, chairs or even architecture. Created for the family of nendo's managing director Akihiro Ito, stairway house is no exception. The dominant feature of this two-generational home is a giant staircase – a conventional building component writ very, very large. Picking up where a public walkway leaves off, its treads ascend dramatically, penetrating the house, and culminating in a large skylight topping the home's second floor. 'My favourite place is the second-floor sofa where I can look up at the sky,' says Ito.

1 More conceptual than functional, the giant stairway visually links the home's three floors.

2 Like a continuation of the public walkway beyond the site, the giant stair is an urban-scaled element running through the house up to the skylight.

Spotlight

Gardens and Courtyards

Careful compositions of plants, rocks and stone ornaments, traditional Japanese gardens are a feast for the eye. Unlike the lush lawns and colourful flower beds of the West, they are not meant for play or even sitting. Given their meticulous upkeep and their consumption of space, these private oases have today become the exception more than the rule. Yet having an outdoor area of one's own remains a priority in Japan.

During the post-World War II period, when the Westernization of the home was in full force, the garden took on a different cast. As Yoshiharu Tsukamoto of Atelier Bow-Wow notes, the era of rapid economic growth spanning 1954 to 1973 brought the proliferation of suburban housing developments consisting of detached houses with private yards. This trend was reversed some twenty years later, when younger people began returning to cities, having been priced out by high land values.[1] The small urban sites that they were able to purchase didn't leave much room for a garden. But outdoor space could be found on top, in the middle or off to the side of the house – enough to enjoy the sun, air-dry the laundry and nurture potted plants. In Japan, where quality does not equal quantity, a single blossom on the front stoop can be more precious than an entire flower bed.

Size really does not matter where courtyards are concerned either. Historically, miniature enclosed gardens known as *nakaniwa* (opposite page) brought light and fresh air into the heart of the house, particularly in the city where homes stood cheek by jowl. Naturally, this concept has been adopted by contemporary architects keen to focus attention inwards or open up the interior. In Japan, where boundaries can be fluid, exterior space can be incorporated into the middle as easily as the edge of a building.

This ambiguity has given rise to a host of transitional spaces, including the entry foyer and the *engawa* porch. An extension of the floor plane protected by the roof eaves, the latter is a narrow slot of space that merges the interior with the outdoors. Traditionally, it was a place to enjoy the garden and, perhaps, the greenery beyond – a concept known as *shakkei* or 'borrowed scenery'. But it is also a place where children played, quotidian tasks were completed and memories were made. Architect Kengo Kuma recalls: 'In front of the *engawa*, I often made *takibi* fires and roasted sweet potatoes in the ash. Especially in the wintertime.'[2]

2020——2023

2020s
Pandemic Panic

Like the rest of the world, Japan was paralysed by the coronavirus pandemic from the start of the decade. But, as other countries rolled out vaccines as quickly as possible, Japan took its time. The shots' efficacy had to be tested in Japanese labs before they could be doled out, first to the elderly and then gradually to a broader swathe of the population. Yet Japan was ahead of the game in terms of prevention because mask-wearing (opposite page) was already an accepted practice – as in other parts of the Asia-Pacific region, the facial coverings are frequently donned to prevent the spread of common colds and mitigate seasonal allergies. Perhaps even more important was the population's willingness to abide by rules and regulations intended for the public good. With infection rates consistently among the globe's lowest, Japan's Covid-19 response was admired and envied.

Naturally, the ripple effect impacted Japan in various ways, including the difficult decision about whether to hold the 2020 Tokyo Olympics in the middle of a pandemic. After postponing for a year, the Japanese government made the controversial choice to go ahead with the games in 2021. But this was not the first problem to plague the event. In 2012, the commission for the main stadium had been awarded to the British-Iraqi architect Zaha Hadid, only to be taken away in 2015 after her design received strong criticism from Japan's architectural community and other commentators. It was deemed too bold, too big, and way too expensive. This led to a second competition, which resulted in the Kengo Kuma-designed, 68,000-seat Japan National Stadium.[1] Though sparsely attended since foreign visitors were prohibited entirely, the games went off without a hitch and did not become the super-spreader event that critics had feared.

Another shocking event occurred in 2022, when former prime minister Shinzo Abe was assassinated. David Sanger, previously the *New York Times* Tokyo bureau chief, called him '[T]he most transformational politician in Japan's post-World War II history.'[2] In Japan, where gun controls are extremely strict and shootings very rare, Abe's violent death shook the nation to its core.

House of Furniture
Tezuka Architects
Tokyo 2020

1

Like a custom-made cabinet, the House of Furniture sits perfectly on its small site in a quiet Tokyo neighbourhood. Here roads are narrow and homes close together. Instead of shutting out these surroundings with a wall or fence, Yui and Takaharu Tezuka embraced them with an expansive, elevated row of operable windows. Defining the home's street front, this vast sweep of glass is as much an urban as an architectural gesture.

Within the house, the windows both open the interior and frame views of the housetops across the road and the sky beyond. Balancing the need for privacy inside with the desire to connect to the environment outside, the windows perch on a solid wall 150 centimetres (59 inches) above the ground plane. This

placement was inspired by a visit to the high-windowed Paris atelier where the painter Zenzaburo Kojima, Takaharu's great-uncle, worked in the 1940s. While the sliding panels recall *shoji* screens, each one weighs a hefty 350 kilograms (770 pounds). 'It's like pushing a truck,' jokes Takaharu. But, thanks to good wheels, the glass panels glide smoothly once moving.

Contrasting sharply with the large windows above, a small door modelled after the servants' entrance at samurai villas, or *mogurido*, is embedded in the wall below. 'I thought it would be fun for the clients' two children,' explains Yui. A more formal entrance is on the home's north side. Both lead into the double-height ground floor, where furniture designates the living and dining zones while *tatami* mats denote a practice area for the *shamisen* – a Japanese-style lute. Tucked beneath a bed-filled mezzanine, the only fixed elements are the kitchen counters and the bathroom, which is loosely enclosed by a combination of glass and opaque partitions.

The two levels are connected by a fresh take on the *hakokaidan*, a traditional built-in box stair also used in Takaharu's ancestral home in Saga Prefecture. Both furniture and architecture, here it provides useful storage, while the largest of its cabinet-like compartments contains an additional toilet. The stair's construction was also integrated with the floor-to-ceiling bookshelves. Embedded in the shelves are random light bulbs, which Takaharu likens to twinkling city lights. Since the clients work in publishing, book storage was a top priority and completely lines three walls, enlivening the home with an array of colourful spines.

❶ The huge scale of the facade's windows contrasts sharply with the diminutive size of the *mogurido* door.

❷ The loft-like interior is wrapped with book-filled shelves.

❸ Plans: (A) entrance, (B) living, (C) kitchen, (D) dining), (E) sleeping, (F) bath, (G) *tatami*, (L) void.

2

GROUND FLOOR

MEZZANINE

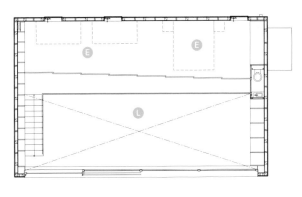

3

1

❶ The mezzanine-level sleeping loft (left) opens to the living and dining areas on the ground floor.

❷ When open, the huge windows fill the interior with light and fresh air, while the *mogurido* door is ideally sized for the clients' son.

❸ Telescoping, sliding panels can be shut to separate the sleeping loft.

2

3

Terada House
Naoki Terada
Tokyo
2021

Terada House evokes the futuristic optimism of the 1960s, but there's nothing nostalgic about this home. Designed by the architect and product designer Naoki Terada as a two-generational home for his own family, it incorporates furniture icons and bright colours from the era of his youth. But the dynamic interior also reflects his current state of mind. 'Everybody is using neutral colours,' observes Terada. 'But for me, the home should give new energy and cheer people up.'

The designer of ice-cream spoons and clocks as well as buildings, the architect noticed this property just a block from his home during his daily commute. It was a chance to build his dream house – within reason. Located in a typical Tokyo residential neighbourhood, the small parcel came with constraints, including a harsh limit on how much land could be covered. Fortunately, legal exceptions enabled the construction of a three-storey house. An independent apartment for Terada's parents forms the base of the building, with two levels above for his immediate family.

Sequestered behind a concrete exterior, the front entrance is the only shared space. It leads both to the parents' quarters (plus his father's painting studio), and to the stairs ascending to the pitched-roof volume containing the architect's home. On the latter's first level are an open kitchen, double-height dining and living areas, and terraces front and back. A spiral staircase leads up to the balconied family room, the master bedroom, and the daughter's room, which includes a cosy loft just big enough for a bed and desk.

Top to toe, the entire building is unified by a massive angled wall that slices dramatically across all three floors before culminating in the roof's ridge line. 'When designing a small home, it is better to have one strong idea,' explains Terada. Drawing the eye upwards, the angled plane enlivens the rectilinear rooms, adding an expansive feel even in the bathroom, a narrow, tile-lined slot of space.

Together with the grey walls and ceiling, this angled surface forms the perfect backdrop for the home's carefully curated furnishings: mid-century classics plus Terada originals. Rendered in sunny yellows, oranges and reds, the selection includes Eero Saarinen's Tulip Chairs, Vernor Panton's Living Tower and Terada's own Miffy Sofa, a homage to the beloved rabbit created by children's illustrator Dick Bruna in 1955.

1

1 The abstract building front is animated by the architect's red vehicles.

2 Brightly coloured furnishings enliven the living-dining room and the family room in the loft above.

3 Plans: (A) entrance, (B) living, (C) kitchen, (D) dining, (E) sleeping, (F) bath, (J) studio, (L) void, (M) terrace.

2

GROUND FLOOR

FIRST FLOOR

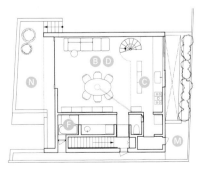

SECOND FLOOR

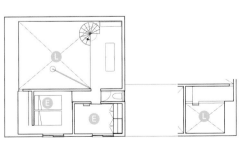

3

Tetusin Design
Re-Use Office/House
yHa architects
Fukuoka
2021

2

In 1928, a splendid Western-style edifice was erected on Kyushu University's Hakozaki campus. But, after years of use as a dining hall and offices, the worn-out wooden building was slated for demolition. Fortunately, the structure was acquired by a local graduate keen to save it. Though he owned land just 800 metres (2,600 feet) away, moving the entire building was not possible given its condition. And size-wise, it would have towered over nearby homes. Instead, he enlisted like-minded architects, Yuko and Yujin Hirase of yHa architects, to harvest bits and pieces and integrate them into a new building containing his home and graphic-design office.

Working closely with the demolition team, the architects removed everything from iron hardware to an entire staircase. Incorporating these elements into their design was both a challenge and starting point. They wanted to repurpose fragments – a process they liken to the re-used building material, or spolia, common in ancient Greek and Roman structures – as well as respect the memory the pieces embody.

Their two-storey building sits on the approach to Hakozaki Shrine, and many passers-by fondly remember the old structure – an effect that the architects attribute to 'urban memory'. The new building is fronted with a three-storey volume, half solid and half void, that echoes the shape and symmetry of the old building, minus its bulk. The void section is defined by a simple three-dimensional frame opening to the garden at the back, while the solid portion leads to an office at ground level and the family home above, the two connected internally by reconstructed stairs. Recalling the original colour scheme and window placement, the new facade is a pastiche of blank panels outlined by blue frames, plus repurposed elements such as weathered wood panels and an ornamental metal grille.

Inside, the home features a long communal area modelled after the central corridor that organized the old building. The interior's smooth surfaces and straightforward geometry are accented by reinstalled doors; a pass-through counter reborn as a Shinto shrine; and the kitchen from the clients' former home, now installed in the office. But most dramatic of all is the original U-shaped stairway, which was rebuilt to meet contemporary standards. 'It was like *kintsugi*,' says Yujin, referencing the practice of repairing broken pottery with gold. Previously, renovations were practically unknown in Japan, but in recent years they have increased. 'Values are changing,' says Yuko. But, as Yujin notes, 'Re-use is still rare.'

❶ Half solid and half void, the new facade echoes the old building.

❷ The facade of the original 1928 building as it stood on Kyushu University's Hakozaki campus.

1

1 Aglow at dusk, the office fills the base of the building, while the home tops it off.

2 Plans: (A) entrance, (C) kitchen, (D) dining, (E) sleeping, (F) bath, (J) studio.

3 In the office, the kitchen from the clients' previous home is re-purposed and a pass-through counter salvaged from the 1928 building is reborn as a Shinto altar.

4 In the home, upcycled doors lead to the bedrooms and bath.

FIRST FLOOR

GROUND FLOOR

2

3

4

House & Restaurant Junya Ishigami Yamaguchi Prefecture 2022

1

Junya Ishigami has a habit of pushing the limits of architecture. He routinely strives to make the roof thinner, the walls lighter or the overall shape more complexly curved. This time his challenge was to make something old.

The origins of this project can be traced back to the start of Ishigami's career, when he designed clean modern furniture for the client's first eating establishment. For House & Restaurant, however, the chef wanted the atmosphere of a wine cellar – rough and age-worn. 'One wouldn't know if it was made today or one thousand years ago,' says the architect. With the help of digital processes and skilled modelmakers, he moulded a submerged landscape consisting of two functional zones – one each for the home and restaurant – with three courtyards in between. In addition to separating work and play, these openings bring light and air to the middle of the building. Approached through independent entrances, each zone contains the usual functions – there are no surprises here. But the craggy, cave-like space is totally unique.

Instead of the usual process of building from the ground up, construction entailed digging deep holes in the dirt that became moulds for poured-concrete columns. Once the concrete solidified, the earth around these stalactite-like supports was excavated, leaving a sequence of connected spaces. Of course, Ishigami did not know exactly how this experiment would turn out. 'Accidental kinks add richness to the space,' he comments. Though the architect planned to smooth down the columns, he liked their earth-crusted appearance so much that their coarse surfaces were left as they were, and simply coated with a natural sealant used for traditional *tsuchikabe* mud walls. Turning the raw space into rooms, Ishigami added a concrete floor, a flat roof, and laser-cut sheets of glass (some fixed and others pivot-hinged for windows and doors), before installing custom furniture made of rattan and iron.

Unquestionably, Ishigami is among the most forward-thinking architects of his generation. He approaches his discipline with freshness and fearlessness. And he uses whatever tools or technology he needs to achieve his goal – even when this results in a combined house and restaurant whose archaic form seems as old as the hills.

1 Within the home, a sunken bathtub looks out towards the courtyard.

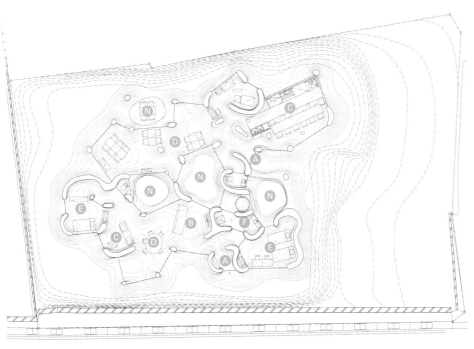

2

3

❷ The restaurant's open kitchen enables patrons seated at the counter to banter with the chef.

❸ Plan: (A) entrance, (B) living, (C) kitchen, (D) dining, (E) sleeping, (F) bath, (N) courtyard.

❹ Beneath its flat roof, House & Restaurant holds a warren of cave-like spaces (overleaf).

4

House
Junya Ishigami
Kanagawa Prefecture
2023

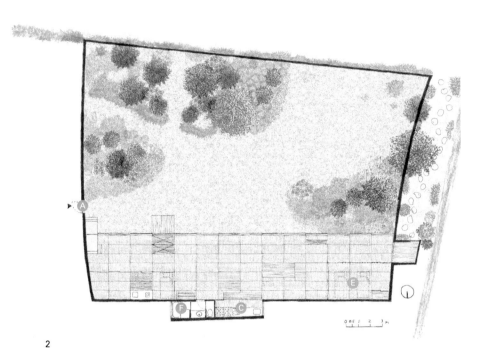

2

Imbued with sights, smells and sounds, a childhood home is a receptacle for many of our earliest memories. For Junya Ishigami, these impressions were born in his grand-parents' home, where he lived until the age of three. Located in a rural village, the house centred on a large, light-filled, *tatami*-floored room on the ground floor. This south-facing space gazed out at a view of rice paddies, clusters of trees and distant mountains – a dreamscape etched on the mind of the architect. Over time, the farms were replaced with generic housing, the greenery was uprooted, and the family homestead wore out. But when it came time to rebuild, it was the idyllic image of his youth to which Ishigami returned.

A perfect marriage of landscape and architecture, the replacement that Ishigami created is essentially one sprawling oblong room open to the garden, a mixture of plantings and paths made from stones recycled from the property's old walls. Instead of closing off the house, Ishigami protected the home's privacy and edited its view by wrapping the large site with walls. Just beyond the edge of the building, the ground plane begins to rise gradually until it completely obscures the perimeter wall at the rear of the property. 'Even if the trees aren't that tall, the upward slope creates a feeling of enclosure,' explains Ishigami. Recalling the traditional concept of borrowed scenery, the trees and mountains beyond the property line pick up where the garden leaves off.

Overhead, the house is topped by a massive, swooping roof that terminates in eaves a mere 1.3 metres (4 feet 3 inches) from the ground. In this shallow space, Ishigami inserted a 25-metre (82-foot) long window. 'When standing inside, it is low, but when sitting you can see out,' explains the architect, who blanketed most of the house's concrete floor with *tatami* mats. Fusing inside and out, the spacious interior floor aligns effortlessly with the exterior ground plane. In place of view-impairing partitions, curtains may be drawn to separate sleeping areas, while the kitchen and bath jut out from the home's concrete north wall. Salvaging bits and pieces from the old house, Ishigami utilized its sliding doors for closets and reinstalled the *getabako* shoe-storage box. Through re-use and remembering, this house merges past and present as it points the way towards the future.

1 This rendering captures the seated view of the garden from the edge of the house, where the swooping roof hovers just 1.3 metres (4 feet 3 inches) above the *tatami*-mat floor.

2 Plan: (A) entrance, (C) kitchen, (E) sleeping, (F) bath.

Spotlight

Furniture and Finishes

For centuries, the divide between architecture and furniture was somewhat ambiguous in Japan. While lightweight building components such as *shoji* screens and *tatami*-mat flooring were as movable as furniture, built-in cabinetry and staggered display shelves were as much architectural elements. Against this backdrop sat the concept of *shitsurai*, which utilized movable furnishings to alter the function of rooms. In addition, living at floor level kept furniture low to ensure that belongings were accessible without needing to get up. This custom led to the 'cockpit effect', a term coined by writer Kyoichi Tsuzuki to describe Tokyo's small contemporary homes, yet one that is also applicable to their historic predecessors.[1]

Straddling the line between portable and fixed, a whole host of wooden *tansu* chests developed. In addition to functional variations and regional styles, some were adorned with intricate metal hardware that showcased the craftsperson's skill and provided a modicum of ornament. In contrast to the carved trims and other flourishes integrated into Western buildings, the Japanese home was all but devoid of applied decoration. Instead, the grain of wood, the textures of paper and the qualities of other natural materials ensured that practicality and aesthetics were combined.

Perhaps the most dramatic shift in furniture and finishes occurred during the Meiji period (1868–1912), when Western pieces began to be adopted, mainly by the wealthy living in hybrid homes. While Western-style rooms were used for formal occasions, *tatami*-floored quarters were for relaxation. Sofas and chairs did not become common fixtures until after World War II, yet it took time for chair-sitting and bed-sleeping to sink in. Blended pieces, such as Riki Watanabe's Rope Chair (opposite page), helped smooth the transition. A simple wood frame with rope webbing, it incorporated familiar *zabuton* floor cushions for its seat and back. '[T]he trend toward Japanization of Western furniture, spurred on by the postwar Westernization of home life, is beginning to culminate in the creation of a genuinely new Japanese style,' observed the designer Masaru Katsumi in 1958.[2]

Indeed, the post-war building boom spawned some of Japan's most iconic home goods, including Isamu Noguchi's Akari Light Sculptures and Sori Yanagi's Butterfly Stool. While many designers took their cues from traditional Japanese forms, crafts and materials, others began embracing new technologies, including moulded plywood, and subsequently such materials as plastic and metal. But even as the new is integrated with the old, the size, scale and feel of its furniture remain particular to Japan.

The Japanese House Today and in the Future

Kumiko Inui

Japanese housing in the modern era has undergone significant changes, reflected in the great diversity of remarkable homes built in the decades since 1945. But looking towards the future, what will define the next generation of Japanese houses?

Today, we can see a productive tension between universality and originality in many of Japan's newly built and planned houses. In a country where the housing sector zealously repeats the 'scrap-and-build' approach, and the appearance and value of housing change continually with the mood and mode of society, it falls to architects to design houses that support the practical needs of the Japanese people. At the same time, architects are individuals with their own points of view. Therefore, a delicate situation has been created in which their residential works must be places to live, reflect societal shifts and also showcase artistic ambitions. Kazunari Sakamoto was already onto this in 1970 when he completed the Machiya in Minase (right), which, like many of his residential works, blends into the everyday Tokyo landscape. By restricting the number of doors and windows facing the busy street – compensated by a skylight that feeds the central corridor with natural light – he gave the house a secluded feel, removed from the pressures of modernization and the world outside. The slight differences in proportions and materials that distinguish all of Sakamoto's buildings from surrounding houses create unique living spaces, free from societal conventions.

A recent trend in residential architecture in Japan is collective design, which has developed against the background of universalism – houses designed to suit the everyday needs of the people who live in them. The driving forces behind works created collaboratively are such ideas as escaping from the market economy, degrowth and a scepticism associated with postmodernity; these notions are gaining traction worldwide as destruction of the environment continues. In addition to global

Kazunari Sakamoto's Machiya in Minase, 1970.

Tokuda House by Ryue Nishizawa, 2016.

Living Pool, Shingo Masuda and Katsuhisa Otsubo, 2014.

climate change, Japan is plagued by the problem of how to dispose of its waste.

The balance between universality and originality – long a feature of Japanese residential architecture – has been replaced by a balance between collaboration with users themselves and the architect's own originality. The creative dialogue between architects and homeowners is crucial for producing and redeveloping houses that are functional, innovative and appropriate for the local community. Supporting these changes are the growing need for renovation rather than new construction, and the increasing number of owners who are opening their homes to the community in a bid to help society, literally sharing their houses with neighbours – a growing trend in Japan.

The increasing popularity of renovation and re-use is driven by a renewed preference for characterful old homes rather than the new ones supplied by the housing industry. As more people feel the cultural draw of living in traditional buildings, renovation projects are becoming more commonplace, such as Ryue Nishizawa's Tokuda House (left), completed in 2016. The meticulous restoration of this century-old Kyoto *machiya*, or wooden townhouse, was carried out by hand by the architect and a team of artisans. Reusing vacant houses – often left unoccupied as their former residents enter homes for the elderly, an effect of Japan's ageing population – is also increasing in popularity. An example of this is Living Pool (below left), Yamagata, a renovation project from 2014 by Shingo Masuda and Katsuhisa Otsubo that aimed to preserve the character of the house while making it feel lighter and airier.

Another recent development in the story of the Japanese house, and one that looks set to continue in the future, is the attempt to distance architecture from the industrialized building complex by using local resources such as wood, straw and soil. The more we try to improve circular building practices, the plainer and simpler the architecture becomes. In this context, rather than bridging the gap between traditional materials and our desire for the conveniences of a contemporary lifestyle through a series of renovations taking place over a long period after construction, instead investment in local methods and sustainable resources is considered by the architect at the outset – when a new building is conceived. For example, Akeno Raised Floor in Yamanashi (overleaf), by Nousaku Fuminori is a recent attempt to transplant the straw-bale method, which originated in the United States and utilizes straw for structural elements or building insulation, to Japan. Here, Fuminori aimed to create a hybrid building by adopting a stilt system to adapt straw-bale techniques to the hot and humid Asian monsoon climate. In addition, the appearance of the whole house floating above the ground – on a raised floor – points to a new model of open housing for the area. It is through innovations like these that architects are pushing the boundaries of creativity, while the balance between originality and universality appears to be manifesting itself with increased subtlety.

Collaborative design, use of local materials, renovation and re-use will be ever more important considerations in the future, as we try to reconcile environmental issues with socially conscious design. In Japan today, even while whittling away their own authority by championing simple design and local resources, architects are still exploring what originality can be exhibited.

Akeno Raised Floor, designed by Nousaku Fuminori in 2021.

Notes

INTRODUCTION

1 Yoshio Uchida, 'The Challenge of PREMOS' in Hiroshi Matsukuma et al. (eds.), *Kunio Maekawa Retrospective*, exhibition catalogue, Bijutsu Shuppan Design Center, Tokyo, 2005, p. 315.

2 Laura Neitzel, *The Life We Longed For: Danchi House and the Middle Class Dream in Postwar Japan*, MerwinAsia, Portland, ME, 2016, p. 33.

3 Shunsuke Kurakata, 'The Japan of a Prophetic Architecture' in Takahide Tsuchiya et al. (eds.), *Japan in Architecture: Genealogies of Its Transformation*, exhibition catalogue, Mori Art Museum and Shimoda Yasunari, Echelle-1, Inc., Tokyo, p. 281.

4 Fumihiko Maki, 'Driving Force of the 1990s', *The Japan Architect*, no. 2, Spring 1991, p. 4.

5 Noboru Kawazoe, *Contemporary Japanese Architecture*, Kokusai Bunka Shinkokai, Tokyo, 1968, p. 35.

6 Shozo Baba, '45 under 45 – Japanese Young Archi-wave' in Adolph Stiller (ed.), *45 under 45 Young Architecture*, exhibition catalogue, Verlag Anton Pustet, Salzburg, 2002, p. 8.

7 Riichi Miyake, 'Japanese Architecture at a Crossroads: Tasks for the 21st Century', *The Japan Architect*, no. 65, Spring 2007, p. 12.

8 Chris Fawcett, 'An Anarchist's Guide to Modern Architecture', *Architectural Association Quarterly*, vol. 7, no. 3, 1975, p. 39.

9 Kazuhiro Kojima, 'What is a "Good House"?' in Takeshi Ishido (ed.), *Contemporary Japanese Houses 1985–2005*, TOTO Shuppan, Tokyo, 2005, p. 14.

1940s
INTRODUCTION

1 David B. Stewart, *The Making of Modern Japanese Architecture: 1868 to the Present*, Kodansha International, Tokyo and New York, 1987, p. 193.

2 Sarah Teasley, *Designing Modern Japan*, Reaktion Books, London, 2022, p. 191.

3 Laura Neitzel, *The Life We Longed For: Danchi House and the Middle Class Dream in Postwar Japan*, MerwinAsia, Portland, ME, 2016, p. 31.

4 Ibid., p. 191.

5 Ibid., p. 137.

6 John W. Dower, *Embracing Defeat: Japan in the Wake of World War II*, W.W. Norton and Company, New York, 1999, p. 534.

HOUSES

1 Naomi Pollock, *Japanese Design Since 1945: A Complete Sourcebook*, Thames & Hudson, London, 2020, p. 10.

2 Kunio Maekawa, *Kenchiku no Zen'ya Maekawa Kunio Bunshu*, Jiritsu Shobo, Tokyo, 1996, p. 39.

3 Terunobu Fujimori, 'Kunio Maekawa and Tradition' in Hiroshi Matsukuma et al. (eds.), *Kunio Maekawa Retrospective*, exhibition catalogue, Bijutsu Shuppan Design Center, Tokyo, 2005, p. 310.

SPOTLIGHT

1 Takeshi Nakagawa, *The Japanese House: In Space, Memory and Language*, International House of Japan, Inc., Tokyo, 2005, p. 240.

1950s
INTRODUCTION

1 Shuichi Matsumura, 'Why Steel is the Mainstay of Prefab Homes in Japan', *The Japan Architect*, no. 75, Autumn 2009, p. 30.

2 Laura Neitzel, *The Life We Longed For: Danchi House and the Middle Class Dream in Postwar Japan*, MerwinAsia, Portland, ME, 2016, p. 24.

3 Ibid., p. 33.

4 Jordan Sand, *House and Home in Modern Japan: Architecture, Domestic Space, and Bourgeois Culture, 1880–1930*, Harvard University Press, Cambridge, MA, and London, 2003, p. 374.

5 Natsuo Okawa and Jun Sato, *Kiseki to Yobareta Nihon no Meisaku Jutaku 50*, X-Knowledge Co., Ltd, Tokyo, 2014, p. 22.

6 Naomi Pollock, *Japanese Design Since 1945: A Complete Sourcebook*, Thames & Hudson, London, 2020, p. 12.

HOUSES

1 Noribumi Kitamura, 'Junzo Sakakura's Modern Movement' in *Une Architecture pour L'Homme: Junzo Sakakura in Architectural Documents*, exhibition catalogue, National Archives of Modern Architecture, Tokyo, 2013, p. 21.

2 Naokazu Kitamura, *Architect Junzo Sakakura*, exhibition catalogue, National Archives of Modern Architecture, Tokyo, 2013, p. 6.

3 David B. Stewart, *The Making of a Modern Japanese Architecture: 1868 to the Present*, Kodansha International, Tokyo and New York, 1987, p. 193.

4 Hiroyasu Fujioka, 'The Architecture of Kiyoshi Seike: Implications of His Approach to the Making of Things' in *Architect Kiyoshi Seike 1918–2005*, Shinkenchiku-sha Co., Ltd, Tokyo, 2006, p. 403.

5 Antonin Raymond, *Antonin Raymond: An Autobiography*, Charles E. Tuttle Company, Tokyo, 1973, p. 65.

6 Ibid., p. 101.

7 Ibid., p. 234.

8 Shin-ichi Okuyama and Sotaro Yamamoto, 'Detail Considered in the Context of Steel Houses', *The Japan Architect*, no. 75, Autumn 2009, pp. 7–8.

9 Saikaku Toyokawa, 'A House' in Takahide Tsuchiya et al. (eds.), *Japan in Architecture: Genealogies of Its Transformation*, exhibition catalogue, Mori Art Museum and Shimoda Yasunari, Echelle-1, Inc., Tokyo, 2018, p. 148.

10 Kiyoshi Ikebe, 'Adventures of the Glass House: An Attempt at Ideal Urban Housing', *Fujin Asahi*, vol. 10, no. 12, December 1955, p. 154.

11 Ibid., p. 155.

12 Ibid., p. 154.

13 'The Cradle of Creativity – Taro Okamoto's Studio', exhibition text, Taro Okamoto Memorial Museum, Tokyo, 2014.

14 Kiyonori Kikutake, 'When Metabolism Was Born of Renovation', *The Japan Architect*, no. 73, Spring 2009, p. 14.

SPOTLIGHT

1 Hirota Yoshizaki, 'Japanese Courts back the "Right to Sunshine"', *New York Times*, 18 July 1976, p. 10.

1960s
INTRODUCTION

1 'Animation: The World's 10 Largest Economies by GDP (1960–Today)', Visual Capitalist, 1 November 2018. https://www.visualcapitalist.com/animation-the-worlds-10-largest-economies-by-gdp-1960-today/.

2 'Tokyo's History, Geography, and Population', Tokyo Metropolitan Government. https://www.metro.tokyo.lg.jp/ENGLISH/ABOUT/HISTORY/history01.htm.

3 Zhongjie Lin, 'City on the Move: Mobility, Structure, and Symbolism in Kenzo Tange's 1960 Plan for Tokyo', *Seeking the City*, Association of Collegiate Schools of

Architecture, Washington, DC, 2008, p. 449. https://www.acsa-arch.org/proceedings/Annual%20Meeting%20Proceedings/ACSA.AM.96/ACSA.AM.96.52.pdf.

4 Tomohiro Hasegawa, 'Introduction to the Building Standard Law', Building Center of Japan, Tokyo, 2013, p. 8. https://www.bcj.or.jp/upload/international/baseline/BSLIntroduction201307_e.pdf.

5 'Senri, Japan, Asia', International New Town Institute, 2017. http://www.newtowninstitute.org/newtowndata/newtown.php?newtownId=227/.

HOUSES

1 Kiyoshi Ikebe, *Sumai*, Iwanami Fujin Gahou, Iwanami Shoten, Tokyo, 1954, p. 132.

2 Kiyoshi Ikebe, 'No. 58 Basic Experiments in Componentization', Ikebe Laboratory, University of Tokyo, Tokyo, 1960.

3 Seng Kuan, introduction to *Kazuo Shinohara: Traversing the House and City*, Lars Müller Publishers, Zurich, and Harvard University Graduate School of Design, Cambridge, MA, 2021, p. 11.

4 Kazuo Shinohara, 'A Theory of Residential Architecture', *The Japan Architect*, no. 93, Spring 2014, p. 30. Reprinted from *The Japan Architect*, no. 135, October 1967.

5 Hiroshi Misawa, 'The Legacy of Antonin Raymond and Junzo Yoshimura for Modern Residential Architecture in Japan', *GA Houses*, special issue *Japan VI*, no. 100, August 2007, p. 57.

6 Shinobu Akahori and Waro Kishi, 'The Chalet Moby Dick/1966', *The Japan Architect*, special issue *Modern Houses II*, no. 29, Spring 1998, p. 110.

7 Ibid.

8 Ken Tadashi Oshima, 'Variations on the Square: Shinohara's Umbrella House' in Seng Kuan (ed.), *Kazuo Shinohara: Traversing the House and City*, Lars Müller Publishers, Zurich, and Harvard University Graduate School of Design, Cambridge, MA, 2021, p. 43.

9 Thomas Daniell, *An Anatomy of Influence*, Architectural Association Publications, London, 2018, p. 29.

10 Naomi Pollock, *Modern Japanese House*, Phaidon Press Limited, London, 2005, p. 15.

1970S
INTRODUCTION

1 Shinji Hamada, 'Japanese Car Design Since 1945' in Naomi Pollock, *Japanese Design Since 1945: A Complete Sourcebook*, Thames & Hudson, London, 2020, p. 267.

2 'Hello Kitty', Hello Kitty Wiki. https://hellokitty.fandom.com/wiki/Hello_Kitty.

HOUSES

1 Hiroyasu Fujioka, 'The Architecture of Kiyoshi Seike: Implications of His Approach to the Making of Things' in *Architect Kiyoshi Seike 1918–2005*, Shinkenchiku-sha Co., Ltd, Tokyo, 2006, p. 402.

2 Chris Fawcett, 'An Anarchist's Guide to Modern Architecture', *Architectural Association Quarterly*, vol. 7, no. 3, 1975, p. 41.

3 Kenjiro Hosaka, 'Interview with Otsuji Seiko and Otsuji Tetsuo' in Seng Kuan (ed.), *Kazuo Shinohara: Traversing the House and City*, Lars Müller Publishers, Zurich, and Harvard University Graduate School of Design, Cambridge, MA, 2021, p. 199.

4 Ibid., pp. 199–200.

5 Tadao Ando, 'Ando by Ando' in *Tadao Ando 1: Houses and Housing*, TOTO Publishing, Tokyo, 2007, p. 85.

6 Aida Takefumi, 'On Playfulness and Toy Blocks', *The Japan Architect*, vol. 60, no. 9, September 1985, p. 43.

1980S
INTRODUCTION

1 'The Bubble Economy and the Lost Decade', About Japan: A Teacher's Resource, Japan Society, New York, 2022. https://aboutjapan.japansociety.org/the_bubble_economy_and_the_lost_decade_2.

2 Alexandra Bregman, 'Forgotten Boom: The Legacy of Japan's 1980s Art Buying Spree', *Nikkei Asia*, 16 October 2020. https://asia.nikkei.com/Life-Arts/Arts/Forgotten-boom-the-legacy-of-Japan-s-1980s-art-buying-spree2.

3 Naomi Pollock, *Japanese Design Since 1945: A Complete Sourcebook*, Thames & Hudson, London, 2020, p. 80.

HOUSES

1 Minoru Takeyama, 'Design Memo' in *Minoru Takeyama: Architectural Record*, Rikuyosha Co., Ltd, Tokyo, 2000, p. 2.

2 Kazuo Shinohara, 'Towards Architecture', *The Japan Architect*, vol. 56, no. 9, September 1981; reprinted in *The Japan Architect*, no. 93, Spring 2014, p. 100.

3 Kazuo Shinohara, 'ModernNext' (originally published in *Kenchiku Bunka* in 1988) in Seng Kuan (ed.), *Kazuo Shinohara: Traversing the House and City*, Lars Müller Publishers, Zurich, and Harvard University Graduate School of Design, Cambridge, MA, 2021, p. 225.

SPOTLIGHT

1 Atsushi Ueda, *The Inner Harmony of the Japanese House*, Kodansha International, Tokyo and New York, 1990, p. 53.

2 Ibid., p. 55.

3 Ryue Nishizawa, 'Discussing the Contemporary Urban Landscape', *The Japan Architect*, no. 66, Summer 2007, p. 11.

1990S
INTRODUCTION

1 Kazuhiko Namba, 'Post Syndrome', *The Japan Architect*, no. 24, Winter 1996, p. 4.

2 Naomi Pollock, 'Designing for the Japanese Public' in John Zukowsky (ed.), *Japan 2000: Architecture and Design for the Japanese Public*, exhibition catalogue, The Art Institute of Chicago, Chicago, and Prestel Verlag, Munich, 1998, p. 34.

3 'Jan 17, 1995 CE: Kobe Earthquake', National Geographic Society. https://education.nationalgeographic.org/resource/kobe-earthquake.

4 Aga Sugiyama et al., 'The Tokyo Subway Sarin Attack Has Long-Term Effects on Survivors: A 10-Year Study Started 5 Years After the Terrorist Incident', *PLoS One*, vol. 15, no. 6, 23 June 2000. https://journals.plos.org/plosone/article?id=10.1371/journal.pone.0234967.

5 Fumihiko Maki, 'Driving Force of the 1990s', *The Japan Architect*, no. 2, Spring 1991, p. 5.

HOUSES

1 Quoted in Thomas De Monchaux, 'Crit: Truly Surreal', *Architect*, vol. 100, no. 3, March 2011.

2 Laura Barnett, 'Kathryn Findlay, Architect – Portrait of the Artist', *The Guardian*, 2 April 2013.

3 Ibid.

SPOTLIGHT

1 Atsushi Ueda, *The Inner Harmony of the Japanese House*, Kodansha International, Tokyo and New York, 1990, p. 108.

2000S
INTRODUCTION

1 'Roppongi Hills: Concept and History', Mori Building Co., Ltd. https://www.mori.co.jp/en/projects/roppongihills/background.html.

2 Naomi Pollock, 'Tokyo Midtown', *Architectural Record*, vol. 195, no. 11, November 2007, p. 124.

HOUSES

1 Tadao Ando, *Tadao Ando 1: Houses and Housing*, TOTO Publishing, Tokyo, 2007, p. 280.

2 Ibid., p. 277.

3 Hiroshi Sambuichi, *GA Houses*, special issue *Japan VI*, no. 100, August 2007, p. 228.

SPOTLIGHT

1 Laura Neitzel, *The Life We Longed For: Danchi House and the Middle Class Dream in Postwar Japan*, MerwinAsia, Portland, ME, 2016, p. 41.

2 Ibid.

3 Kiyoshi Ikebe, *Sumai,* Iwanami Fujin Gahou, Iwanami Shoten, Tokyo, 1954, p. 62.

4 Naomi Pollock, *Japanese Design Since 1945: A Complete Sourcebook*, Thames & Hudson, London, 2020, p. 395.

2010S

INTRODUCTION

1 Eri Sugiura, 'Japan Gets More Than It Bargained for with Tourist Boom', *Nikkei Asia*, 17 April 2019. https://asia.nikkei.com/Spotlight/The-Big-Story/Japan-gets-more-than-it-bargained-for-with-tourist-boom.

2 'Cool Japan Strategy Public-Private Collaboration Initiative', Cool Japan Strategy Promotion Council, 17 June 2015. https://www.cao.go.jp/cool_japan/english/pdf/published_document2.pdf.

3 'Japan's Emperor Akihito Abdicates', Sky History, 30 April 2019. https://www.history.com/this-day-in-history/japanese-emperor-akihito-abdicates-throne.

SPOTLIGHT

1 Yoshiharu Tsukamoto, 'Redefining the Gap' in Hiroyasu Fujioka, Kenjiro Hosaka et al., *The Japanese House: Architecture and Life After 1945*, exhibition catalogue, The National Museum of Modern Art and Shinkenchiku-sha Co., Ltd, Tokyo, 2017, p. 139.

2 Naomi Pollock, 'Kengo Kuma', *Kinfolk*, vol. 32, Summer 2019, p. 37.

2020S

INTRODUCTION

1 Tom Ravenscroft, 'Five Architecture and Design Controversies that Rocked the Tokyo Olympics', *Dezeen*, 6 August 2021. https://www.dezeen.com/2021/08/06/tokyo-2020-olympics-controversies-architecture-design/.

2 David E. Sanger, 'Shinzo Abe's Influence Was Still Evident Long After He Left Office', *New York Times*, 8 July 2022. https://www.nytimes.com/2022/07/08/us/politics/shinzo-abe-influence.html.

SPOTLIGHT

1 Kyoichi Tsuzuki, *Tokyo Style*, Kyoto Shoin Co., Ltd, Kyoto, 1996, p. 19.

2 Masaru Katsumi, 'Furniture of Today' in Iwao Yamawaki, Kunihiko Yamakosi and Masaru Katsumi (eds.), *Japanese Houses Today*, The Asahi Shimbun Press, Tokyo, 1958, p. 234.

Further Reading

Biographies

Author Acknowledgments

Engel, Heinrich, *The Japanese House: A Tradition for Contemporary Architecture*, Charles E. Tuttle Company, Inc., Rutland, Vermont, and Tokyo, 1964

Fujioka, Hiroyasu, Kenjiro Hosaka et al., *The Japanese House: Architecture and Life After 1945*, exhibition catalogue, The National Museum of Modern Art and Shinkenchiku-sha Co., Ltd, Tokyo, 2017

Ishido, Takeshi (ed.), *Contemporary Japanese Houses 1985–2005*, TOTO Shuppan, Tokyo, 2005

Morse, Edward S., *Japanese Homes and Their Surroundings*, Charles E. Tuttle Company, Inc., Rutland, Vermont, and Tokyo, 1972. First published by Harper & Brothers, New York, 1885

Nakagawa, Takeshi, *The Japanese House: In Space, Memory and Language*, International House of Japan, Inc., Tokyo, 2005

Neitzel, Laura, *The Life We Longed For: Danchi Housing and the Middle Class Dream in Postwar Japan*, MerwinAsia, Portland, Maine, 2016

Nuijsink, Cathelijne, *How to Make a Japanese House*, NAi Publishers, Rotterdam, 2012

Pollock, Naomi, *Jutaku: Japanese Houses*, Phaidon Press Limited, London, 2015

Pollock, Naomi, *Modern Japanese House*, Phaidon Press Limited, London, 2005

Sand, Jordan, *House and Home in Modern Japan: Architecture, Domestic Space, and Bourgeois Culture, 1880–1930*, Harvard University Press, Cambridge, Massachusetts, and London, 2003

Souteyrat, Jérémie, *Tokyo No Ie*, Le Lézard Noir, Poitiers, 2014

Stewart, David B., *The Making of a Modern Japanese Architecture: 1868 to the Present*, Kodansha International, Tokyo and New York, 1987

Tsuchiya, Takahide, et al. (eds.), *Japan in Architecture: Genealogies of Its Transformation*, exhibition catalogue, Mori Art Museum and Shimoda Yasunari, Echelle-1, Inc., Tokyo, 2018

Ueda, Atsushi, *The Inner Harmony of the Japanese House,* Kodansha International, Tokyo and New York, 1990

NAOMI POLLOCK is an American architect and author whose writing has appeared in numerous publications on both sides of the Pacific, including *A+U*, *Dwell*, *Jutakutokushu*, *Kinfolk*, *Wallpaper** and *Architectural Record*, for whom she is the Special International Correspondent. She has also written numerous books, including *Modern Japanese House*, *Made in Japan: 100 New Products*, *Jutaku: Japanese Houses*, *Sou Fujimoto* and *Japanese Design Since 1945: A Complete Sourcebook*. In addition, she was the editor of *NUNO: Visionary Japanese Textiles*. In 2018, she was invited into the College of Fellows of the American Institute of Architects.

TADAO ANDO was born in Osaka, Japan, in 1941 and is entirely self educated. He established Tadao Ando Architect & Associates in 1969 and won the prestigious Pritzker Architecture Prize in 1995. He has taught at Yale University, Columbia University, Harvard University and the University of Tokyo, where he is currently a Professor Emeritus. His works include Church of the Light, Modern Art Museum of Fort Worth and the Bourse de Commerce / Pinault Collection.

HIROYASU FUJIOKA was born in Hiroshima, Japan, in 1949. He graduated from and taught at the Graduate School, Tokyo Institute of Technology, where he is now professor emeritus. His book, *Sutemi Horiguchi: The Seeker for Total Art* (2011), won the Architectural Institute of Japan Award.

KUMIKO INUI was born in Osaka, Japan, in 1969. In 1992, she graduated from Tokyo University of the Arts, gaining a Master's at Yale School of Architecture in 1996. Inui worked at Jun Aoki & Associates between 1996 and 2000, before founding Inui Architects in 2000. She was associate professor at Tokyo University of the Arts from 2011 to 2016; in 2016, she undertook a professorship at Yokohama National University Faculty of Urban Innovation. Her works include Shichigahama Junior High School, Nobeoka Station Area Project and Miyajimaguchi Passenger Terminal.

The creation of this book would not have been possible without the assistance of many people, starting with my team at Thames & Hudson. Lucas Dietrich, Augusta Pownall, Helen Fanthorpe and John Jervis all helped me in so many different ways. I am especially appreciative of Anabel Navarro, who relentlessly chased down photos and drawings, and book designer Stefi Orazi for her elegant vision.

A big thank you to all of the architects, as well as their staff, family members and clients, who generously shared ideas and information. In addition, numerous critics, academics and photographers supported my research, writing and image-gathering. I am particularly indebted to Takefumi Aida, Koji Aikawa, Shiro Doi, Terunobu Fujimori, Isao Hashimoto, Miho Kida, Noribumi Kitamura, Shuko Koike, Jin Motohashi, Shin-ichi Okuyama, David B. Stewart and Junko Takatsuki. Thank you also to the guest essayists, Rie Azuma, Hiroyasu Fujioka, Konomi Ikebe, Mana Ikebe, Kumiko Inui, Yuki Kikutake, Yoko Kinoshita, Naomi Kobayashi, Fumihiko Maki, Katsuhiro Miyamoto, Takaharu Tezuka, Yui Tezuka, Michiko Uchida, Makoto Shin Watanabe and Takako Yoshimura. Each of you contributed important texts that have expanded the scope of this book. I am especially appreciative of Tadao Ando's wonderful foreword.

In closing, I would like to thank my family. I am grateful to my sister, Beth, for her unflagging interest and encouragement. And to my brothers Raphael, Daniel and Benjamin, who all supported me through this endeavour. I am grateful to my daughters, Abigail and Eve, for listening, reading, finding humour when desperately needed and accompanying me on site visits way back when. And I am grateful to my husband, David, for so many things. Your thoughtful insight, keen eye, clever wit and superior translation skills were essential to the realization of this book. For many reasons I could not have written this book without you beside me.

It is with the utmost pleasure and appreciation that I dedicate this book to Abigail, Eve and, most of all, David.

Index

Page numbers in *italics* refer
to the illustrations.

Picture Credits

a = above; b = below; c = centre; l = left; r = right. Sources of illustrations by page number:

9: ©Jun Aoki; 10: ©Osamu Murai; 11:Toshiyuki Yano Photography; 12a: Photo Masao Nishikawa; 12b: Photo Makoto Yoshida; 13: Photo ©Daici Ano; 16a: Published in Kingo Hirabayashi & Hideo Inagaki, Suzuki Shoten, 1920; 16c: Published in Reimondo No Ie, Kouyousha, 1931; 16b: Photo Hiroyasu Fujioka; 17: The National Archives of Modern Architecture, Agency for Cultural Affairs (NAMA); 18a: Published in Tanabe Heigaku, Tanabe Heigaku sensei juusan-kaiki kinen jigyoukai, 1966; 18c: Yukihiro Masuzawa; 18b, 19a, 19b: Photo Hiroyasu Fujioka; 20: World History Archive/Alamy Stock Photo; 22: Photo F. Nishizawa. The National Archives of Modern Architecture, Agency for Cultural Affairs (NAMA); 23: Photo Francis Haar; 24: Photo F. Nishizawa. The National Archives of Modern Architecture, Agency for Cultural Affairs (NAMA); 25a, 25b: The National Archives of Modern Architecture, Agency for Cultural Affairs (NAMA); 26, 27, 28–9, 30, 31a, 31b: Maekawa Associates; 32, 33a, 33b: Courtesy Ikebe Family; 34: Woradanue Nakdee/Alamy Stock Photo; 36: Paul Popper/Popperfoto via Getty Images; 38, 39, 40, 41: The National Archives of Modern Architecture, Agency for Cultural Affairs (NAMA); 42: Courtesy Design System Archive; 43, 44a: Photo Chuji Hirayama. ©Jiro Hirayama; 44b, 45: Courtesy Design System Archive; 46, 47, 48a, 48b, 49: Raymond Collections, The Architectural Archives, University of Pennsylvania; 50, 52a, 52b, 53a: Photo Chuji Hirayama. ©Jiro Hirayama; 53b: Masuzawa Architect & Associates; 54, 55, 56: Photo Chuji Hirayama. ©Jiro Hirayama; 57a: Hirose Kenji Archives; 57b: Photo Chuji Hirayama. ©Jiro Hirayama; 58: ©Osamu Murai; 59, 60a, 60b, 61a, 61b, 62, 63a, 63b: ©Michiko Uchida (Kenzo Tange Archive); 64: Photo Saeki Yoshikatu. Courtesy Design System Archive; 65a: Photo Naomi Maki. Courtesy Design System Archive; 65b: Photo Chuji Hirayama. ©Jiro Hirayama; 66: Photo Saeki Yoshikatu. Courtesy Design System Archive; 67: Courtesy Design System Archive; 68, 69, 70a, 70b, 71, 72, 73a, 73b: Courtesy Ikebe family; 74, 75: Photo Chuji Hirayama. ©Jiro Hirayama; 76: The National Archives of Modern Architecture, Agency for Cultural Affairs (NAMA); 77: Photo Chuji Hirayama. ©Jiro Hirayama; 78, 79a: Photo ©Eiji Kitada; 79b: Takamasa Yoshizaka and Juichi Otake; 80, 81a: ©Akio Kawasumi; 81bl: Photo Nobuyuki Akiyama; 81br: Tokyo University of the Arts. Reproduced by permission of Takako Yoshimura; 82–3: ©Akio Kawasumi; 83, 84, 85a, 85b: ©Osamu Murai; 86: The National Archives of Modern Architecture, Agency for Cultural Affairs (NAMA); 87: ©Osamu Murai; 88: Mave/Alamy Stock Photo;

90: MeijiShowa/Alamy Stock Photo; 92: Photo Fumio Murasawa. ©Shokokusha; 93, 94a, 94b, 95; Courtesy Ikebe family; 96, 97, 98a: ©Osamu Murai; 98b: Kazuo Shinohara Estate; 99: ©Osamu Murai; 100, 101a, 101bl: Photo Tahira Toshio. The National Archives of Modern Architecture, Agency for Cultural Affairs (NAMA); 101br: The National Archives of Modern Architecture, Agency for Cultural Affairs (NAMA); 102, 103, 104a: Photo Tsuneo Sato; 104b: Tokyo University of the Arts. Reproduced by permission of Takako Yoshimura; 105: Courtesy Yoshimura Takako; 106, 107, 108, 109a: Raymond Collections, The Architectural Archives, University of Pennsylvania; 109b: Raymond Architectural Design Office, Inc.; 110, 111a, 111b: ©Osamu Murai; 112a, 112b: Mayumi Miyawaki Architectural Laboratory; 112–3, 114, 115: ©Osamu Murai; 116a, 116b: Kazuo Shinohara Estate; 116–7: ©Osamu Murai; 118, 119a: Photo Yutaka Suzuki; 119b: ©Makoto Suzuki; 120: ©Osamu Murai; 121: Azuma Architect & Associates; 122a, 122b: ©Osamu Murai; 123: Courtesy Rie Azuma; 124, 125, 126: Photo ©Shigeo Ogawa; 127: Courtesy Katono family; 128: Japan Stock Photography/Alamy Stock Photo; 130: Robert Balayan/Alamy Stock Photo; 132, 133a, 133bl: Photo Akiyama Minoru. Courtesy Design System Archive; 133br: Courtesy Design System Archive; 134, 135: ©Osamu Murai; 136a, 136b: Mayumi Miyawaki Architectural Laboratory; 136–7: ©Osamu Murai; 138: Photo Tomio Ohashi; 139, 140a: Photo Shinjiro Yamada; 140b: Capsule Architecture Project; 141a: Photo Shinjiro Yamada; 141b: Capsule Architecture Project; 142: ©Shokokusha; 143l: Photo ©Kozo Mozuna; 143r: ©Kiko Mozuna; 144: Photo Shuji Yamada; 145, 146a: ©Miyamoto Ryuji. Courtesy the artist; 146b: The National Archives of Modern Architecture, Agency for Cultural Affairs (NAMA); 147: ©Miyamoto Ryuji. Courtesy the artist; 148, 149, 150a: Photo Hiroshi Ueda; 150b: Kazuo Shinohara Estate; 151: Photo Hiroshi Ueda; 152, 153, 154a: Photo ©Tadao Ando; 154b: Tadao Ando Architect & Associates; 155: Photo ©Tadao Ando; 156: Courtesy Toyo Ito & Associates, Architects; 157, 158a: ©Koji Taki; 158b: Courtesy Toyo Ito & Associates, Architects; 159: ©Koji Taki; 160l: Photo Mitsumasa Fujitsuka; 160r: Photo Itsuko Hasegawa Atelier; 161a: Photo Mitsumasa Fujitsuka; 161b: Itsuko Hasegawa Atelier; 162a, 162b: ©Riken Yamamoto & Field Shop; 163a, 163bl: Photo Tomio Ohashi; 163br: ©Riken Yamamoto & Field Shop; 164, 165, 166a: ©Osamu Murai; 166b: Courtesy Maki and Associates; 167, 168a, 168b, 169: Courtesy Naomi Maki; 170, 171, 172a, 172b, 173a: Photo Mamoru Ishiguro; 173b: Shoji Hayashi & Masako Hayashi; 174l: ©Aida-Doi-Architects; 174r: ©Takefumi Aida; 175l, 175ar, 175br: ©Aida-Doi-Architects; 176: Anthony Brown/Alamy Stock Photo;

178: yannick luthy/Alamy Stock Photo; 180, 181: Photos Tomio Ohashi; 182a: Itsuko Hasegawa Atelier; 182b, 183a, 183b: Photos Tomio Ohashi; 184, 185al, 185ar: ©Katsuaki Furudate; 185br: ©Minoru Takeyama; 186, 187a: Photo Yoshio Shiratori, ZOOM; 187b: Shoei Yoh Archive, Kyushu University; 188, 190al, 190ar: Photo Tomio Ohashi; 190b: Kazuo Shinohara Estate; 191: Photo Tomio Ohashi; 192, 193, 194al: Photo ©Tadao Ando; 194ar: Tadao Ando Architect & Associates; 194b: Photo ©Mitsuo Matsuoka; 195a: Tadao Ando Architect & Associates; 195b: Photo ©Tadao Ando; 196, 197a: Photo Tomio Ohashi; 197b: Kazuo Shinohara Estate; 198, 199a: Photo Tomio Ohashi; 199b: Courtesy Toyo Ito & Associates, Architects; 200, 201a, 201b, 202, 203: Osamu Ishiyama/Studio GAYA; 204, 205: Photo Tomio Ohashi; 206l: ©Riken Yamamoto & Field Shop; 206–7: Photo Tomio Ohashi; 208, 209, 210, 211a: Photo ©Tadao Ando; 211b: ©Katsuaki Furudate; 211b, 212, 213: Courtesy Yoko Kinoshita; 214: Photo Tomio Ohashi; 216a, 216b: Kazunari Sakamoto Architectural Laboratory; 217a: Photo Tomio Ohashi; 217b: Kazunari Sakamoto Architectural Laboratory; 218: Masa Uemura/Alamy Stock Photo; 220: Photo Hiroyuki Hirai; 222, 223: Photo ©Mitsuo Matsuoka; 224l: Toru Murakami Architect & Associates; 224–5: Photo ©Mitsuo Matsuoka; 226: Photo Hiroyuki Hirai; 227: ©Waro Kishi + K.Associates/ Architects Co., Ltd; 228al, 228ar: Photo Hiroyuki Hirai; 228b: ©Waro Kishi + K.Associates/Architects Co., Ltd; 229: Photo Hiroyuki Hirai; 230, 231a: Katsuhisa Kida/Fototeca; 231bl: Eisaku Ushida & Kathryn Findlay; 231br: Katsuhisa Kida/ Fototeca; 232, 233, 234a, 234b, 235a, 235b: Courtesy Kazuyo Sejima & Associates; 236, 238a: Photo Hiroyuki Hirai; 238b: Shigeru Ban Architects; 239, 241, 242a: Photo Hiroyuki Hirai; 242b, 243a: Shigeru Ban Architects; 243b: Photo Hiroyuki Hirai; 244, 245, 246l, 246–7, 248, 249l, 249r: Courtesy Katsuhiro Miyamoto & Associates; 250, 251, 252a: Photo Shunichi Atsumi; 252b: Hitoshi Abe; 253a, 253b: Photo Shunichi Atsumi; 254, 255, 256al, 256ar, 256b, 257a, 257b: ©Atelier Bow-Wow; 258: Photo Shigeru Hiraga. Courtesy Taira Nishizawa; 259a: Photo Heiner Schilling. Courtesy Taira Nishizawa; 259b: Courtesy Taira Nishizawa; 260: imageBROKER/Alamy Stock Photo; 262: Valery Hache/AFP via Getty Images; 265a, 265b, 266a: Katsuhisa Kida/FOTOTECA; 266b, 267: Courtesy Tezuka Architects; 268: Hiroyasu Sakaguchi, A to Z; 269: Courtesy Endoh Masaaki; 270, 271: Hiroyasu Sakaguchi, A to Z; 272, 273a: Photo Hiroyuki Hirai; 273bl: Shigeru Ban Architects; 273br: Photo Hiroyuki Hirai; 274: Photo ©Mitsuo Matsuoka; 275, 276l: Tadao Ando Architect & Associates; 276–7: Photo ©Mitsuo Matsuoka; 278, 279a, 279b, 280, 281: ©Kazuyo Sejima & Associates; 282, 283a, 283b: ©Sambuichi Architects; 284, 285a: Photo Hiroyuki Hirai; 285b: Courtesy Architecton;

286, 287, 288, 289a, 289b: ©Atelier Bow-Wow; 290, 291, 292: Photo ©Daici Ano. Courtesy Kengo Kuma & Associates; 293a: Kengo Kuma & Associates; 293b: Photo ©Daici Ano. Courtesy Kengo Kuma & Associates; 294, 295a: Photo Yoshiharu Matsumura; 295b: Shuhei Endo; 296: ©Shinkenchiku-sha; 297a, 297b: ©Sambuichi Architects; 298: Go Hasegawa & Associates; 299a, 299b: Photo Takumi Ota; 300, 301a: Photo ©Daici Ano; 301b: ©TNA; 302, 303a: Photo ©Daici Ano; 303b: Jun Aoki; 304: Photo Akihisa Masuda; 305a: Terunobu Fujimori; 305b: Photo Akihisa Masuda; 306, 308a: Photo Iwan Baan; 308b: Sou Fujimoto Architects; 309a: Photo Iwan Baan; 309b: Sou Fujimoto Architects; 310, 311, 312a: Photo Ryota Atarashi; 312b: Mount Fuji Architects Studio; 313: Photo Ryota Atarashi; 314, 315a, 315b: Photo ©Shinichi Ogawa; 316: directphoto.bz/Alamy Stock Photo; 318: Mark Pearson/Alamy Stock Photo; 320, 321, 322a: Photo ©Tadao Ando; 322b: Tadao Ando Architect & Associates; 323: Photo ©Tadao Ando; 324: Photo ©Kai Nakamura; 325, 326a, 326b: Courtesy o+h; 327: Photo ©Kai Nakamura; 328, 329, 330a, 330b, 331: Office of Ryue Nishizawa; 332, 333, 334a: Photo Iwan Baan; 334b: Sou Fujimoto Architects; 335: Photo Iwan Baan; 336, 337a: Photo Kenichi Suzuki; 337bl: Tato Architects; 337br: Photo Yohei Sasakura/ Sasanokurasha; 338: Nacasa and Partners Inc.; 339al: Hiroshi Nakamura & NAP; 339ar, 339b: Nacasa and Partners Inc.; 340, 341a, 341bl: Photo Ikunori Yamamoto; 341br: Yuko Nagayama & Associates; 342, 343 : Photo Yasutaka Yoshimura; 344l: Yasutaka Yoshimura Architects; 344-5: Photo Yasutaka Yoshimura; 346, 347: ©Shinkenchiku-sha; 348: Taichi Mitsuya & Associates; 349: ©Shinkenchiku-sha; 350, 351a, 351bl: ©Takumi Ota; 351br: Courtesy DGT; 352, 353al: Photo ©Daici Ano; 353ar: Inui Architects; 353b: Photo ©Daici Ano; 354, 355, 356a: AVH. Atelier Vincent Hecht; 356b: ©Akihisa Hirata architecture office; 357: AVH. Atelier Vincent Hecht; 358, 359a, 359bl: Yuna Yagi (atelier now/here); 359br: ©Atelier Tsuyoshi Tane Architects; 360: Koji Fujii/ TOREAL; 361a: Hiroshi Nakamura & NAP; 361b: Koji Fujii/TOREAL; 362, 363, 364a: Photo ©Daici Ano; 364b: n e n d o; 365: Photo ©Daici Ano; 366: Scott Sim/ Alamy Stock Photo; 368: Aflo Co. Ltd./ Alamy Stock Photo; 370, 371a: Katsuhisa Kida/FOTOTECA; 371b: ©Tezuka Architects; 372, 373a, 373b: Katsuhisa Kida/FOTOTECA; 374, 375a: Photo ©Ben Richards; 375b: Terada Hirate Sekkei; 376: Photo Yousuke Harigane; 377: Photo yHa architects; 378a: Photo Yousuke Harigane; 378b: yHa architects; 379a, 379b: Photo Yousuke Harigane; 380, 381a, 381b, 382-3, 384, 385: ©junya.ishigami +associates; 386: Metropolitan Gallery Inc., Tokyo; 388: Atelier and I, Kazunari Sakamoto Architectural Laboratory; 389a: Photo Hisao Suzuki; 389b: Photo Kazuhiro Ishiyama; 390: Jumpei Suzuki.

First published in the United Kingdom in 2023 by
Thames & Hudson Ltd, 181A High Holborn, London WC1V 7QX

First published in the United States of America in 2023 by Thames &
Hudson Inc., 500 Fifth Avenue, New York, New York 10110

British Library Cataloguing-in-Publication Data
A catalogue record for this book is available from the British Library

Library of Congress Control Number 2023934015

ISBN 978-0-500-34373-9

Printed and bound in China by C&C Offset Printing Co. Ltd.

Be the first to know about our new releases,
exclusive content and author events by visiting
thamesandhudson.com
thamesandhudsonusa.com
thamesandhudson.com.au